A STATE OF WAR EXISTS

A STATE OF WAR EXISTS

REPORTERS IN THE LINE OF FIRE

MICHAEL NICHOLSON

Biteback Publishing

First published in Great Britain in 2012 by
Biteback Publishing Ltd
Westminster Tower
3 Albert Embankment
London
SE1 7SP
Copyright © Michael Nicholson 2012

Michael Nicholson has asserted his right under the Copyright, Designs and
Patents Act 1988 to be identified as the author of this work.

Every reasonable effort has been made to trace copyright holders of material
reproduced in this book, but if any have been inadvertently overlooked the
publishers would be glad to hear from them.

ISBN 978-1-84954-180-0

10 9 8 7 6 5 4 3 2 1

A CIP catalogue record for this book is available from the British Library.

Set in Caslon Pro and Orator by Selina Swayne
Cover design by Namkwan Cho

Printed and bound in Great Britain by
CPI Group (UK) Ltd, Croydon CR0 4YY

To Diana,
Best friend and wife,
Who understands.
And to my sons Tom and Will,
whose idea it was.

CONTENTS

ACKNOWLEDGEMENTS

My thanks to my old friend Robin O'Connor for his patience and research. It would have taken so much longer otherwise.

With the Kimberley relief column after the Battle of Speyfontein, 1900, by Frederic Villiers

PROLOGUE

This is a book about the trade, the art, the business of war reporting and some of its greatest practitioners. But as the title might suggest, it is not only about reporting war but the parallel war relentlessly waged against correspondents by those who would prefer, and even demand, that only their own versions of events are published: the military, the establishment and the many and various fighting factions.

From the Crimea and the Somme to Iraq and Afghanistan, war reporters fight on many fronts. It has always been so.

The war reporters I have chosen have no special placing in the league of the Greats. They are simply my favourites, paragons if you like. You probably have your own listing.

❧

I went to my first war, or rather it came to me, when I was only three years old. My family lived in Essex, about three miles from the Thames, which meant we were directly under the Luftwaffe's nightly bombing runs into the London docks. Our nights were spent in an underground Anderson shelter at the bottom of the garden, dank and smelly and lit by a single paraffin lamp when there was paraffin, and by a single candle when there was not. My mother would sing Bing Crosby's 'You Are

My Sunshine' and pause and hold a finger to her lips as we listened to the distant explosions. When we dared, which was not often, we would peek out to see the orange pink of fires over London and the criss-crossing beams of searchlights, like immaculate white marble columns, as they probed the blackness for the invaders. In the park, less than half a mile away, the ack-ack guns, the anti-aircraft batteries, followed their beams, hoping to hit something all those thousands of feet up.

My mornings were spent with the other boys in the street collecting bomb shrapnel and shell splinters and, just the once, a jagged piece of grey-painted aluminium, part of a German bomber that had been hit by our guns. I still have it. One morning, as my mother was hanging out her washing, a Dornier flew over so low I swear I saw the Luftwaffe Iron Crosses on its wings.

In between, we children went to war with our little lead toy soldiers, the British painted khaki, fighting the enemy in grey, the garden our battlefield. Mounds of earth became our mini-fortresses as entire battalions were slaughtered. We Brits always won; that was the rule.

Then, like thousands of other children from the cities of Britain, I was suddenly without a home or a mother. That autumn morning in 1940 she took me to Paddington station, settled me in the carriage of my first train and tied a manila label around my neck with my name and registration number scrawled on it. With my gas mask on my lap and jam sandwiches in my jacket pocket, she left me without a hug or kiss goodbye. I saw only the back of her as she hurried away sprayed by the locomotive's steam; a mother, like so many, returning to an empty Anderson shelter and the lonely nights of fear, sans children, sans husband, sans everything. None of us cried. I seem to remember only laughter. We must have thought we were simply off on holiday.

I was an evacuee on my way to a farm in Somerset, one of the youngest in 'Operation Pied Piper', and it would be three years before I saw my mother again.

Many of us were returned home before the war ended and, for some, it was too soon. The bombing was less frequent but we were not safe, night or day. The air raid sirens were not silenced. In 1944 the Germans sent us something new, the V1 flying bomb; we nicknamed it the 'Doodlebug'. We could hear it coming, a low growl, growing louder until it was overhead. Then, as the last of its rocket fuel was burnt, silence. We held our breath for a minute or more, praying. Would it drop like a stone and hit us or glide to end others' lives? It was a hateful wait.

I remember our 'end of war' street party, the commotion and the banter and the painted banners strung across the lamp-posts. I did not know then what the initials V.E. meant except that they were making everybody happy and drunk. Within a month my father came back but not for long. He was a major in the Royal Engineers and had been one of the first to land in Normandy. Now he was part of what was called the C.C.G., the Control Commission of Germany, and he was in charge of repairing and regenerating a section of the Dortmund–Ems Canal. When he returned to Germany in the winter of 1946 we went with him, the first British family to arrive in Emden, Westphalia.

A nine-year-old English boy was suddenly in the country of the people who only six months before had been the feared and hated enemy. In the years that followed, he saw things that are indelible and remain the most prominent in a grown man's lockerful of memories. Emden, a city the size of Leicester or Canterbury, flattened by Allied bombing from horizon to horizon, so that not one building stood intact. That winter, the survivors lived among the ruins, the more fortunate in their cellars. There were makeshift crosses in the rubble and every so often, along the verges of the country roads, an upturned rifle, the barrel dug into the ground with a German helmet on the butt, which marked a soldier's shallow grave; signposts of the dead.

One day, my father was supervising the exhumation of the British dead who had been hastily buried in a mass grave. I cannot remember why I was with him; we must have been en route to somewhere else. He forbade me to leave the car but a small boy's curiosity edged me closer to a place to watch. It was the smell that overwhelmed me and I vomited then and for some days afterwards. The doctor said it was mild dysentery but my father knew it was not.

My boarding school, Prince Rupert in Wilhelmshaven for the children of servicemen, had been a training base for U-boat officers. The Royal Air Force had attacked and sunk every submarine in their pens and at lunchtimes we schoolboys, quite nonchalantly, watched Royal Navy divers, in their brass helmets and lead boots, bring up the bodies of those who had been trapped for so long inside their metal coffins.

A few childhood memories of war.

And war has remained with me all my life. Exactly thirty years ago, at the end of that very bloody conflict, I left the Falklands and did not expect ever to return.

I should have known better. How many times in over forty years of a reporting career have I said that about so many places only to be contradicted by events.

Returning to a war zone is the oddest mix of excitement and sadness, and I have been back to many. But nostalgia can be a very assorted package and in the Falklands it is especially so.

All the other wars I have covered have been wars in foreign places, other people's wars. But in 1982, in those ten weeks of a Falklands spring, I was reporting a war among my own people, British soldiers fighting on behalf of those who were defiantly, obstinately, British.

Last Christmas I went back to the Islands to take part in an ITV documentary to commemorate the thirtieth anniversary of the war. I found them in good health and booming and not at all fussed by the distant sound of rattling sabres.

Those of us who witnessed it, and those of us who have been privileged to return, do not doubt that the war had to be fought and we had to win it.

You will understand that a British war for a British correspondent remains a very special war and the Falklands a very special place.

Archibald Forbes, by Frederic Villiers

INTRODUCTION

'The worst moment in a war was my fear I would not be sent to it.'

I wrote that over twenty years ago when I had already gone to
nine of them. Now, as I hang up my boots, the final tally is
eighteen. The expectation of the sight and sound of war never
failed to exhilarate me. Risk spiced my life. But then I had the return
ticket, the paper promise to lift me, whenever I chose, away from the
killing fields to a safe haven.

There was only one response to that repeated question: why?
A self-deprecatory shrug of the shoulders and the simple and generally misunderstood one-liner – it was because I wanted to. I simply
could not resist the invitation and it was easily done because, except
for the once, it never occurred to me I would not come back. James
Cameron, my paragon, once wrote that it was against the rules to
have a war without him. I know the feeling well.

War reporters belong to an exclusive club of globetrotters. They
are issued a privileged passport to travel this world and witness
astonishing happenings. It is usually only when they are together that
they talk of their wars and even then warily. Their adventures seem so
unlikely in retrospect. Who else would believe them?

Is it machismo or masochism that encourages us so compulsively
and repeatedly to risk our lives? Probably both. There is no choice.

Having done it once, you have to do it again and few of us would have the cheek to deny that the chase becomes an end in itself. We are all slave to the same impulse a gambler must feel when his luck is running. To some it is like sex.

One of the greatest television combat cameramen, Tasmanian Neil Davies, was a good friend of mine. He spent more time covering the wars in Vietnam and Cambodia than anyone from any network. He was quite fearless, believing, as many of us did, that he was invincible.

He wrote these lines on the flyleaf of every working diary he kept in all his years in South East Asia:

> *Sound, sound the clarion, fill the fife!*
> *To all the sensual world proclaim.*
> *One crowded hour of glorious life*
> *Is worth an age without a name*

It says it all and that message was his daily mantra until the day he was killed by a stray bullet in an attempted coup in Bangkok.

War has glamour. You win no friends admitting it. Walter Cronkite, the doyen of American broadcast journalists, once wrote that there is nothing in the field of journalism more glamorous than being a war correspondent. He said the public stereotype them as handsome derring-do swashbucklers, dashing from one crisis to another in romantic criss-crossings, flamboyant, brave and exhilarated by danger.

Ernest Hemingway reported the Spanish Civil War and Jack London, reading reports of General Gordon's last stand in Khartoum, decided he too would become a war reporter for the thrills. In 1904 he travelled to Japan to cover the Russo-Japanese War with 'gorgeous conceptions'. Disillusioned, he quickly returned home and, like Hemingway, confined himself to novels.

The *New Yorker* once described war reporters as 'congeries of eccentrics and prima donnas, not so much serious as cynical'. Michael Herr wrote in his Vietnam masterpiece *Dispatches:*

> We have been called many names; war-junkies, thrill freaks, wound-seekers, ambulance-chasers, hero-worshippers, dope addicts, closet queens, ghouls, seditionists, traitors, career prostitutes, fiction writers, more nasty things than I can remember.

War is entertainment. Most people only know it courtesy of Hollywood. Actors play soldiers as heroes in simplified, formulaic scripts where the good guys beat the bad guys in the ultimate sacrifice, defending right against wrong, liberty against tyranny.

There is the iconic scene in Ford Coppola's *Apocalypse Now*. American helicopters laden with napalm, flown by junkies led by a mad colonel, playing Wagner's 'The Ride of the Valkyries' over loudspeakers, obliterate villages and all who were once alive in them. It crystallises not just the insanity of war but the glorious black romance of being part of such a mighty killing machine. It remains Hollywood's darkest vision yet in its continuing fascination with war and all its attendant horrors.

Correspondents belong to an association of Cassandras. We spend a career in the energetic hope that what we report will do good, that it can somehow change the world for the better. We travel from conflict to conflict, from one human misery to another and, like the cameramen and photographers who are our brave companions, we suffer from an overdose of everything. The world's woes are perverse and self-inflicted and in time we become saturated with them.

Yet we are supremely privileged. We have a seat in the spectator stands of great events, both witness and juror as history is being made. We write the first drafts.

It is an odd occupation, a war profiteer with death and destruction as the matter-of-fact reason for being there. It is difficult to catalogue the wars we have known and not begin to doubt their recall. The temptation to embellish is always at the shoulder and sometimes difficult to resist.

Who would believe how many wars this world has lived through in one lifetime? Two World Wars are indelibly recorded. We are coming to terms with the bloody aftermath of the Iraqi invasion and the futility of taming Afghanistan. Television's catalogue of events in the so-called Arab Spring is still vivid. But who remembers the others, the little wars?

Can you recall the starving, emaciated face of Biafra? The Palestinian grenade rolling down the aisle of a Pan Am jet? The pits full of rotting corpses on the birthday of Bangladesh? The faceless napalmed babies of Vietnam?

Do you remember Idi Amin's Uganda, the House of Death in the Congo, the cannibals of Cambodia, the decapitated nuns in Rhodesia, the blacks bleeding red in Soweto? Cyprus and war, Israel and war, Nicaragua, El Salvador, Sri Lanka, Algeria. War on war.

War reporters, then as now, confess to inner conflicts. How do we mark the foggy line between sincerity and technique, the imperative from the glib, a line so fragile that one can tread all over it in those anxious minutes to a tight deadline, or a ringing phone, a nagging producer, a thirst? How do we explain or excuse that final decision on what to report and what not to?

James Cameron wrote that never in his life had he made any claim to be an objective journalist, if objectivity meant the uncritical presentation of wrong or foolish events. To him it was dispassionate reporting, cold-blooded, bystander journalism. His trademark was to show emotion, humanity, disgust, despair, impotence.

It has been called the journalism of the repressive self-righteous. But veterans of war will ask how else can you respond, surrounded by the carnage of a mortar attack on a crowded Sarajevo market place or walking through hospital wards full of mutilated crying children in Rwanda? Is it possible to be anything but subjective in war?

There are newspaper reporters with long-established reputations, well known for their emotional writing of war and their dedication to a cause. They break the taboos of journalistic impartiality, writing what they see without the least restraint, and they do not spare their readers the horror in the detail: soldiers do not die without bleeding, anti-personnel mines take away their genitals, mortar shrapnel opens up the stomachs of pregnant mothers. Unlike so much television news, their reports are printed unfiltered, unsanitised.

This is one account by Robert Fisk of the massacre by Christian militia of Palestinian refugees at the Chatila camp in Lebanon in 1982:

> They were everywhere, in the road, in laneways, in backyards, beneath crumpled masonry and across the tops of garbage tips. Blood was still wet. When we had seen a hundred bodies, we stopped counting the corpses, women, young men, children, babies and grandparents, lying together in lazy and terrible profusion where they had been knifed or machine-gunned down. A child lay on the roadway like a discarded flower, her white dress stained with mud and dust, the back of her head had been blown off by a bullet fired into her brain.

And this from John Pilger describing the Veterans' March in Washington in 1971, at the height of the Vietnam War:

> Never before in this country have young soldiers marched in protest against a war they themselves have fought and is still going on. They have stopped Mr and Mrs America in the street and told them what they did, about the gore and the atrocities, a battalion of shuffling stick figures.
>
> A former quartermaster, shouting through a loud hailer, described to rush hour shoppers how he helped raze a Vietnamese village.

'Listen to this friends ... the whole village was burning but the spotter planes reported people fleeing across open fields, so we switched to fragmentation shells and began to chop them up. Then we began firing phosphorus shells and watched them burn.'

They belong to what is often called 'attachment journalism', what one critic of it eloquently, if cynically, describes as the journalism of 'sanctimonious moral perfectionism motivated by a social conscience that too often overwhelms'. They are accused of being flagrantly partisan, anti all wars, each intent on persuading readers that his or her opinion should be theirs too. They do not deny it. It remains their conviction that absolutely nothing in the tide of human affairs cannot be explained, given time and enough column inches; that war ends in defeat and the sure knowledge that more horror will follow. It is no secret.

In Britain, at the start of nationwide broadcasting in the 1920s, there were no rules governing impartiality. There was no need. BBC radio was funded at the discretion of the government and generally did its bidding. Reporters addressed politicians as 'Sir' and no one ever dared interrupt a minister in full flow however economical he was with the truth.

Only in 1955, with the birth of commercial television, did impartiality become a legal requirement. Impartiality meant balance. Tip the scales and you were in trouble and even the most scrupulous reporters, attempting that balancing act, fell foul.

In August 1965, the BBC's Washington correspondent Charles Wheeler reported the rioting in the Watts district of Los Angeles. It followed the arrest of a black man suspected of drink-driving and provoked some of the worst racial violence in modern American history. It lasted six days, fourteen thousand police and National Guardsmen were involved and martial law was declared.

Wheeler's commentaries in that week were condemned by

sections of both the American and British media. He was accused of bias, of justifying the violence of the black rioters and of allowing his personal opinion to colour his reports.

In fact, all he had done was to remind his viewers of why black Americans felt such hostility to the white man's law and its enforcers and why violence might indeed be their only redress. To his critics, Wheeler had crossed the line and it was unforgivable.

In 1968, during the Nigerian Civil War, Frederick Forsyth was reporting from Biafra for BBC television. Ignoring warnings and complaints from his editorial masters that his commentaries were blatantly biased towards the Biafrans, he was finally ordered back to London and sacked. Months later he returned to Biafra in full military uniform to act as its public relations officer.

Another BBC television veteran, Martin Bell, was publicly accused of slanting his commentaries during the Bosnian War in favour of direct military intervention by America as a way of ending it. He later admitted he had become emotionally involved in the conflict to such an extent that it excused his biased stance and was unrepentant.

ITN's Sandy Gall experienced much the same, reporting the war in Afghanistan during the Soviet invasion. He too became an emotional casualty. Despite his insistence that he had not deliberately favoured the British-backed mujahideen leader Ahmed Masud in his commentaries and that he had not transgressed the rule of impartiality, he was later on record admitting that Masud was an honourable man and his rival 'a murdering thug'.

Global television and the World Wide Web have merged to undermine the entire principle of impartiality. The recently entitled 'social media' enables anyone with a camera or mobile phone to record a news event as seen from their own perspective and submit it to any news channel around the world. Given competitive demands, most news organisations, including the BBC, invite them to do so.

The Internet has provided us with spectacular methods of collecting and consuming news. Speed is once again more important than integrity and impartiality less of an issue. In newspapers, factual news is losing column inches to the opinion of celebrity columnists. Journalists have become bloggers on their days off. We casually accept information from anonymous contributors whose reputations are unknown, whose reliability is untested and of whose beliefs and allegiances we know nothing. And yet our media barons and their editors rubber-stamp them and ask us to believe them.

The first principle of war reporting is that the public's right to know must always be subordinate to the soldier's right to live. A correspondent should not presume to be an apostle of the absolute, to freely publish what he knows. The military consider that to be an incontrovertible truth. They have a point.

But it is an unsavoury fact that people will accept lies more readily than truth and in war there is an unlimited supply of lies. The manipulated millions are easily aroused or soothed by lies, something Mr Goebbels and his master knew to their advantage.

There is a popular myth that journalism is all about getting it either right or wrong. But as Max Hastings of the *Evening Standard* wrote at the time of the Falklands War:

> You know very well that in fact what you are actually trying to do is have a sort of stab at the truth, in which case if you are getting it right about half the time you are doing rather well. In war that drops to about thirty per cent.

The military's ideal war reporter, and this is true of the military worldwide, is one who writes what he has been told, questions nothing and can be cajoled into writing what he knows not to be true. It is also considered to be the reporter's first duty to support the war effort.

In 1956, at the time of the attempted invasion of the Suez Canal, the Ministry of Defence printed a booklet that was given to each of the accredited war reporters who were to accompany the British invasion forces. Twenty-six years later, that very same booklet, unaltered, was handed to every one of the correspondents who went to the Falklands in 1982. It began:

> The essence of successful warfare is secrecy; the essence of successful journalism is publicity. No official regulation can bridge the gap between the two. A satisfactory liaison calls for complete frankness on the one hand and loyal discretion on the other and mutual cooperation in the task of leading and steadying public opinion in times of national stress or crisis.

Few journalists then or now would consider it a duty or even a priority to lead or steady public opinion in a time of national stress or crisis. Max Hastings, however, swum against the tide. The Falklands was his twelfth war but it was, like many of us there, his first alongside British troops in a British campaign. Because of it, he considered it his patriotic duty, when necessary, to distort the facts to hide the truth.

> In the task of leading and steadying … was I deliberately deceitful, yes! The night the *Atlantic Conveyor* and *Coventry* were sunk, morale on the beachhead was low. But I continued to file stories about how well the build up was going, writing more optimistically than I knew it to be. I wouldn't have wanted to have filed a dispatch that was likely to the give the Argentineans any hope or comfort.

Hastings knew he was ditching all the rules in order to 'aid and abet' the British invasion. He had become, by his own admission, something of a propagandist. Hastings suffered no self-delusions then and has been unrepentant since.

I sought to convey the impression that it was all going splendidly well. The Argies had taken some pretty severe losses themselves and if they had received a second-hand dispatch from one of us on the beachhead saying we were in real trouble it might have made them feel it was worth another crack. I knowingly distorted the feeling as I knew it to be.

Hastings wore a Territorial Officer's battle tunic once he was ashore and even pinned up a daily copy of his dispatches wherever he could, *pour encourager les autres*. It did boost troop morale and it certainly did him no harm with his military minders.

David Norris of the *Daily Mail* was another who put patriotism above all:

> I can honestly say that I did not write a single word that would have been against the British operation. I felt I had to do that. It was my country at war. I had no choice.

It was contrary to professional ethics but it comforted his editor. From the very moment the British armada sailed for the South Atlantic, jingoism was the unwavering theme of the *Daily Mail*'s Falklands coverage.

We have all, at some time or some place, witnessed bizarre censorship. During the war in South Vietnam, an American military press information officer gave a daily briefing in Saigon to the collected international correspondents. He would recite a list of the communist dead, the kill ratio and American successes. He did not believe them and neither did the press corps. We called them 'The Five o'Clock Follies'. They were entertaining and an outrage to our intelligence.

During the Indo-Pakistan War in 1971, those of us who were holed up during the siege of Dacca, including Don Wise, Clare Hollingworth,

Gavin Young and John Humphrys, were briefed by a Pakistani officer who, with some passion, told us what he would have us believe was happening in the war. He cited victories that had never happened and such sessions were followed by our polite but mischievous enquiries.

> Question: You say you killed five hundred Indians today. How is it you have no dead?
> Answer: In our army we believe no soldier dies in battle. He goes straight to paradise.
> Question: Can he still shoot Indians from paradise?
> Question: The Indians claim they have established a bridgehead at the Ganges. Is this true?
> Answer: There is no bridge there so how can there be a bridgehead?

The elegant Donald Wise immortalised this nonsense with the phrase: 'I feel I am shovelling fog into a bucket.'

In the century and a half since William Russell reported the Crimea War, the contradictory principles of the military and the war reporter have set them apart and they will remain so. Since the Falklands, when correspondents were handed that same unaltered Suez booklet, many attempts have been made to reconcile the irreconcilable. In recent times millions of pounds of taxpayers' money has been spent on media training where all three Services can meet the press in congenial seminars sometimes beguilingly entitled 'Let's get to know each other'.

But the military's real focus has been to discover how we work, not how we can work together. From the beginning of the Bosnian War in 1992, the British and American military introduced something new into their media relations, something their political masters had been successfully doing for some time. Spin had become censorship by omission.

British soldiers in Bosnia were discouraged from talking to the press. But they were given a pamphlet instructing them how to handle reporters just in case we caught them by surprise. They were to remember that:

The media are not necessarily hostile.
Handled well, they will promote the unit's image.
Poorly treated the opposite applies.
Things unsaid are rarely regretted.

If he was in any doubt, an anxious soldier was to make the following statement and he was to learn it by heart: 'We are here to help supplies get through to those in need. We do not support any side. That's not our job.'

Little of any real significance in the relationship between the two opposing sides has changed. Nor, given the intransigence that exists, can there be change in any radical way. Such a compromise has obvious narrow limits.

The least subtle of all the military's manipulation of the international media in recent years is the introduction of the 'embedded' strategy. Unsubtle because it has always been so. It is simply in a new disguise. Under it, reporters, photographers, television crews, all become an integral part of a military unit, be it a platoon, a squadron or a ship. They are kitted out in full military gear and given 'unprecedented' freedom to witness events as they unroll, to see what they want to see unhampered and write what they see uncensored. Such is the theory.

The strategy outlaws the lone maverick reporter who can be dangerously disruptive. Instead the press is herded into one pen. It was developed much more extensively in the Gulf Wars and news organisations, especially the American television networks, were delighted with live coverage of their correspondents seemingly in the line of fire right on the front line.

It was only afterwards that they realised that their men had effectively been held captive. Editorial post mortems revealed it was a reversal of what they had been promised. They had been taken where the military wanted them to go, to see what the military wanted them to see in order that they wrote what the military wanted them to write. Some reporters did try to re-route themselves, to break free but once embedded there was seldom a way out. There was almost total control of movement and information and both the military and the political establishment were very satisfied with themselves.

The sheer numbers that make up the modern press corps and the new technology (mobile phone, BlackBerry, iPod and the lightweight wireless laptop) they carry as their essential hand luggage promise to free the press from the military's stranglehold. The DBS (direct broadcasting satellites) are each capable of carrying twelve television channels enabling multiple live pictures to be transmitted from one side of the globe to the other twenty-four hours a day. High frequency radio transmitters can bypass censorship and receivers can monitor insecure military communications.

All this has given war reporters the ability to transmit directly to their news desks unhindered. That is unless or until governments outlaw it or the military find ways to disrupt it.

Those academics who choose to monitor the course of journalism believe we are witnessing the fast erosion of the kind of war reporting we took for granted even ten years ago, a generation gap marking the end of a tradition.

No one can deny that reportage is now confronted with accelerating commercial and political restraints, the budgets, the insurance premiums, the cost of air travel, the cunning of the spin doctors, the unchanging self-protective military censorship, the public sector PR barrage of misinformation, the Special Interests. Editors can seldom afford to send their correspondents or their television crews to far-away places as they once did, on a hunch, without hesitation. Except for war or some other major event or catastrophe, they have no option but to accept this state of affairs tamely and too often rely instead on second-hand inputs from second-rate news agencies who may well be in the pay or in fear of their government or the warring factions.

People get to know what war looks like from their television screens. They learn to trust those familiar faces and the well-honed reputations earned after years of covering conflicts. Many of the stars of yesteryear learnt their trade in newspapers or from the disciplines in news agencies like Reuters, Associated Press and UPI. Gone are those long and thorough apprenticeships. Now there are short cuts through broadcast journalism degree courses and what passes as media studies.

Unlike the print journalist, today's television reporters work under the restrictions of a British law that demands they will not offer opinion or the mildest comment on air lest it be interpreted as bias. The compliance lawyers are the latest, severest and best-paid censors and they pretend to be on our side. Too many of the current generation of television reporters see their job in the simplest terms: to report the facts, to report a war as if it was a crime story and to fit words to pictures as economically as possible in their allotted bulletin slot. They do it as well and as honestly as such legal and editorial strictures permit. They struggle with new technology, their reports are measured in seconds and they must succumb to the final tyranny of the round-the-clock news agenda.

They are frequently caricatured as editorial eunuchs playing theatrical bit parts, dressed in helmets and customised Kevlar flak jackets, standing on top of hotel roofs, reciting lines as if they believed them, reporting events they themselves have not witnessed, repeating hearsay, dependent on the technology that promotes them and held hostage by the propaganda of the side they report from. They do their best to fill a vacuum. But television news has an insatiable appetite and it nowadays looks very lean.

There was a time when carrying a press card or having PRESS scrawled across your car would, in most circumstances, be some guarantee of safe conduct. You were, after all, a non-combatant, on nobody's side, a spectator. The shrapnel was not meant for you. You also fondly believed that survival anyway was a fluke, which enabled you to live with colossal and comforting fatalism, like the Marines in Vietnam who boasted that they only worried about the bullet with their name on it. Those with more battle experience would instead warn them to be wary of the one simply inscribed 'To whom it may concern!'

In today's wars the words 'PRESS' or 'PRESS-TV' are more likely to kill you. At St Bride's in the City of London there is a memorial to journalists who have lost their lives in war zones. There is a similar memorial in Arlington Cemetery, Virginia, erected by the Freedom Forum. Cut into its stone are the names of over nine hundred international reporters killed doing their job. More ominous is the large empty space waiting to be filled.

In the last three years alone, over two hundred reporters and cameramen have been killed covering conflicts worldwide. For those who live within a war, those whose homes and families are in war zones, survival can often mean living like an anonymous fugitive. They know well enough that honest reporting can alienate the correspondent on one side in the conflict from the other. They live under constant threat, their entire existence often defined by their home, their newsroom, and travel between the two. The risks are greater, the rewards less. Now they are shooting the messenger.

War reporters fight on many fronts. Top priority is to survive the present one in readiness for the next. Then, when it is all over, to be able to erase from the memory all that should be forgotten and finally draw the curtain tight.

After the day's work: British ambulance cars on their way to Boulogne, 1915, by Frederic Villiers

ONE

THEN AND NOW

Who is the war reporter? Who qualifies? How many wars must he or she have covered before gaining entry to that exclusive club of privileged globetrotters?

Was Herodotus the first? The Greek historian born two and a half thousand years ago, who travelled extensively through Europe and recorded what he saw in *The Histories*, considered one of the seminal works in Western literature? Cicero claimed him as the 'Father of History'. His graphic, often eyewitness, reports of the continuing wars between the Persians and the Greeks may well qualify him as the world's first war correspondent.

He was present at the Battle of Marathon, one of history's most famous military engagements and one of the earliest to be recorded. He reported it thus:

> So when the battle was set in array, the Athenians charged, the distance between the two armies was little short of two furlongs. The Persians saw them coming on at speed, made ready to receive them, although it seemed to them that the Athenians were bereft of their senses and bent upon their own destruction, a mere handful of men without either horsemen or archers. But the Athenians fell upon them and fought in a manner worthy of being reported.

Celebrating the Greek victory, he records that the Greeks lost some two hundred men, the Persians over six thousand. Being a country-man of the winning side his statistics are understandably questionable.

According to legend, a messenger was sent from the battlefield to carry news of the victory to Athens. His name was Pheidippides and having run the twenty-six miles non-stop in three hours, made the announcement and promptly fell down dead from exhaustion. The present day marathon of that distance continues to celebrate his feat.

Towards the end of his life Herodotus wrote words that have reso-nated through the ages of war to this day. They are the consummate epitaph for all wars, for those who fight and die in them and for those who suffer their loss.

In peace, sons bury their fathers
In war, fathers bury their sons.

To enter the lion's den, to go where no other reporter has dared go, to have the ingenuity as well as the courage to seek out an interview with a war-crazed general, a ruthless dictator, a political tyrant and survive to tell the story would rate as a scoop in any language of any newsroom today.

The Greek writer Priscus did just that in 448 AD. He sought out and had dinner with Attila the Hun.

Priscus followed the long and arduous path of Attila's armies as they marched and plundered from Constantinople to Scythia, a terri-tory the Huns had just conquered in the lower Danube. Finally he found and entered their fortified compound. He waited anxiously until he was granted the first recorded interview with Attila. He describes seeing him for the first time.

He came forth with a dignified strut, looking left and right, and stood in front of his house. Many persons came up to be given his judgement and he received ambassadors of barbarous peoples.

2

I was invited to a banquet at three o'clock and when the hour arrived I stood in the threshold of the hall in the presence of Attila. The cupbearers gave us cup, according to the custom, so that we might pray before we sat down.

Attila ate nothing but meat on a wooden trencher and his cup was of wood while the guests were given goblets of gold and silver. He showed himself temperate, his dress quite simple, affecting only to be clean. The sword he carried at his side, the ratchets of his shoes, the bridle of his horse were not adorned, like those of the others, with gold or gems or anything costly.

As evening fell, torches were lit and two barbarians came forward in front of Attila and sang songs celebrating his victories and deeds of valour.

Bartholomé de las Casas was among the Spanish Conquistadors who, in the early sixteenth century, invaded and colonised in what we know today as the West Indies. His father had sailed with Columbus and the family had settled in Cuba.

In his mid-thirties, sickened by the barbarity of his fellow countrymen towards the Taino and Arawak Indians, las Casas became a priest. He wrote at length about what he saw and he became the war reporter of his age. His descriptions of the atrocities were relayed back to the Spanish King Charles V.

The Spaniards entered villages with their horses and spears, sparing neither children nor the women, nor the old. They ripped open their bellies and cut them to pieces as if they were slaughtering lambs. They made bets with each other over who could thrust a sword into a man's middle or who could cut off a head with one stroke. They took the little ones by their heels and crushed their heads against the cliffs.

I saw four native chiefs roasted and broiled upon a makeshift grill.

They cried pitifully and it troubled the captain so he ordered them to be strangled.

I vouch that some six thousand children have died of exhaustion and starvation working as slaves in the gold mines.

I have all these things seen and others infinite by men who are empty of all pity, enemies of mankind. I saw there so much cruelties that never any man living either have or shall see the like.

In the first ten years of the Spanish occupation of the islands, an estimated ten million Taino and Arawak Indians were slaughtered. By the time Bartholomé's repeated entreaties to the Spanish throne succeeded in bringing in new laws to protect them, it was already too late. They were all but extinct.

The word genocide had not been invented then but how familiar las Casas's description is to those of us who, five hundred years on, witnessed the Hutu genocide of the Tutsis in Rwanda, or those reporters who entered the Palestinian refugee camps at Chabra and Chatila in the aftermath of the massacre by the Lebanese Christian militia. Or Dachau. Or Pol Pot's Killing Fields, or any of the roll call of atrocities that have been repeated in our own lifetime.

One of the earliest known eyewitness accounts of an historical event in England was an undated pamphlet reporting the Battle of Flodden in 1513. It was signed by one Richard Faques.

Henry Crabb Robinson claimed to be the first British war reporter. He was a well-travelled diarist and his friends included Goethe, Schiller, Lamb, Coleridge and Wordsworth. On his journeys through Europe as a young man, he had sent occasional articles to the London *Times* and so impressed was the editor that, in 1807, he was sent to report the Napoleonic campaigns along the Elbe. His reports made impressive reading until it became evident that Crabb had not visited any of the battlefields.

In the Peninsular War he witnessed Sir John Moore's victory at

Corunna and again he was complimented on his dispatches. It was later revealed that he had not personally witnessed it but had compiled his reports from hearsay, articles in local newspapers and invention. He returned to London quite expecting to be offered a regular post on the *Times* but by then his deceptions were known by his editor and he was told that 'he did not have the talent or training to be on the staff'. Instead, he became a barrister in the Middle Temple and was a founder member of the Athenaeum Club and University College, London.

The first newspaper correspondent to write his report from the scene of a battle was Charles Guneison for the *Morning Post* during the Spanish Civil War in 1835.

The war reporter came of age with the invention of the telegraph in 1843. Eighteen years later it was used for the first time in a major conflict with the outbreak of the American Civil War. Reporters were able to transmit their stories from the front line to the front page on the same day.

At the outbreak of hostilities between the Union and the Confederates in 1861, the London *Times* sent William Russell to report it. He did not stay long. He 'had no heart for it'. He did not disguise his sympathies for the North and his dispatches did not sit well with the newspaper's pro-Southern editorial line. Professionally he could not or would not adapt to the telegraph. It speeded up communication and therefore shortened deadlines, which did not suit his style of reporting the detailed analysis of military strategy. He returned to London with his reputation tarnished, which delighted the British military establishment, who would never forgive him for his critical reports from the Crimea.

The only other journalist worthy of replacing him was the Irish correspondent Edwin Godkin, who had reported the Crimea War for the London *Daily News*. He had since emigrated to America to publish *The Nation* but he was suffering a long illness and did not fully recover until the war was almost over.

Russell and Godkin had both become journalistic icons as a result of their reporting from the Crimea. That neither were now available at such a critical time created a vacuum.

The American Civil War offered great opportunity for stardom but there were few British reporters talented enough to grab it. Those who did go were voted 'infantile, ignorant, dishonest, inflammatory, inaccurate, unethical and partisan'. Almost to a man, they were consistently hostile to the North, which in turn seriously affected Britain's later relationship with the later reconciled United States. The British reporter, like his editor and proprietor, failed to recognise the historical momentum of what was happening on the far side of the Atlantic and their dismal coverage of it reflected this.

The American public's appetite for news of the war was insatiable and new newspapers opened every day, some consisting only of one side of a page. Upwards of five hundred home-based correspondents covered the war on the Union side. The Confederates were less well served and, as the war progressed and the South retreated, most of their newspapers were destroyed or closed. The *Memphis Appeal*, the *Chattanooga Rebel* and the *Stars and Stripes* followed the army columns with their printing presses in wagons and, as they ran out of newsprint, published on the blank side of wallpaper.

But the new technology did nothing to improve accuracy. In the race to file first, reporters on both sides were notorious for sending stories that were all too often make-believe. This was the New World's first war and like all newcomers to the battlefield they were fired by its excitement and the glamour of seeing one's name splashed across the front page. It was laissez-faire journalism, motivated by ambition, sensationalism and jingoism. They had no problem describing defeat as victory and vice versa, reporting battles that had not taken place, towns invaded by armies that had yet to reach them. There were few independent observers to contradict them. Their stories were eagerly devoured and the telegraph daily brought them congratulations from their editors.

Wilbur Storey, editor of the *Chicago Times*, even famously ordered his reporters at the front to 'telegraph fully all the news you can get and when there is none, send rumours'.

There is the story of one reporter who, trying to interview a mortally wounded soldier, demanded he kept himself alive until the interview was finished. The soldier was told that his dying words would 'be published in the influential and widely-read journal that I represent'.

The advent of the telegraphed dispatch gave rise to two famous newspaper by-lines: *By telegraph*, signalling immediacy, urgency, and *From our own correspondent*, giving the story the appearance of being an exclusive, whether it was or not.

Given the freedom correspondents had to roam the battlefields at will and their ability to write whatever pleased them, even if it might be of some strategic use to the other side, it should not have surprised them that the military would sooner or later try to control them. Or at least contain them.

Out of the antagonism that quickly developed between the two – the reporter whose business it was to fill a newspaper and the generals who job it was to win a war – came censorship. It has ever since been the albatross hanging around the reporter's neck.

General Sherman made no secret of his hatred of the press and did his best to keep them away from his soldiers. He publicly called them 'dirty scribblers who have the impudence of Satan and the day will come when the press must surrender some portion of its freedom or perish in the wreckage with the rest of us'.

He issued a directive that any war reporter who wrote anything that might be of use to the enemy would be treated as a spy and in Sherman's army, spies were summarily shot. One such unfortunate accused of espionage was William Swinton of the *New York Times*. He was saved from the firing squad by the last-minute intervention of General Grant.

The Union government prosecuted newspaper proprietors who printed information that, in its opinion, compromised military security. President Lincoln even ordered the closure of the *Chicago Times* for simply publishing a leader article criticising him. As the war progressed, reporters found themselves ever more confined. Censorship had now become a military priority. All dispatches had first to be read and anything deemed in the least sensitive or contrary to the military's own interpretation of events was erased. Any correspondent who had written unflattering stories, true or not, was banned from the front and any breach of the regulations was considered a criminal act and dealt with accordingly. Even private letters home were scrutinised in case the writer was trying to bypass the censor's red marker.

Given an increasingly hostile press and a readership egged on by the newspaper proprietors, the military finally conceded that there had to be some compromise. Sherman, with his own career in mind, said: 'So greedy are the populace for war news that it is doubtful that any commander can exclude all reporters without bringing down on himself a clamour that may imperil his own safety.'

But it was the politicians who effectively ended the worst journalistic excesses. Lincoln introduced strict new libel laws with crippling penalties for any breach of them. As a consequence, reporters, their editors and the men who owned the newspapers quickly became more circumspect. For self-preservation, self-censorship became the rule of the day.

But it was not to last. When Americans had stopped fighting Americans in 1865, the old rules no longer applied. In 1898, they went to war with a foreign enemy and it was back to a journalistic free-for-all.

The Spanish–American War introduced a new and more sinister way of sensationalising a conflict and another name was added to the media's vocabulary: the 'Yellow Press'. William Randolph Hearst was crowned its father.

He was the multi-millionaire owner of the New York *Morning Journal*, immortalised by Orson Welles in his film *Citizen Kane*. He had ruthlessly bought out or neutralised all but one of the opposition. His only remaining competitor was Joseph Pulitzer, owner of *The World*.

These two press barons, fighting their own circulation war, together plunged America into the conflict against Spain for control of Cuba. Never in the history of war reporting was the adage 'The pen is mightier than the sword' so aptly as with Hearst's *Journal* and Pulitzer's *World*.

Hearst himself accompanied the initial American invasion force and filed sober, accurate reports. But when he returned he decided that simply reporting the facts was not enough to sell newspapers. He reckoned that his readers wanted something extra: for truth to inter-mingle with untruths, for actuality to be spiced with dramatic fiction. It worked spectacularly and has done so ever since, the world over.

He ordered his staff to write stories that had no basis in truth whatsoever. Headlines splashed imaginary reports of Spanish concentration camps, of American civilians tortured, of cannibalism by Spanish soldiers, atrocities that might well have been copied from the priest Bartholomé's sixteenth-century reports. It is said that it was Hearst who first decreed: 'Never let the facts get in the way of a good story.'

He hired the most talented artists to draw front-page pictures, dramatic depictions of the war and its carnage that were entirely of the illustrator's own imagination. One front page featured a nude surrounded by Spanish soldiers. The caption beneath said that the woman, an American, had been strip-searched by the men. It enraged America as no other front page had ever done before but it later transpired that no American woman had ever been treated that way. It mattered not and Hearst promoted the man who drew the picture.

He sent his chief illustrator to Havana to capture 'dramatic images'. Some days later the man cabled him to say that he could find no war. Hearst replied:

Remain. You furnish the pictures. I will furnish the war.

The strategy paid off. Within a year, circulation of the *Journal* had quadrupled. So jubilant was Hearst that at the end of that year and with the American forces clearly winning, he published the headline: 'HOW DO YOU LIKE THE JOURNAL'S WAR?'

For good reason, it was known as the journalists' war. Unlike the restrictions imposed in the American Civil War, reporters were pampered by military commanders who had come of age. They knew how important newspapers were in maintaining public support in the winning of the war.

Reporters were allowed freedom of movement and similarly freedom to write how they pleased. If occasionally some were considered too reckless, a local commander might impose his own censorship but in a less obvious way, like re-routing the reporter's dispatches by the longest telegraphic route so that, by the time they reached the news desks, the story was already history.

If there was criticism it came from where it mattered least to the newspaper editors: from academia and the intellectual elite. They accused reporters of feeding on popular myths, of exaggerating minor events as hugely significant and 'seeing an outbreak in every breeze and a bloody encounter in every rustling bough'.

No one was listening, least of all the war correspondents themselves. Their cavalier style of reporting, the drama of their self-congratulatory tales of derring-do at a front line, which was often miles from the actual fighting, made them famous, coast to coast. Impartial objectivity had yet to become a guiding principle. In the eyes of the readers, the war reporter had become a glamorous adventurer and as much a brave hero as the soldiers he was writing about.

The age of the 'Yellow Press' had arrived and it got its name from a strip cartoon called 'The Yellow Kid' in Joseph Pulitzer's *World*. There is some irony in the fact that he, who like his competitor Hearst had done so much to debase journalism, should later establish the Pulitzer Prize, still awarded annually for journalistic excellence!

The Second Boer War in 1899 was the first 'media war', the first major conflict covered by what is nowadays termed the mass media. The *Morning Post* sent Winston Churchill. There was no indication then or later that he ever had any intention of making journalism a career. What attracted him was the adventure, the excitement that war offered. In 1895, only twenty-one years old and a lieutenant in the 4th Queen's Own Hussars, he took leave on the pretext of holidaying in the West Indies. In fact he went to Cuba for a dual purpose, to see combat and observe the tactics of the Spanish army and to report the war for the *Daily Telegraph*. In a letter to his mother from Havana he wrote: 'It's better making the news than taking it ... to be an actor rather than the critic. It is an adventure ... to begin with it's a toy, an amusement. Then it becomes your mistress and finally your tyrant.'

In one of his first dispatches to the *Daily Telegraph* he describes his first experience under fire as the Spanish General Valdez attacked Cuban rebels:

> The General in a white and gold uniform riding a grey horse drew a great deal of fire upon us and I heard enough bullets whistle and hum past to satisfy me for some time to come. We rode right up to within five hundred yards of the enemy and there we waited until the fire of the Spanish infantry drove them from their position. We had great luck in not losing more than we did.

In a second article, sent to the *Saturday Review* in March 1896, he was contemptuous of the rebel army, saying that if they ever came to power:

> They would be corrupt, capricious, unstable. Revolutions would become periodic, property insecure, equity unknown. Their army consists of coloured men, they neither fight bravely nor use their weapons effectively. They cannot win a single battle or hold a single town. They are an undisciplined rabble.

He was fiercely criticised for his failure to report the war impartially. But he was young, it was his first war as well as his first assignment as a war reporter. His youth, inexperience and family background might excuse his naïve explanation at the time that being under fire with the Spanish on his twenty-first birthday and roughing it with people who provided him with food, shelter and safety bred a comradeship that made objective reporting near impossible. He was to apologise later, leaving the most important sentence as a practising journalist to the last:

> I reproach myself for having reported a little uncandidly and perhaps done injustice to the insurgents. I rather tried to make out a case for Spain. It was politic and did not expose me to the charge of being ungrateful to my hosts. What I wrote did not shake thrones or unheave empires but the importance of principles does not depend upon the importance of what involves them.

Just over forty years later, Churchill tried to dissuade his son from going to the Spanish Civil War as a correspondent for the *Daily Mail*. He reminded him of his own experiences and how difficult it would be to write objectively about a war when you were confined to one side of it.

Churchill had by now decided he would leave the army. His earnings from the *Daily Telegraph* were five times what he had been paid for his three years as a lieutenant on fourteen shillings a day. The *Morning Post* had paid him £300 for his dispatches from the Sudan, including his eyewitness account of the Battle of Omdurman and its famous cavalry charge. His occasional unsigned letters to various newspapers sent from India's north-west, where he was attached to the 7th Lancers, earned him three times his daily army pay.

Once back in England, he wrote a weekly article, 'Letter from London', for the American periodical *Pioneer*, who paid him £3 for each of them. Then, with the outbreak of the Second Boer War in 1898, Oliver Borthwick, editor of the *Morning Post*, offered him a contract as senior foreign correspondent, all expenses paid, for £250 a month, the highest of any senior British reporter. Soon after, he joined the *Dunottar Castle* bound for South Africa. He took with him what he considered to be essential for the hazardous assignment ahead, items supplied by his favourite wine merchant, Rudolph Payne and Sons of St James's. The invoice is dated 6 October 1899:

6 bottles Vin d'Ay Sec.
18 bottles St Emilion.
6 bottles light Port.
6 bottles French Vermouth.
18 bottles Scotch Whisky (10 years old).
6 bottles Very Old Eau de Vie.
12 bottles Rose's Cordial Lime Juice.

His first assignment was almost his last. On his arrival in Durban, he boarded an armoured train carrying troops to Ladysmith. But the Boers now controlled the line and just as the train was leaving Chievely it was ambushed. He described it in one of his most graphic war reports:

A huge white ball of smoke sprang into being only a few feet above my head. It was shrapnel, the first I had ever seen and very nearly the last. The steel sides of the truck tanged with the patter of bullets. Then suddenly there was a tremendous shock and the train travelling at forty miles an hour was thrown off the rails and I could see scores of figures running forward and throwing themselves down on the grass from which came accurate and heavy fire. It was continuous and there mingled with the rifles the bang of field guns and the near explosion of their shells.

Another shrapnel burst nearby and the train driver ran from his cab, his face cut open by shell splinters streaming with blood. He was dazed and it looked as if all hope of escape was cut off as only he knew the machinery. So I told him that no man was hit twice in a day, that a wounded man who continued to do his duty was always rewarded for his distinguished gallantry and that he might never have the chance again. On this he pulled himself together, wiped the blood from his face, climbed back into the cab and thereafter obeyed every order I gave him.

Some hours later, Churchill, surrounded by Boers, surrendered, no doubt encouraged by Napoleon's advice that when one is alone and unarmed a surrender may be pardoned. His dramatic escape from the Boers soon after was reported in the world's newspapers:

> Lieutenant Churchill managed to slip away from his guards at night by scaling the wall. He boarded a train which ran from Pretoria to Delagoa Bay just as it was moving from the platform and concealed himself under coal sacks. A close search was made but he was not discovered. For several days he lived simply on chocolate.

On his return to England he was feted as a national hero but his career as a war reporter was finally at an end.

In 1897 Frederic Villiers, a celebrated British war artist, was the first to take a film camera to war in the brief campaign between Greece and Turkey. The following year he mounted his tripod on one of Lord Kitchener's gunships sailing up the Nile for the relief of Khartoum. As the guns fired the camera went overboard and the film was ruined. But Villiers's attempt to record the war on celluloid heralded a new era of war reporting.

During the Spanish–American War in 1898, the Edison Company claimed to have filmed the funeral procession of the victims of the American ship *Maine* that had been sunk by the Spanish. Its authenticity has since been questioned but there is genuine film stock of Teddy Roosevelt's Rough Riders of Santiago and American troops invading Baiquiri in Cuba. The Vitagraph Company also accompanied Roosevelt to Cuba and filmed the Rough Riders' assault on Juan Hill.

In 1900, William Dickson of the British Mutoscope and Biograph Company was sent to cover the Boer War and brought with him the latest film camera called the Bioscope. He confidently expected to record the first dramatic moving images of the fight between the British Redcoats and the Boer commandos. His Bioscope was large, encased in a cumbersome elm box supported by a sturdy oak tripod and so heavy it had to be transported in an ox wagon. He apparently considered himself to be uniquely defined by this brand new medium and in his semi-fictional novel *Ladysmith*, Giles Foden portrays him as someone who deliberately set himself apart from the rest of the media because he was not of them.

> He wished he was elsewhere ... these silver tongued correspondents, they were another breed. Even the way they held their bodies was different. Look at Churchill now ... even when he was not the centre of attention and listening as another of them blathered on, he had a patronising air.

He wished he had his camera with him, with its armour in front of him, its sturdy wooden box, its glass plate and hood … he felt protected, in control, unassailable.

But Dickson was not prepared for the war he had come to cover. He had been trained to film at a leisurely pace, to rehearse and re-shoot scenes, to light difficult shots. But war is not static and this was not a conventional one. Opposing armies were not facing each other in regimented formation. There was no front line, no pitched battles out in the open. This was a war in the bush and in the veldt with General Botha's commandos, so well camouflaged they were invisible, perfecting what were to become classic guerrilla tactics of sniping, ambush, and hit and run.

At first Dickson had to be content filming armoured troop trains, field headquarters, marching columns, campsites. Then, with so much of his own money and reputation at stake, he simply made it up and the army was keen to oblige on the understanding that they called the shots. Commanders provided him with rehearsed simulated attacks on make-believe Boer outposts and reconstructions of British Redcoats repeating a previous encounter. There is evidence that the military even confided with him their plans of operations so that he could set up his equipment in advance. The footage he sent back to London was, with a few exceptions, illusory. But it fooled the 'newsreel' audiences, fascinated and captivated and convinced that the camera did not lie.

There was one aspect of the Boer War that did suit Dickson's static camera and that was the 'concentration camps'. To deny Botha's men food and intelligence from the civilian population, Lord Kitchener ordered his army to 'sweep the Transvaal and Orange territories clean' of all women, children and the elderly, as well as Africans and young Afrikaners of fighting age. They were herded into these camps and thousands died from malnutrition and disease.

But Dickson did not film them. He must have known about them; their existence was common knowledge to the journalists he so despised. No doubt the military forbade it.

The first of the best newsreel war coverage was in the Mexican Revolution of 1911. But if the camera did not lie, it was used to great effect in helping those who did. For the first time it was used as a powerful weapon of propaganda. Pancho Villa, one of the more famous Mexican leaders, decided he would only fight his battles during daylight hours so that film cameras could record his campaigns. Two years into the war, he offered motion picture rights to any producer who wanted exclusive coverage. The Mutual Film Company promptly signed the contract, paying Pancho Villa $25,000 and 50 per cent of the royalties. He was as good as his word. He delayed his attack on the city of Ojinaga until he was satisfied the camera crews were in place.

Make-believe propaganda techniques were employed by the British government in the First World War. In the absence of actual front-line coverage, much of what was shown to British newsreel audiences of troops in action, 'going over the top', was simply men in training far from the action.

But it was the Chinese–Japanese War in 1930 that provided the most graphic images of war, when combat cameramen were allowed to cover it on both sides. Harrison Forman of *The March of Time* filmed the Japanese bombing of Shanghai. The Hearst cameraman Wong Hai Sheng, known as Newsreel Wong, shot one of the most memorable images of all wars: the solitary baby crying amidst the rubble in the aftermath of the Shanghai attack. Like so many iconic war pictures since, there remains the suspicion that such a thing could only have been staged.

In 1974 the trick was copied again. The crossing of the Suez Canal by Egyptian troops at the start of the War of Yom Kippur was an extraordinary military feat by any standards but it was not filmed by a single Egyptian cameraman. Perhaps their High Command feared the debacle of defeat and did not want that recorded. But it was a success of such enormous proportions that a year after the war had ended and despite their ultimate defeat, the Egyptians repeated the crossing with the same full commitment of armour and troops and the international media were invited to record it. It was subsequently repeated on Egyptian television as the real thing.

With the outbreak of the First World War and with Lord Kitchener as Minister for War and Munitions, the portents were not good for those hoping to report it. Kitchener had been vehemently hostile to journalists ever since his cantankerous experience of them in the Sudan, where he saw no reason for them to be there. He was then outraged by the slightest criticism of the way he was conducting his war against the Dervishes, the Mahdi's army. 'Get out of my way, you drunken swabs!' he shouted at them on his arrival in Khartoum.

Within months of the declaration of war in 1914, he introduced blanket press censorship, the most severe by any British commander yet. In the first year of the war all press accreditation was refused. The British public, anxious to understand the reason for British involvement in a Continental conflict, had to be satisfied with clumsy propaganda from the government's newly formed Press Bureau, which censored even military communiqués before passing them on for publication. Its mantra could be summed up as: 'Do nothing. Say nothing. Keep off the front pages.'

David Lloyd George, who was soon to become Prime Minister, told C. P. Snow, editor of the *Manchester Guardian*, that if people really knew what was going on in the trenches the war would be stopped immediately. At the time, the government even denied trenches existed. As Lloyd George said: 'But of course they don't know. And they shan't know. The correspondents do not write, and the censors would not pass, the truth.'

Kitchener was adamant. There would be no press anywhere near the action. Instead, he appointed Colonel Ernest Swinton as the official war correspondent, later joined by the conscripted journalist Henry Tomlinson. Only military cameramen were allowed near the front. Their filming was amateur, under-exposed, grainy and, as was later proven, often faked.

So British journalists, as well as those from other countries based in London, were obliged to write stories of a war that was less than a hundred miles away across the English Channel, relying on the barely believable and infantile releases from the Press Bureau. It prompted Winston Churchill, then at the Admiralty, to complain about 'The Fog of War', a phrase that has echoed down the corridors of every news organisation everywhere, ever since.

It could not continue. The truth of what was happening on the Western Front was filtering back by other means, much of it from returning wounded troops. The British public, saturated by the daily barrage of government propaganda, became more suspicious, more inquisitive and newspaper editorials more vociferous. In 1915 Theodore Roosevelt wrote to the British Foreign Secretary, Sir Edward Grey, warning him that barring journalists from the front 'was harming Britain's cause in the United States'.

Prime Minister Asquith and Kitchener bent to the President's will. In March that year four journalists were invited, under strict supervision, to visit the British Field Headquarters during the Battle of Neuve-Chapelle, among them Frederic Villiers, both war artist and correspondent. As a result, their dispatches reached London in days rather than weeks, albeit heavily censored. Others, including Henry Nevinson, joined the fleet on its way to the Dardanelles.

Two months later, permanent accreditation was given to five more carefully chosen reporters but on a 'pooled' basis, the five pooling or sharing their information for general distribution to all news outlets in the United Kingdom and abroad.

In another – more sinister – development, kept secret at the time, an official register was kept by the War Office of reporters 'whose patriotism was in no doubt, were on the military's side and could be trusted to comply with regulations and not betray military information to the enemy either by accident or design'.

But the breakthrough came at a cost. Journalists sacrificed much for the privilege of visiting battle areas as censorship was ratcheted up. Correspondents were accompanied at all times by a 'minder', usually a junior officer who despised the press and made it his business to obstruct them at all times. Their dispatches were first examined by a senior staff officer who had the authority of immediate veto before they were relayed to the War Office. There a press officer, usually a minor bureaucrat and suffering no crisis of conscience, moulded the story to suit the official version of the day. These dispatches were then sent by special couriers to the newspapers but with no indication to the editors that what they were about to print bore little resemblance to the stories their reporters had initially written.

Philip Gibbs was sent by the *Daily Telegraph* to France soon after the outbreak of the war and he quickly became critical of the British command and its determination to suppress the truth of what was happening there. He did manage to smuggle some of his reports, uncensored, back to his newspaper and those describing conditions in the trenches appalled his readers. But when Gibbs revealed the bitterness and hostility that existed between officers and other ranks, sometimes bordering on mutiny, Kitchener decided enough was enough. Gibbs was arrested on charges of 'aiding and abetting the enemy and warned he would be put up against the wall and shot'.

Instead he was given a military escort back to England and told he would not be allowed to return to France. But he was not out of favour for long, such was the influence of the newspaper. A month later he was given full military accreditation and returned to the front, where he stayed for the rest of the war. His output was prodigious but he paid the price, submitting, as most did, to ever sterner censorship. This note to his editor was never published: 'Journalism has been throttled. We are so desperate for information that we will report any scrap of any description, any glimmer of truth, any wild statement, rumour, fairy tale or deliberate lie, if it fills the vacuum.'

He had his revenge when the war was over, publishing his memoirs *The Realities of War*, in which he gave a very caustic portrait of Haig.

There were other honourable exceptions, those who would rather write nothing if all they were allowed to write were government untruths. Some found ingenious ways to avoid the military's control. Henry Hamilton Fyfe of the *Daily Mail*, having angered the generals with a smuggled dispatch home, was threatened with arrest and deportation back to England. Instead he joined the French Red Cross as a stretcher bearer and continued his reporting as before.

Another was Charles à Court Repington. He was a former lieutenant colonel in the Rifle Brigade and had served in Afghanistan, in Burma, in the Sudan under Kitchener and as a staff officer in the Boer War. After an affair with a fellow officer's wife became public, he was forced to resign his commission but was offered the post of military correspondent for Lord Northcliffe's *Times*. With his background, he had privileged access to senior officers and diplomats which enabled him to bypass the restrictions that so frustrated his colleagues. His high-ranking contacts fed him valuable titbits of information, assuming that as an officer and a gentleman they could depend on his discretion and confidentiality. This cosy relationship abruptly ended with his scoop, remembered as the 'Shells Crisis' story.

In May 1915, in conversation with the British Expeditionary Force Commander-in-Chief General Sir John French, Repington was told that the shortage of artillery shells had contributed to the failure of the British attack on German positions at Neuve-Chapelle and Aubers Ridge two months earlier, which had resulted in appalling

British casualties. Repington wrote: 'The want of an unlimited supply of high explosive shells was a fatal bar to our success.'

The story caused a furore which forced Prime Minister Asquith to dissolve his Liberal government and form a coalition. General French was replaced by Haig and newspapers, including *The Times*, demanded the resignation of Lord Kitchener. He kept his seat in Cabinet but was replaced as minister responsible for munitions by Lloyd George.

Kitchener exacted his revenge on Repington by ensuring he was promptly barred from visiting the Western Front, an order not reversed for another year and then only under pressure from the new government.

Repington became a campaigner for a national army, what was later to become known as the Territorials. Towards the end of the war, he resigned from *The Times* after a disagreement with Northcliffe over his style of reporting and promptly joined the *Morning Post*. He was later arrested and charged under the Defence of the Realm Act with disclosing classified military information in one of his articles. After he was found guilty and fined he wryly commented that the military had a long memory and a revengeful, unforgiving nature.

Despite all the humiliation they had to endure, there was little resistance from the editors or proprietors of the national newspapers. Their reporters seemed resigned to a form of journalism that demanded they tamely exchanged their professional integrity for the limited access the military provided. Many defended themselves, arguing that being near the battlefront, whatever the restrictions, was better than sitting at their desk in London turning War Office hand-outs into readable copy.

But they had become a small, selfish, privileged coterie, joined together in the conspiracy of lies, propaganda and the suppression of truth. Henry Nevinson, who had been a colleague of Churchill in the

Boer War, wrote this: 'We lived chirping together like little birds in a nest, wholly dependent on the military to feed us.'

They had become allies in deceit. Their stories often portrayed the war like a football match, which nauseated the men in the trenches. On the first day of the Battle of the Somme, some reports omitted to mention the twenty thousand British dead. They were even willing to lend their names to absurd government propaganda atrocity stories: that the Germans ate Belgian babies, that the Germans were boiling their dead in vast vats to produce glycerine for munitions.

They had conspired to hide the truth of the mass slaughter in Flanders fields, the continuing and shameful shortage of ammunition, the decisions made by Kitchener and General French, and later Haig, that led to the mass slaughter of entire battalions in one day's fighting. Initially, and to their everlasting disgrace, even the Somme was initially reported as a victory. Reporters hid from their readers, whose fathers, sons and brothers were fighting, the sheer scale of the casualties.

After the war some wrote of how deeply ashamed they were at what they had written, a shame compounded when the government offered them knighthoods and many accepted. There were honourable exceptions, including Nevinson and Repington, who saw it as a bribe to keep their silence. Had they the courage to break that silence when it mattered most, how different it might have been.

Wine bottles in place of crosses, 1915, by Frederic Villiers

TWO

THEN AND NOW — II

The Spanish Civil War, which began in July 1936, heralded what is frequently described as the golden age of war reporters. The world's literary elite, over one thousand of them, descended on Spain and became participants, even combatants, on either side in the fight between the Republicans and the fascist Nationalists. They brought with them an altogether new kind of war reporting which hastily abandoned the old-established style of non-attached, objective, fact-and-figures journalism. They had a compulsion to be there, to bear witness, to report in the first person, to dispense with the ethics of professional impartiality, their mantra being: 'I must not just write what I see but write what I feel.'

They came not just to cover this war but to report the ideological battle of the time: Church against State, rich against poor, aristocracy versus the classless, democracy fighting fascism. What was happening in Spain was everybody's fight and they brought their colours with them. Like the leftist Martha Gellhorn: 'I went to Spain and didn't have the slightest idea of doing anything except being there. It was an act of solidarity, it was the only place fighting fascism.'

The French author and aviator Antoine de Saint-Exupéry flew his own aircraft. Kim Philby was already spying for the Kremlin, using his position as reporter for *The Times* as cover. He was almost killed in a Republican ambush and General Franco gave him a medal for bravery!

Harold Cardozo of the *Daily Mail* was a constant travelling companion of the General and was not troubled by accusations of complicity. It was an association that provided his newspaper with many exclusives.

George Orwell, writing for the *New England Weekly*, was shot through the neck but it did not stop him sending his weekly dispatches back to London. In one article, 'Spilling the Spanish Beans', he exposed the divide between the various factions of the Republicans, between those fighting against Franco and those fighting for the Soviet Union: 'As for all the newspaper talk about this being a war for democracy ... well that's just plain eyewash.'

Ernest Hemingway, looking every inch the battle-scarred adventurer, posed for the *New Republic* holding a rifle in a mock firing position. He had excellent contacts on both sides, and they kept him well supplied, not only with story lines but with food, brandy, a car and petrol. This did not make him popular with the rest of the international press corps, who had few of these luxuries. He lived in style, insisting he had breakfast brought to his hotel bedroom every day.

It was here that he wooed Martha Gellhorn and where she launched her career as a war reporter with a four-page article for *Collier's Weekly*.

On Wednesday 26 April 1937, reporters were having dinner in Bilbao's Presidencia Hotel when they heard the news of the bombing of the ancient Basque town of Guernica. Reuters filed the story first but it was the South African correspondent George Lowther Steer whose dispatch made the front pages of *The Times* and the *New York Times*, the two most influential newspapers either side of the Atlantic.

Steer had identified the black crosses on the tails of the aircraft and named the types of German bombers. It was proof, long suspected, that the Nazis were actively supporting Franco's fascists. It was the first time in war that civilians had been attacked in such devastating force from the air, the first blitzkrieg and a warning of things to come.

The newspapers headlined his report: 'The Most Appalling Air Raid Ever Known'.

> The most ancient town of the Basques has been completely destroyed by insurgent raiders. For three and a quarter hours, a powerful fleet of German Junkers and Heinkel bombers did not cease unloading their bombs on the town. Fighter planes plunged low from above the centre of the town to machine-gun those who had taken refuge in the fields. The whole town is flaming from end to end, the reflection could be seen in the clouds of smoke above the mountains. This raid is unparalleled in military history. In the centre of the town flames were gathering in a single roar. There were people to be saved they said but nothing could be done. We put our hands in our pockets and wondered why on earth the world was so mad and warfare become so easy.

Knowing that Franco and Hitler would deny all complicity, Steer brought out of the wreckage incontrovertible evidence: three shiny aluminium tubes with the remains of silver white powder inside. They were thermite incendiary bombs stamped with the German Imperial eagle.

One reader of Steer's dispatch would make it immortal: Pablo Picasso. Within a month of it, he began painting a giant canvas, twelve feet by twenty-five, and on 4 June, his *Guernica* was shown for the first time in Paris. The Germans were furious with Steer's revelations and the name 'Steer, G. L.' was put on the Gestapo Special Wanted List of people to be immediately arrested once the Nazis had successfully invaded England.

War correspondents in the Second World War were known throughout the Armed Services as WARCOs. Photographs show them fitted out with uniforms, Sam Browne belts and the insignia

C for Correspondent. They were forbidden to carry arms but could, if captured as prisoners of war, assume the rank of captain.

Some were later to admit, shame-facedly, that they had behaved like the spoilt children of very wealthy parents. They took it for granted that they should be lodged in the best houses or hotels, to have army cars and drivers at their disposal and be served the best food available. In return they were expected to be 'onside' with the military, obey without question their restrictions and not hanker after freedom from the censor. They were blithely considered by military and government alike to be instruments of the war effort, subjected to precisely the same rigid editorial control as the genera-tion of reporters before them. Most had little choice but to console themselves, realising how dependent they were on the military for access and information. The poet Humbert Wolfe wrote these lines to describe them:

> *You cannot hope to bribe or twist,*
> *Thank God, the British journalist.*
> *But seeing what the man will do*
> *Unbribed, there's no occasion to.*

He was clearly not an admirer of the British war reporter and at the outbreak of war, it is not surprising that he was employed by the War Office to compile a list of writers who could serve as propagandists for the British army.

The Germans, who had been quietly gearing up for another war ever since their humiliation at Versailles, had also perfected their media strategy. When war began, their journalists were conscripted into the three Services along with film and radio producers, printers, artists, writers and cameramen. They had been given basic mili-tary training, with orders to fight if necessary. They were in effect Hitler's propaganda shock troops. Every army unit had its reporter and photographer, every squadron and every ship the same. It explains why so much of the archive of the war we have today is of German origin.

The Minister of Propaganda, Joseph Goebbels, wooed the foreign press with special privileges, like free transport, extra food rations and generous rates of exchange. Yet he ensured that all communication out of Germany was fastidiously monitored and any foreign reporter who filed negative copy might find himself arrested on charges ranging from 'soliciting' to espionage. But in the early stages of the war it was certainly simpler and more profitable to be filing from Berlin than London where British reporters were kept on a tight leash, starved of information, denied access.

The reins were loosened a little when the British Expeditionary Force landed in France on 9 May 1940. Four British war reporters were allowed to accompany them but their 'pooled' reports were so heavily censored that even verbs had been erased and copy that arrived back in London made little sense. The newspaper proprietors complained and the *Daily Express*, in a sarcastic editorial, suggested that the Royal Air Force should drop leaflets over Britain informing people what was happening on the other side of the Channel. The government promptly responded by recalling the newspaper's correspondent O. D. Gallagher, who was condemned to spend the rest of the war reporting domestic stories.

Reporting by 'wireless' came into its own with the outbreak of the war and it loosened the bounds of censorship. Throughout the early 1930s the BBC had been experimenting and developing various methods of outside broadcasting which included the Blattnerphone in 1931. It recorded sound magnetically onto a large steel tape at three feet a second. In 1935, the corporation experimented with a gramophone machine that cut grooves on to a magnetic aluminium disc, ready for immediate playback. It was cumbersome and unreliable but it relieved producers of having always to present every programme live.

BBC technicians were also converting standard saloon cars into mobile recording studios featuring a single turntable called 'the Mighty Midget', capable of four minutes' uninterrupted recording. It was a critical breakthrough because these recordings could be relayed back to Broadcasting House over the telephone line or the less reliable short-wave transmitter. The Corporation also fitted out a large van, nicknamed Belinda, which was capable of multiple record-ings and able to transmit lengthy reports on the same day. A brand new way of reporting war was launched with an authenticity no other medium then could possibly match. It was called 'Spoken News'.

From the day war was declared, the BBC began broadcasting dispatches from its many overseas correspondents. Long before D-Day it was airing over a hundred reports a month on its *Combat Diary* for the Allied Expeditionary Forces Network, *Radio Newsreel*, transmitted on its world service, and *War Report* on the Home Service. But it was the prospect of the Second Front, the invasion of Europe, that propelled the BBC news gatherers forward.

In March 1943, a military exercise codenamed 'Spartan' was held across southern England to test new equipment and new battlefield tactics in preparation for D-Day. The BBC was granted the oppor-tunity to use these manoeuvres to develop its reporting of war. Their technicians were attached to the two 'opposing' armies; engineers recorded elaborate sound of the sham fighting, there were eyewitness running commentaries, feature writers dramatised particular events and ongoing news dispatches were flashed to Broadcasting House.

The BBC set up a mock unit where the mass of material was censored before being edited into dummy newsreels and bulletins. Everything was done for real, even to the extent of rushing items through at precisely the scheduled time. It was the first time that all the various news departments at Broadcasting House had been brought together as one team. 'Spoken News' was re-christened 'Sound Photography'.

When the results were played back to the Secretary of State for War and the Commander-in-Chief Home Forces they agreed that, come the day, the BBC would have the 'fullest co-operation of the army ... indeed of all three Services in the forthcoming invasion of Western Europe'.

Selected correspondents, some recruited from newspapers and periodicals, many from within the BBC, were obliged to attend courses on censorship. It was easy for the censor to delete a sentence or change the emphasis in a written dispatch but impossible if those words had been recorded on disc. To introduce them to the dangerous nuances in a hastily written dispatch, they were taken to a 'plausibly German headquarters where a plausibly Nazi Intelligence Officer played some specially-prepared recordings by a British correspondent. The "German" then converted seemingly innocent remarks into more significant military information.'

It was their first lesson in self-censorship. Finally the recruits faced their toughest test. They began months of special training to equip them for the hardships they would face as they accompanied troops at the front. They went on an intense physical training course which earned them the nickname 'BBC Commandos'. They were instructed in gunnery, signals, reconnaissance, aircraft and tank recognition and map reading. They went on assault courses, crossed rivers on ropes and crawled through netting under live fire. Some were attached to regular army units and shared every exercise and route march with them.

Those who survived the ordeal won the respect of the army. Correspondents would no longer be regarded in the field as civilians in khaki fancy dress; they knew army jargon and service discipline. At its most senior level the army came to regard them as an extension of their own public relations machine, which was to have mixed benefits. Correspondents were indeed often taken into the confidence of field commanders but they were also assumed to be onside, a family member, which threatened to compromise editorial integrity.

On D-Day, 6 June 1944, the BBC launched its nightly *War Report*. It followed the nine o'clock news bulletin and continued uninterrupted, from the initial landings to Germany's final surrender. An estimated fifteen million listeners tuned in to hear the familiar, trusted voices of Chester Wilmot, Frank Gillard, Wynford Vaughan-Thomas, Godfrey Talbot, Richard Dimbleby and Stanley Maxted.

They communicated directly and intimately to families gathered around their wireless sets, to soldiers at the front, to sailors in the warships, to the merchant seaman in the supply convoys, to the French, Belgian, and Dutch underground resistance and saboteurs listening secretly under the shadow of the Gestapo. When, on 24 March 1945, Joseph Goebbels tuned in to the BBC World Service, as he did every night, he heard Richard Dimbleby aboard a Dakota aircraft describing the British glider landings at the Battle of the Rhine.

The Rhine lies left and right across our path shining in the sunlight and the whole of this mighty airborne army is filling the sky. A Dakota has just gone down in flames. Above us and below us are the tugs as they take their gliders in. Down there is the smoke of battle. Our skipper is talking to the glider pilot, warning him that we're nearly there, preparing to cast him off. Ahead is a pillar of smoke where another aircraft has gone down ... it's a Stirling, a British Stirling, going down with flames coming out of its belly ... parachutes are coming out ... one, two, three, four billowing parachutes, out of the Stirling.

'Stand by and I'll tell you when to jump off.' Our pilot is calling up, telling the glider pilot that in just a moment we shall have to let go. All over the sky ... here comes his voice ... NOW! We've let her go ... we've turned hard away in a tight circle to port ... sorry if I'm shouting but this is a tremendous sight.

In the glider he was describing was Dimbleby's colleague Stanley Maxted:

Just a few feet off the ground and a wicked snap of Spandau machine-guns, mixed with the bang of 20mm incendiaries. There was an explosion that appeared inside my head, the smell of burnt cordite. I went down on my knees, then something hot and sticky was dripping into my right eye and off my chin. I saw the Bren carrier go out of the nose of the glider and wiping two signallers off the top of it like flies … I saw a man pinned against the wreckage as bullets kept crashing through the fuselage. The ground was a mist of smoke from our artillery bombardment. I saw crashed gliders, burning gliders and the great courage of men going into fight.

Maxted proved his own courage. He was wounded in the landing but carried on to report the battle that sealed Hitler's defeat.

The BBC's War Reporting Unit established the corporation's high reputation as a serious news provider, which has been maintained to this day.

On the Normandy invasion and the subsequent Allied push through Europe, there were 558 accredited WARCOs from Britain and America. American reporters fought British censorship from every angle. Their army saw public relations and news management as a vital part of their overall strategy. General Dwight Eisenhower allocated considerable resources to accommodating and controlling the growing American press corps, concerned that there should be a working balance between the two. It was, he said, 'a matter of policy that accredited correspondents should be accorded the greatest possible latitude in the gathering of legitimate news and be given all reasonable assistance'.

It was, of course, the military's prerogative to define what was 'legitimate news' and dispatches were routinely if lightly censored. But American reporters were allowed easy access to the fighting, field commanders were less suspicious of them and the minders that accompanied them were often former journalists themselves and more ready to compromise. British reporters looked on with envy.

The British army in the north Africa campaign was more media friendly because, like Eisenhower, its commander there understood the importance of media exposure both for himself and for the war he was fighting. General Bernard Montgomery was a self-confessed master of self-promotion and manipulated the press to his and to his troops' advantage. To him, the press was an essential arm of warfare.

He regarded them as part of his staff. No other British general in any other theatre of the war had his charisma and he exploited it shamelessly. In the north Africa campaign, his 'Desert Rats' loved him and so did the WARCOs who accompanied him. Their stories read like adventurous fiction. His running 'duel' with Rommel, the 'Desert Fox', made him a living legend.

He knew the power of the newsreels and according to those who filmed him, he was wary of them, selective, manipulative, artfully posing. It was said that Monty never rode on a tank unless there was a camera to record it. A WARCO wrote at the time that ' every journalist should sit on a tank if he wants to be loved ... really loved!'

He recognised that radio was his best and most immediate weapon for invigorating troop morale as well as galvanising support on the home front. He was not content for his successes to be reported second-hand in the newspapers; he also wanted to be heard. Whenever he had anything to say he would invite the BBC reporter to his caravan to record it. His voice was listened to by his troops of the 21st Battle Group and by their families back home and in that way, he knew he could win the confidence and loyalty on both fronts.

Frank Gillard spent much time with him.

I enjoyed his strong support. He was always willing to broadcast but there were occasions when I thought it best not to and he accepted my decision without quibble. And he always respected the BBC's editorial independence.

Monty sent Gillard an unusual request:

> I got a message from his ADC that the Field Marshal would like a puppy. He thought I might mention it on one my broadcasts. Of course such a mention, supposing it got past my editors, would have produced thousands of puppies with ghastly consequences. So I scoured our narrow beachhead and in a devastated little village I found a tiny Scotch terrier puppy. Monty received it with delight and instantly named him Hitler. But this Hitler too, did not survive the war. He was run over by one of Monty's tanks in the final advance. But during his short life, I know he gave companionship to a man who inwardly was a very solitary person.

With exceptions that can be counted on the fingers of one hand, all British WARCOs were men. In the entire British press corps covering the five years of the war only five were women. American women correspondents and photographers totalled nearly two hundred, among them Margaret Bourke-White and Martha Gellhorn.

Despite their insistence on being treated as equals, British women reporters were barred from active combat zones. Phillip Ashley, head of the 8th Army's Press Division, a junior lieutenant, which is a measure of the importance the military attached to the job, had decided that women reporters should only be given 'special visitor status and only then after full consideration for their safety and well-being'. This at a time when nurses were braving the bombs and saving lives in the wreckage of the Blitz. And others, some barely out of their teens, were ferrying Spitfires and Lancasters to aerodromes around Britain, under constant threat from the Luftwaffe. Amy Johnson, who had flown single handed in a record-breaking flight to Australia in 1930, died doing that job.

In the Korean War, the American General McArthur decided not to impose formal censorship and instead shifted the burden of responsibility onto the reporters themselves, trusting them not to compromise military security. But without clearly defined ground rules the reporters found the lines of transgression were too vague and they floundered. The disclosure of sensitive military information by correspondents became a daily occurrence and when the Chinese army began to turn the tide of the war in their favour in mid-September 1950, there was a very rapid return to the familiar censor's veto and the physical containment of the correspondents.

Ever since their Civil War, the Americans have maintained their military and political manipulation of the media to a greater or lesser degree. This despite the First Amendment to the Constitution, which states: 'Congress shall make no law abridging the freedom of speech or of the press.' It is a remarkably unambiguous statement and yet successive administrations have delivered their own interpretations of it when at war.

In Vietnam the military command offered unprecedented access to the battlefields yet at the same time relentlessly tried to bamboozle the international media. They boasted of their success in it, and for years concealed the extent of their defeats and the scale of their casualties. Their generals displayed astonishing arrogance in their dealing with reporters, unaware or unconcerned about the effect this would have.

They offered unparalleled freedom of movement and information. If a reporter went to MACV, the American Military Press Liaison Centre in Saigon, and requested a trip to a battle zone, by evening a helicopter would have dropped him there. He could speak to whom he liked and there was no censor's blue pencil to alter his dispatch. A waiting Huey was ready the next day to fly him back to safety. Yet at the same time the Pentagon's media relations gurus actively encouraged a strategy of denial and secrecy to such an extent that from 1968, in the aftermath of the Têt Offensive, they were dealing with both an American and an international press corps that had become chronically hostile and disbelieving.

This has since become known as the Vietnam Syndrome: that it was the media not the generals who lost the war. It was Marshall McLuhan who said that 'television brought the brutality of the war into the comfort of the living room. Vietnam was lost in the living rooms of America not on the battlefields of Vietnam.' It was a convenient myth, but it has dictated the political and military attitudes to the media in all countries ever since.

When the Israelis invaded Lebanon in 1982 they imposed a total news blackout. Until then, the system of press relations and censorship they operated was a model that worked well for both military and journalists. It had worked, to much acclaim, in the Yom Kippur War nine years earlier. Access then had been everything, the censors' niggling came later. But as their troops crossed their northern border in 1982 they invoked what became known as the 'Battle Fog Policy'. Correspondents were not allowed into Lebanon until six days later by which time Israeli troops were in control and news was already history.

The Americans did the same when they invaded Grenada. Code-named 'Operation Fury', ten thousand US Marines landed on the beaches to depose the military dictator Hudson Austin. Meanwhile, over four hundred reporters were queuing up at the American Embassy in Barbados demanding accreditation and transport to Grenada. They had to wait another week before the American military allowed the first to fly in. Their containment had been absolute.

In 1982, Sir John Fieldhouse, Commander-in-Chief of the British forces en route to the Falklands, declared that reporters accompanying the fleet were 'bloody inconvenient. If I had my way I wouldn't tell anyone there was a war going on until it was over. Then I would simply tell them who'd won!'

It is fact that even before the tiny British armada had left the English Channel, a coded message was sent from Royal Navy head-quarters in Northwood to the flagship HMS *Hermes* which simply read 'DIET'. Decoded it read: 'Starve the press'. The Navy was more than happy to obey.

The British military in the Falklands, as in all its previous wars, blithely considered correspondents to be handy instruments of propaganda and misinformation. The Chief of the General Staff, Sir Terence Lewin, later admitted that 'journalists had been very useful with our deception'.

It all changes when a war reporter is among his own people. When I was with the British forces in the Falklands, I made the naïve assumption that I was among a military I could trust and would trust me. I had by then already reported from nine wars but they had all been other people's wars, foreign wars. But the Falklands was my first alongside my own people, men who came from towns and cities I knew, speaking in accents that were fondly familiar to me.

Despite all the lessons I had learnt in those foreign wars, that lies become truths simply in the saying, that nothing and no one is quite what they seem, I ditched my usual caution and cussedness that had stood me in good stead for so long. I wanted to believe what I was told. The absurdity of that confession now embarrasses me.

William Howard Russell

THREE

WILLIAM HOWARD RUSSELL

1820–1907

He called himself 'the miserable parent of a luckless tribe'.

And to this day he is arguably Britain's most influential war reporter.

His life reads like a history of Great Britain in the years of its greatest global power. He was acquainted with famous contemporaries. He gossiped with Lincoln in the White House, he quarrelled with Bismarck at Versailles and his personal friends included the Prince of Wales, Dickens and Thackeray.

It could be said that, single handed, he brought down a British government.

He was an extrovert, a convivial clubman with a ready wit, as might be expected of a Dubliner. He was always ready to provide his listeners with a fund of anecdotes and, suitably refreshed, could render any number of popular music hall ballads in a pleasing baritone voice. He was a tolerant, affectionate, if absentee, family man who adored his many children and doted on his wife, the shy and timid Irish girl, Mary. He inherited his father's optimism and something of his grandfather's temper and from his mother's side he relished the absurd and the eccentric. Yet, accepting the mores and conventions of his time, he was the personification of a typical middle-class Victorian. His weaknesses, frequently admitted to, were an over-fondness for good living, vast meals, good wine, wasteful afternoons at billiards, embarrassing losses at whist and a maverick attitude to spending. He was always in debt.

His success was due to the simple tenets of Victorian England: hard work, respect for the truth, and a keen moral conviction of what was right and what was wrong. Many of his rivals were better educated, better positioned, but he outclassed them all with the eloquence, clarity and detail of his writing as well as his courage on and off the battlefield. He was never afraid to speak his mind, whoever or whatever he might offend.

No other man was eyewitness at such close quarters to the Victorian age in all its aspects. Although he was a 'man of war', he had great humanity and is remembered and revered as the first in his profession and of his generation to see 'the pity of war'. No other journalist, poet or writer of his time conveyed the horrors of war, the suffering of the soldiers, the mutilation of man by man, describing in his reports the gory detail of what happens to the human body when it is torn apart by bayonet, bullet and shell fire. It is said that, reading his reports of the slaughter in battle, men would leave their breakfast table, unable to read more. Or, in their fury reading Russell's critical description of a costly British military blunder, tear their newspaper to shreds.

But he was at odds with much of the age, especially the concepts of slavery and colonialism. Victoria's reign marked the apogee of Britain's empire and Russell was its fiercest critic. He saw no glory or gain in the enforced subservience of other peoples. He regarded colonialism as a moral outrage, simply commercial mercantile greed aided and abetted by political ego, the jingoism of the hoi polloi and a military class always at the ready. He wrote: 'Queen Victoria's reign has been an incessant record of bloodshed.'

He spent much of his life on one-man campaigns arguing against the exploitation of Egyptians, Zulus, Indians, Maoris, Boers, Burmese and Afghans. The British, he said, would eventually pay dearly for their colonial adventures.

This conviction was not surprising. He had lived his first twenty years in Ireland and had seen at first hand the arrogance and brutality of British rule there. He was among the first to report the wretchedness and deaths from starvation during the Irish potato famine in 1846. He did not know who was to blame but the images haunted him for the rest of his life.

> In all my subsequent career, supping the full horrors in full tide of war, I never beheld sights so shocking as those that met my eyes in that famine tour of mine. They were beyond not merely description but imagination, here at our doors, a whole race ... perishing round Christian churches ... children digging up roots, miserable crones and the scarecrow old men in the fields. They were bestial to behold.

He spent his apprenticeship as a reporter covering much of the political and religious upheaval in Ireland and Britain's attempts to control it. It was a sadness that never left him – that the two countries he loved most were so irreversibly divided.

As *The Times* correspondent for thirty years he reported every major story of his time: the Irish famine, the Crimea, the Indian Mutiny, the American Civil War, the Franco-Prussian War and the Sudan and Zulu wars.

※

He was born William Howard Russell in Tallaght, County Dublin on 28 March 1820. When his father and mother emigrated to Liverpool, they left him behind to be brought up by his grandfather Captain

John Kelly, a retired officer. He endured his early schooldays at the hands of a sadistic teacher and later at the Rev. Geoghegan's much admired Academy in Dublin.

After his grandfather died, the young Russell dithered; a decision on a lifetime's career commitment was scary for a man barely out of his teens. He toyed with becoming a teacher and for a while was tutor at a school in County Leitrim. He studied for the entrance examinations to Dublin's Trinity College but failed to win a scholarship. He then decided that law might better suit his style and temper and he set about studying for the Bar.

A cousin, John Russell, unexpectedly arrived at his doorstep from London and introduced himself as a 'special correspondent' for *The Times*. He had come to Ireland to report the forthcoming elections but, realising that he could not cover the entire countrywide campaign on his own, was recruiting educated young men who would write reports under his direction. William was offered a pound a day, good pay for a beginner, plus hotel expenses; he did not hesitate. His subsequent reports caught the attention of the newspaper's editor, John Delane, who asked Russell to contribute regularly to the newspaper as a freelance. Then in 1842 Delane offered the 22-year-old a permanent staff position. It was the launch of a momentous career and the die was cast. Within a year it came perilously close to ending.

Russell was sent back to Ireland where events were moving to yet another crisis by virtue of the Republicans' demands for self-rule, led by the man idolised as the 'Great Liberator', Daniel O'Connell. Days before a banned mass meeting was due to take place at Clonarf, O'Connell was arrested. Russell was to report the court proceedings with the repeated imperative from the editor's office that *The Times* must be the first to report the final verdict. Meticulous preparations were already under way to make sure he would deliver it personally at Delane's office way ahead of his competitors.

A special train was kept in readiness at Dublin's Westland Row station. A steamship, the *Iron Duke*, was berthed in Kingstown harbour and another special train stood by at Holyhead for the run to London. A cab was on permanent hire at Euston station for the final journey to Printing House Square. All were waiting for their single passenger, the young, eager *Times* correspondent.

Russell had to wait twenty-three days for the jury to find O'Connell guilty before his race home could begin. It was not uneventful.

> At Westland Row station there was a delay as the engineer had gone off to sleep or to a beer. But at last the express rattled out of the dirty suburb. I stepped out on the platform at Kingstown with all my baggage and a large notebook but there was no one to receive me, no boat at the stairs. Presently a boat came for me and as I stepped aboard the steamer I was received with the remark 'We'd gave you up after midnight but we'll be off in half an hour'. But the *Iron Duke* made a rapid run across the channel and a few minutes after landing I was on my way to London, the bearer of exclusive news.

So fatigued had he been in the train from Holyhead that he had taken off his boots. Getting them back on again in a moving horse-drawn cab proved all but impossible and he arrived at *The Times* offices carrying his large notebook in one hand and a boot in the other. This might help excuse what, in his confusion, happened next.

> The messenger opened the cab door. 'I'll tell the editor you've come,' he said and vanished through a door, outside of which stood some men in their shirt sleeves. As I alighted one of them in my ear said, 'We are very glad to hear they've found O'Connell guilty at last.' I did not reflect ... thought it was one of the office people ... and answered, 'Oh, Yes! All guilty but on different counts.' And then, with one boot under my arm, I entered the editor's office.

But Russell was tricked. The man who had spoken to him as he had arrived, a seemingly idle bystander, the man in shirtsleeves, was in fact a reporter from the *Morning Herald*. Russell had given the game away. An extravagantly expensive scoop had been lost and the fledgling Russell might well have thought his job had gone too. But Delane held fire.

> The confounded miscreants, but it was sharp of them. Now, my young friend, let me give you a piece of advice. As you have very nearly severed your connection with us by your indiscretion, let me warn you to keep your lips closed and your eyes open. Never speak about your business but commit it to paper for your editor and for him alone. We would have given hundreds of pounds to have stopped your few words last night.

It had been Delane's original intention to make Russell a parliamentary reporter, confining him to the monotonous duties in the press gallery. But for the next few years he spent much of his time back in the courtrooms of Ireland, on one occasion witnessing the conviction of four Sinn Féiners found guilty of treason and sentenced to be hanged, drawn and quartered. There is no evidence that Russell's impassioned report of it affected the judgment but the sentence was later commuted to transportation for life.

Despite his albeit limited success as a reporter, he never quite abandoned his original determination to become a lawyer. Maybe his many visits to court proceedings encouraged him to believe he was better suited to a wig than a pen. Maybe it was the uncertainty that troubles all journalists, the nagging anxiety of insecure employment. And so, between his assignments, he resumed his legal studies and was finally called to the Bar at the Middle Temple in June 1850. Editor Delane attended the celebratory dinner at the London Tavern and even applauded speeches predicting Russell's future as an eminent barrister, which might have seemed odd given how much he now valued his young protégé. It mattered not, for a month later Delane sent the promising lawyer to cover his first war.

In July, Russell was sent as *The Times*'s 'Special Correspondent' to Schleswig-Holstein. In the scheme and scale of world events it was not an important war; perhaps it is better described as a conflict. It lasted one day and Prime Minister Lord Palmerston dismissed it thus: 'The Schleswig-Holstein question is so complicated only three men in Europe have ever understood it. The first was Prince Albert, who is dead. The second was a German professor who became mad. I am the third and I have forgotten all about it.'

For centuries, Danish kings had also coveted the title of Duke of Holstein, governor of the twin plots of land bordering the neck of the Danish peninsula. But the people there were German by language and by custom and had long resented Danish rule. That year, 1850, a volunteer army of some thirty thousand were ready to confront the incumbent Duke and he, in turn, decided it was time to re-assert his authority.

What passed as a battle took place in the village of Idstedt. Russell came under fire for the first time in his life, nursed a slight flesh wound, concluded that, with the rebels in full retreat, the Danes had won the day, filed his story and returned home the following morning.

Nothing he had experienced and certainly nothing he had written suggested he had the makings of a war reporter. The title as such did not exist then and when it was first suggested that it might apply to him, Russell replied that he had no more idea of being one as he had of becoming Lord Chancellor.

For the next four years, with no wars in prospect and given the fluency of his descriptive prose, he was mostly tasked to cover ceremonial events. He was sent to cover Napoleon's naval review at Cherbourg. He wrote at length of the Duke of Wellington's funeral, sixteen thousand words in all, his description of the cortège appearing as seven unbroken columns in the following day's newspaper.

Yesterday the mortal remains of Arthur, Duke of Wellington, were conveyed from the Horse Guards to the Cathedral of St Paul's and there buried by the side of Nelson. A million and a half people beheld and participated in the ceremonial. When the independence of England was assailed … Providence sent us a champion and should the days of darkness come again and this land of freedom once more be threatened, God grant us another to lead our armies and win our battles.

For that to happen, Russell would not have to wait long. Within eighteen months England was at war again, a war bloodier than Waterloo, a war beyond Europe, the first 'modern war' and the one that would make Russell Britain's first war correspondent and a legend thereafter.

The war in the Crimea began as an obscure quarrel between Christian monks over who should hold the keys to a shrine in Jerusalem. It developed into an international contest between the Russian Tsar Nicholas, who backed the Greek Orthodox monks, and Napoleon, who capriciously upheld the Roman Catholics' claim. Both in turn demanded the support of the Sultan of Turkey, whose territory extended into the Holy Lands. But, as Karl Marx had predicted years before, war between Russia and the crumbling Ottoman Empire was inevitable.

Turkey was considered the 'sick man of Europe' and the Tsar had long planned to grab as much of the Balkans as he could. So threatened, Turkey declared war and in a pre-emptive strike attacked and defeated the Tsar's forces at Oltenitza.

No immediate British interests were threatened, but if Russia succeeded in defeating Turkey it would capture territory bordering the eastern Mediterranean and Britain's route to India might well be threatened. Napoleon feared the prospect of Russian armies coming so close to his borders and decided France's best interests lay with the British.

When Russian warships attacked and sank the Turkish Black Sea fleet off Sinop, Britain and France, after months of dithering, declared their support for the Sultan and war was declared against Russia on 28 March 1854. It was Russell's thirty-fourth birthday.

His departure to the Crimea appears too casual to be real. But this is what he wrote in his diary on the eve of his departure:

> Mr Delane has arranged a very agreeable excursion for me to go with the Guards. The government had resolved to show Russia that England was in earnest in supporting the Sultan ... and that I was the best man to represent the paper on the occasion. The Commander in Chief of the British army has given order for my passage and everything would be done to make my task agreeable. My wife and family could join me, handsome pay and allowances would be given, in fact everything was painted '*couleur de rose*'. Mr Delane says it will be a pleasant trip for a few weeks and I'll be back by Easter.

No correspondent then or since was promised so much and provided with so little. The army turned its back on him, offering neither succour, protection nor co-operation, his wife and children did not join him, and he was away not for two weeks but two years.

His coverage of the Crimea campaign remains his most enduring legacy. He reported the stark, brutal realities of war to his readers' breakfast tables, diminishing the distance between home and the remote battlefields in a way that had never been done before.

True to form, the British military High Command was adamant: no correspondents would be allowed to travel on the troopships sailing east. So Russell had to find his own way to the army's first port of call, Malta, and from there he sent his first report. From the very beginning, he and his editor preferred to call them 'Letters'.

The French contingent had already arrived and Russell told his readers that the *entente* remained *cordiale*, that the Guards were

practising with their new French rifles and that there was good
English beer to be had. But he criticised the unsuitability of the
British uniform for battle service, the rigid parade ground discipline
demanded by senior officers and what he considered the absurd order
banning beards and moustaches. And he added a rider, almost as an
afterthought. He warned that the army's most dangerous enemy was
not the Russian artillery. It was disease.

> What we have most to fear … is an enemy that musket and bayonet
> cannot meet or repel. We have a fearful lesson in the records of the
> Russo-Turkish campaign of 1828 in which 80,000 men perished by
> plague, pestilence and famine. Let us have plenty of doctors … an
> overwhelming army of medical men to combat disease. Do not let
> our soldiers be killed by antiquated imbecility.

It was an early warning and a prophecy ignored. Time and time
again in his Letters he repeated his appeal that unless there were
adequate medical teams accompanying the army, including stretchers and ambulances, more British soldiers' lives would be lost to
disease than on the battlefront. And so it was and the final tally
was horrific.

Faced with the blank refusal permitting him to travel with the
troops, he schemed his way aboard the steamer *Golden Fleece* en route
to the army's next destination, Gallipoli in the Dardanelles. He had
hired a Maltese servant to accompany him but as the ship left port,
he was nowhere to be found. The man had jumped ship together with
Russell's baggage and a month's advance in wages. The omens were
not good.

Russell landed with the army in the first week of April but without rations or shelter. He borrowed a tent but the army commander,
Sir George Brown, refused to let him pitch it within the camp. So he
lived in a pigsty and fed on brown bread, eggs and onions.

The army ignored his complaints, senior officers shunned him. Russell's anger seethed into his Letters and created the antipathy that was to endure throughout the two years of the campaign.

Within days he very quickly began to unravel the army's key weaknesses, firing broadside after broadside, each one fiercer and more critical than the last. He ridiculed Sir George's preoccupation with regulations, better suited to manoeuvres on Salisbury Plain than at Gallipoli. He noted that the French had planned their arrival well while British soldiers were ill-fed and the sick were without mattresses or blankets.

He was now getting into his stride but as the army's animosity towards him increased, so his following back in Britain compounded day on day. His biographer, Alan Hankinson, wrote:

> For his readers it was like getting long letters from a soldier son who was fair-minded and fearless, who had an insatiable appetite for information ... and a lively no-nonsense way of putting it down on paper. The very fact that Russell was always ready to correct any mistakes he made in subsequent Letters, increased the trust of his readers. This reliability was his strongest weapon.

For the first time, readers at home were being told the truth about a British army overseas. As never before, the Letters cut straight through the garbage of government propaganda and favoured military myths. It was too early for Russell to recognise it himself but as the principal correspondent of the country's, indeed the world's, greatest newspaper, he was in an immensely powerful position. The army commanders might detest him, do their best to disarm and depress him, but within weeks of landing in Gallipoli, his daily Letters home were essential reading for those in and out of the corridors of power.

He wandered the camps at will, scribbling in his notebook every detail that described the chaos of the British camps. He worried away at them in every one of his Letters: the abysmal planning; the inadequate transport; the lack of field hospitals, doctors, nurses, medicines; a soldier's simple request for a decent diet. And proper weapons for those soldiers to win their battles! This complaint is among one of his most despairing and vitriolic:

> There are no fuses for such shells that we have. We have plenty of fuses for shells we have not. There are lots of 13-inch shells and no fuses for them and there are lots of 10-inch fuses and no shells for them. Who sent them out or who kept them back? Who are the traitors, or knaves or the fools?

Such was the torrent of his complaints that in May *The Times,* in a leader article, warned its readers there was a real danger the military was about to expel all correspondents. That leader ended with words that should echo in every newsroom of the world:

> We can easily understand why a certain class of officer should like no tale told but their own and why Government should wish a veil to be thrown over its possible neglects. But the people of England will look for safety in publicity rather than in concealment.

It would have been circumspect for the British High Command to have taken notice, but it did not. Lord Raglan was now in command and, like his former commander the Duke of Wellington, he loathed the press. Russell wrote to his editor that he had been informed that Raglan was determined not to recognise the press in any way, nor to give them rations or any assistance. Censorship had yet to creep into the British vocabulary but it comes in many disguises and they were present then.

But Russell did not need the help of Raglan or any of his officers. He relied instead on a journalist's cunning, the skill, if such it is, to ease information out of people, to soothe away their reserve, to loosen their tongue; call it the art of gentle persuasion. Russell had it in abundance. He wrote that but for his Irish nature, he would not have got on so well. Captain Ronald Clifford wrote of him as

> A vulgar low Irishman but he has the gift of the gab, uses his tongue as well as his pen, who sings a good song, drinks any one's brandy and smokes as many good cigars as foolish young officers will let him. He is looked upon by most in the camp as a Jolly Good Fellow, just the sort to get information, particularly out of youngsters. I assure you that more than one 'Nob' has thought it best to shake his hand rather than the cold shoulder for he is rather an awkward sort of man to be on bad terms with.

Colonel George Bell wrote: 'Russell comes in from the stable loft where he dwells, to our den of an evening to have a chat, a glass of brandy and cigar. He tells some droll stories, is a jolly good fellow and sings a good song.' Among his favourites were the ballads 'We will catch the Whale, Brave Boys' and 'O, save me a lock of your hair'. Fellow correspondent Lawrence Bodkin remarked: 'He was a welcome guest at every mess table from the moment of his arrival in camp ... a real power before which generals began to quail.'

His reputation of using any means he considered necessary to obtain information led to him being blacklisted by the military. Lord Raglan ordered his officers not to speak to him and not once in the entire campaign did he acknowledge Russell's presence. But in private correspondence he did his best to damn him. In one letter he accused Russell of being as valuable to the Tsar's armies as a paid spy and, in another, accused Russell of endangering British lives by publishing details of British military movements and the location of artillery batteries.

Russell replied that although it might be dangerous to communicate facts likely to be of service to the Russians, it was certainly more hazardous to conceal the truth from the British people. What he wrote next should surely have been written in stone for all the generations of journalists and military that followed him:

> No power on earth can now establish a censorship in England or suppress or distort the truth. Publicity must be accepted by our captains, generals and men-at-arms as the necessary conditions of any grand operation of war. Otherwise the truth will reach home so distorted that it will terrify and alarm.

How right he was and how naïve to believe it could ever happen. His appeal fell on deaf ears. If the military reluctantly accepted that it may be right in a supposed democracy to give the British people the fullest information, they ought to be aware of the price they pay for it and the advantage it gives the enemy. Generals were fond of quoting Napoleon: that he considered British correspondents his best spies. The more Russell pressed for greater cooperation from the military, the more it opposed him.

He was soon to realise the extent of their loathing of him. *The Times* newspaper sent out a young reporter, W. H. Stowe, to Balaclava but within weeks he was sick with cholera. The army medics refused him treatment, denying him even a hospital bed. Russell attended him, helped nurse him but Stowe died soon after.

If Russell despaired of Raglan and his staff, he had scant respect for his fellow correspondents. He considered that most were little better than lazy clerks, lotharios and drunkards who did what they were told by the military and wrote what they were told.

> The *Morning Post* correspondent lives on board the *Caradoc* and comes ashore now and then after a battle to view the ground. The

Daily News correspondent lives on board another ship and, I believe, never comes ashore at all. The *Morning Advertiser* is represented, I believe, by a Mr Keane, who chiefly passes his time in preparing cooling drinks.

Even today, there is an assumption that there is great camaraderie among foreign correspondents, that they belong to a keenly shared membership of an exclusive club of globetrotters. It is a myth. Information and valued contacts are closely guarded and socialising is usually just another way of finding out what the others are up to. The only thing to share with a rival is his whisky. Delane's advice to Russell at the very beginning of his career is as pertinent today as it was then: 'Never speak about your business, commit it to paper for the editor and him alone.'

Russell's private letters home to his wife Mary reveal how guilty he felt at leaving her and their four children. She was his opposite, a timid woman, shy of company, a doting mother but never able to come to terms with being the wife of so eminent a journalist. His letters home are full of affection and concern for the family. He used a dozen or more nicknames for her, like Deenyman, Bucky, Dot and Dotty, and he would sometimes lapse into baby talk or gently chide her for her cold nose and for growing stout. In one letter, he expresses his guilt at being angry with his sons:

> I have often thought of the wrong I did poor little Willie when I thought he and Johnnie had told a fib and of his exclamation when I asked him why, he cried 'Because I thought you were going to beat me'. I want to efface from their minds the idea that I am a cruel papa.

In his first Letter to Delane from Malta, Russell had warned that disease would be more lethal than the bullet. His prophecy was about to come true. Towards the end of July, the French reported that cholera was rampant in their camps. It quickly spread to the British and by the end of the first week of August over seven hundred men were buried in shallow graves.

Unknown to the British commanders, the campsite they had chosen was known locally by the Turks as the Valley of Death.

> The meadows nurtured the fever, the ague, dysentery and pestilence in their bosom, the lake, the stream exhaled death and at night fat unctuous vapours rose from the valley and crept in the dark and stole into the tent of the sleeper and wrapped him in their deadly embrace.

The armies delayed until September but at last the allied commanders were now agreed. It was time to leave, not only to escape the cholera but to confront the Russians. That place would be on the banks of the river Varna, twenty-five miles north of Sebastopol, where some fifteen thousand troops of the Imperial army were waiting to do battle.

It would be Russell's first real test. His only experience of war had been a single day's action four years back in Schleswig-Holstein. Now he asked of himself the questions every war correspondent has repeated since. How will I cope under fire? Where should I be? Where do I run to? Forward? Back? Why on earth am I here? God help me!

Soldiers were trained for this but Russell had no such skills. He had to be in the thick of the action and if he survived there would be no medals, no commendations. If he was killed and joined the others rotting in the bloodied earth, there would be no pension for his wife and children. He wrote that he was 'nobody's child'.

Advice came unexpectedly from a brigade commander, Sir John Pennefather:

> 'By Gad Sir!' exclaimed the General when I told him who I was. 'I'd sooner see the devil. What on earth do you know of this kind of work?'

I answered, 'It is true I have little acquaintance with this business but I suspect there are a great many here today with no greater knowledge of it than myself.'

He laughed: 'Well goodbye. Go to the rear. There will be wigs on the green today my boy so keep away from the front if you don't wish to have your notes cut short.'

The Russians were well dug in, secure on steep rising ground above the river with no natural cover for the advancing allies. So confident was the Russian commander, Prince Menshikov, that he had invited his officer's wives from Sebastopol to picnic on the heights and enjoy the slaughter below.

The battle was fought on 20 September. It was soon over. As British shells cascaded on the forward ranks of the Russian infantry, the Light Division, the Guards and then the Highlanders stormed their way up the hill and broke through the Russian lines with musket and bayonet. The Russian Prince, his army and his picnicking ladies fled and were not pursued. Russell had expected a prolonged battle and could not believe it could end so quickly, so decisively.

How was I to describe what I have seen? My eyes swam as I tried to make notes. I was worn out with excitement, fatigue and want of food. I had been ten hours in the saddle, my wretched horse, bleeding badly, was unable to carry me. I could not remain where the fight had been closest and deadliest. I longed to get away.

Too spent to write and too excited to sleep, he lay awake all night in his tent, the images of the battle magnifying themselves. Outside his tent at dawn he stumbled over the corpse of a Russian. Stretcher parties wandered about the plain turning over the blankets covering the wounded to see whether they were still alive or already food for the worms. As soon as it was light enough and using a quill pen and the yellowed pages of a Russian account book he had found, he began his Letter home. It was his very first account of a great battle.

> An immense mass of Russian infantry were seen moving down towards the battery ... it was the crisis of the day. Sharp and angular they looked as if cut out of solid rock. Lord Raglan saw the difficulties and asked for guns to bear on them. The first shot missed but the next and the next and the next cut through their ranks so cleanly that a clear line could be seen ... leaving behind six or seven lines of dead ... marking the passage of the deadly messengers.

Within weeks, the Russians had regrouped and began their offensive to take Balaclava and cut off the British from the port they were dependent on to bring in their supplies. Russell was now better prepared for battle and had positioned himself high on a ridge overlooking the valley. On his horse nearby, ready to direct his forces, was Lord Raglan. Russell raised his hat to him. Raglan did not respond.

As the Russian cavalry, guns and infantry began their advance, Russell, notebook resting on his saddle, began writing the opening paragraph of what was to become his legendary account of the charge of the Light Brigade. It belies the carnage that was to come.

> Never did the painter's eye rest on a more beautiful scene than I beheld from the ridge. The fleecy vapours still hung around the mountain tops and mingled with the ascending volumes of smoke; the patch of sea sparkled freshly in the rays of the morning sun but its light was eclipsed by the flashes which gleamed from the masses of armed men below.

The Russian advance was repulsed first by the Highlanders and again by the horsemen of the Heavy Brigade. There was a long pause as each army regrouped. It was mid-morning when the military disaster for which this day is remembered began.

The charge of the Light Brigade has been told many times in paintings and in literature. Tennyson immortalised it with his 'Into the Valley of Death rode the six hundred'. But none compares to Russell's eyewitness description in his Letter dated 25 October.

At ten minutes past eleven, our Light Cavalry Brigade advanced. As they rushed towards the front, the Russians opened upon them …with volleys of musketry and rifle. They swept proudly on past, glittering in the morning sun with all the pride and splendour of war. We could scarcely believe our senses. Surely that handful of men is not going to charge an army in that position? Alas! But it was true.

They advanced in two lines, quickening their pace as they closed on the enemy. A more fearful spectacle was never witnessed than by those who, without the power to aid, beheld their heroic countrymen rushing to the arms of death.

The enemy belched forth, from thirty iron mouths a flood of smoke and flame through which hissed the deadly balls. With a halo of flashing steel above their heads and a cheer that was many a noble fellow's death cry, they flew into the smoke of the batteries. But ere they were lost from view, the plain was strewed with their bodies and with the carcasses of horses. We could see their sabres flashing as they rode up to the guns and dashed between them, cutting down the gunners as they stood.

Wounded men and dismounted troopers flying towards us told us the sad tale. Demi-gods could not have done what they failed to do … miserable remnants of that band of heroes. At thirty-five minutes past eleven not a British soldier, except the dead and the dying, was left in front of those bloody Muscovite guns.

The Balaclava Letter was sent next morning and reached Printing House Square twenty days later. It created a national sensation. It is said that the British celebrate their defeats almost as much as their victories and Raglan's ill-fated cavalry charge was certain to appeal to the British reader's appetite for glorious failures. He was not the first correspondent to realise that death and calamity made first-rate copy. His news report became, in the inevitable process of myth making, a legend and one of English literature's epic poems:

> *Half a league, half a league,*
> *Half a league onward.*
> *All in the Valley of Death*
> *Rode the six hundred.*
> *'Forward the Light Brigade!*
> *Charge for the guns!'*

The doomed charge against the mighty Russian artillery provided British readers with an example of military derring-do on a colossal scale and barely believable suicidal heroism.

> *Theirs not to reason why,*
> *Theirs but to do and die.*

Russell's description of them as a band of heroes elevated the horsemen of the Light Brigade to celebrity status and his minute-by-minute account provided his readers with word pictures so vivid they could imagine they could see the colours of the uniforms and the sound of the guns. Never before had the British public been so close to battle. Never were the glorious dead so posthumously revered. Epic canvases of that day have become national treasures. There were well publicised annual reunions of the survivors, the last in 1913.

Russell yearned to be home with Mary and his children. He knew, as every soldier knew, that there were still battles to be won before the war with Russia was over. Delane, his editor, implored him to stay and, turning the screw as editors do, he arranged for Mary to join her husband for a marital respite in Constantinople. A month later Russell returned to the Crimea and continued to follow the campaign, reporting the battles of Inkerman and finally Sebastopol.

No foreign correspondent today would or could have endured Russell's tour of duty. Nor would any editor have the temerity to expect it. Only in his diaries, altogether fifty of them, did he complain of his own personal distress and of all he was being forced to witness. This in one letter home to his wife.

> Oh Mary, the kind good friends I have lost, the dear companions of many a ride and walk and lonely hour. I have seen them buried as they lay all bloody on the hillside amid ferocious enemies and I could not but exclaim in all bitterness of heart 'Cursed is he that delighteth in war'. Our generals, from Raglan down, are not worth a button. I could not sleep in my tent last night owing to the groans of dying Russian prisoners outside. They are as thick on the field as sparrows on a hayrick. They literally die in heaps and are buried thirty together. The air stinks with blood...

The length of his Letters to the newspaper often ran into many thousands of words, often covering an entire page. He was meticulous in recording the minutiae of military strategy, naming every relevant brigade, every regiment, its officers, the numbers of men, the gauge of their artillery shells, the firing patterns of their infantry. He would devote an entire column to critical observations of a general's failing strategy. But what endeared him most to his readers was his concern for the lower ranks, what Kipling called his Tommy Atkins.

He showed compassion for them far beyond that of any other correspondent.

> It is now pouring rain, the skies are black as ink, the wind is howling over the staggering tents, the trenches have turned to dykes ... in the tents, the water is sometimes four feet deep. Our men have not either warm or waterproof clothing ... they are out for twelve hours at a time in the trenches ... they are plunged into the inevitable miseries of a winter campaign and not a soul seems to care for their comfort or even their lives. The prevalent diseases are fever, dysentery and diarrhoea and there are no less than 3,500 sick men in the British camp. These are hard truths and the people of England must hear them.

And again in a Letter from Sebastopol:

> There is no excuse for the privations to which the men are exposed ... obliged to dig holes over their tents to drain away the water. Not one of them could have on a dry stitch and so they perished miserably, murdered slowly and in accordance with military discipline. And yet the commanders are all apathy. Raglan one never sees and there is a joke in camp that there is a dummy up at headquarters to look out of the window while the Commander-in-Chief is enjoying incognito in Malta.

Queen Victoria raged against his 'infamous attacks which have disgraced our newspapers' and Albert her Prince Consort, very much involved in the affairs of the army, was furious that 'the pen and ink of one miserable scribbler is despoiling the country of all advantages which the heart's blood of twenty thousand of its noblest sons should have earned'.

Russell had upset the Ttrone but his persistence had etched its way into the nation's conscience. Another *Times* reporter had more shocking news. Thomas Chenery was in Scutari at the army hospital receiving the Crimea wounded. There were few doctors and the only nursing orderlies were Chelsea Pensioners, some so old they were in need of nursing themselves.

> It is with feelings of surprise and anger that the public will learn that no sufficient preparations have been made for the care of the wounded. There are not sufficient surgeons, no dressers, no nurses, there is not even linen for bandages. Not only are men kept in some cases for a week without the hand of a medical man coming near their wounds ... they are left in agony to die.

Reaction from the British public was instant and generous. *The Times* launched an appeal for funds to finance additional doctors and supplies and received £20,000. Florence Nightingale and thirty-eight other nurses were quickly on their way to Scutari and Alexis Soyer, head chef at London's Savoy Hotel, volunteered to go the Crimea to supervise and improve army rations.

In another article Russell asked why it was that an enterprising merchant had not thought it worth his while making the journey out to open a store so close to the army camps. 'There is demand and a living to be had'. Only one person responded, a Jamaican woman named Mary Seacole, who opened a store in Balaclava and a 'resting house for wounded and convalescing officers'.

Later that October, Delane received a private letter from Russell sent from Sebastopol.

> The army has melted away almost to a drop of miserable, washed out, spiritless wretches who are not fit to do duty against the enemy. My occupation is gone, there is nothing to record more of the British Expeditionary Force except its weaknesses and its misery. I cannot tell the truth now ... it is too terrible.

Delane did not delay. At its thundering best, *The Times* published a leader article which had an unpredictable and historical result.

> The noblest army sent from these shores has been sacrificed to the grossest mismanagement. Incompetence, lethargy, aristocratic hauteur, perverseness and stupidity reign and revel and riot. There are people who think it a less than happy consummation of affairs that the Commander-in-Chief and his staff should survive on the heights of Sebastopol, decorated, ennobled, duly named in dispatch after dispatch, and return home to enjoy pensions and honours amid the bones of 50,000 British soldiers.

Following this, such was the force and extent of public outrage that the government of Lord Aberdeen resigned. He blamed the appalling weather conditions, he blamed the military but he could not hide his government's own failing, its indifference and incompetence.

As the year 1855 was near to ending and with no prospect of an end to the stalemate in the campaign, Delane ordered Russell home, hoping he would make it in time for a family Christmas. He missed it by a few days, ahead of a letter he had posted to his wife from Sebastopol three weeks earlier: 'Right or wrong. I'll leave the camp ... and fly straight to your dear arms, if I'm not too stout to get into them! I can scarcely believe it. It is like a dream.'

During the late summer of 1857, as Russell was preparing his proposed book on the Crimea campaign, British newspapers were preoccupied with another conflict, this time in India. Soldiers of the Bengal army employed by the East India Company had mutinied, shot their British officers and attacked British civilians. Delhi was taken by them, then Cawnpore, where they had massacred many British families. They had then moved on to Lucknow where fifteen hundred British troops, together with over five hundred British women and children, were now besieged. The rebellion was spreading fast and there were fears that it would engulf all of India from Bombay in the west, south to Madras and to Calcutta in the east. The Queen was alarmed. Her empire was threatened but her Imperial army was already on its way to restore order and re-establish colonial authority. Delane was determined that his newspaper should be the first to report it.

He made Russell an offer he could not refuse, but the timing caused him grief. Mary had given birth to their fifth child and was convalescing. Nevertheless, the temptation to return to war was too great. He left their house in London with Mary still too weak to leave her room and the children playing, quite unaware he was off again. He could not bear to say goodbye to them. 'My dear Mary, looking at me with such mild grief in her dear old eyes. I could not bear to be much with her.'

There were many explanations for the unexpected rebellion by what, until then, had been a compliant, subservient India. The army had just been issued with the new Enfield rifle and rumours emanating from bazaars and brothels said that its cartridges were greased with a mixture of cow and pig fat. The cow was sacred to the Hindus, the pig was unclean for the Muslims and such rumours were bound to create alarm. It was not true and soon after his arrival in Calcutta, Russell was quick to discover and anxious to explain other reasons, not all of them popular with his readers.

> It is not a pleasing or popular task to lay bare the defects of one's countrymen ... but I have been struck with the arrogance and repellent manner in which we treat natives. I cannot believe the men who tell me it is essential to our rule that we should use brute force on all our dependants.

He gave numerous examples of acts of brutality by the British that went unpunished because the victims did not report it for fear of recrimination. It became a regular feature in all his future reporting, continually urging restraint, arguing for moderation in dealings with the rebels and fearful that the British army would revenge itself on the mutinous Indian soldiers, the sepoys, in the most brutal way.

He travelled first to Cawnpore, which had just been retaken, and then, on 27 February, moved with the troops under the command of Sir Colin Campbell, towards Lucknow. The caravanserai of marching men, of camels and horses and covered litters hung from bamboo poles, moved across the Ganges and into Oudh, now called Uttar Pradesh, where the rebellion had first started. Russell was pleased that his travelling arrangements were a great improvement on the Crimea. He had his own servants and noted that every fighting man had half a dozen attendants to carry his equipment and provisions, pitch his tents, bring his water and care for his horses. At breakfast, Russell found the mess tents ready, the tables covered in snow-white cloths, the curries smoking and lines of servants waiting, arms folded, ready to serve. It was a fondly established colonial etiquette that the sahib should be spared all labour.

After five days marching they sighted Lucknow. Russell was over-whelmed, inspired and at his supreme, descriptive best.

> A vision of palaces, minars, domes azure and golden, cupolas, long facades of fair perspective in pillar and column, terraced roofs, all rising up amid a calm still ocean of the brightest verdure. Look for miles and miles away and still the ocean spreads and the towers of the fairy-city gleam in the midst. Spires of gold glitter in the sun. Turrets and gilded spheres shine like constellations. There is nothing mean or squalid to be seen.

Until three days later, when the Black Watch and a battalion of Sikhs attacked. Russell went in with them. In forty-eight hours of fighting, more than two thousand mutineers had been slaughtered. He watched, in the aftermath of the bloodbath, the wanton destruction as the soldiers plundered and destroyed the very city Russell had so eloquently described. They entered the ancient white stone palaces, British and Sikh alike, setting fire to vast embroideries, ripping down valuable silk paintings, smashing vast crystal chandeliers, revelling in the destruction, delirious with the smell of blood and the scattered dead around them.

In the Kaiser Bagh palace they forced open caskets full of diamond bracelets, emeralds, rubies, opals and pearls and carried them off in bundles wrapped in lace shawls. One soldier, unable to believe it was for real, offered Russell a handful of jewels for a hundred rupees but Russell had no money on him.

He was even more shocked by the ferocity of the soldiers towards the few surviving sepoys. He had seen many stiffened corpses hanging from trees on the march but he was not prepared for what was now happening in this city. Prisoners were tied across the muzzles of guns and blown apart. Others were butchered, their genitals and stomachs ripped apart by bayonet. The Sikhs even roasted some alive over fires. Russell recorded the savagery of one young British officer.

A boy came towards the post leading a blind and ancient man and throwing himself at the feet of the officer, asked for protection. That officer, as I was informed by his comrades, drew his revolver and snapped it at the wretched supplicant's head. The men cried shame on him. Again he pulled the trigger, again the cap missed. Again he pulled and once more the weapon refused its task. The fourth time, remember thrice had he time to relent, the gallant officer succeeded and the boy's lifeblood flowed at his feet, amid the indignation and the outcries of his men.

Russell, unlike so many war correspondents since, was never a maverick, never a chancer. But he did possess that single quality that separates a great war reporter from the lesser ones. He had the gift of repeated good luck and he took it for granted as lucky people do. But towards the end of his assignment in India his run of luck almost ended and he never came closer to death in all his career than on that day.

It was mid-April and he was travelling with Sir Colin Campbell as his army moved north to suppress the Sowar rebels in Rohilcund. As Russell was about to mount, he was kicked by his horse in his rump and thigh. He was knocked unconscious, bled profusely and was confined to his tent. But early the next morning, the camp was attacked and Russell, dressed only in his night shirt, fled.

> Naked to my shirt, leg bleeding, bare head, I scrambled into the saddle and rode towards the road. I was exhausted and just sinking back when there was another panic ... again the Sowars charged up. One cut down a bullock driver twenty yards off me ... headlong flight ... awful confusion. As I rode on I felt as if cut down ... a Highlander caught me. 'Where are you hit, sir ... a doctor ... a doctor!' I remember nothing more ... screaming from spasms in my lungs, felt I was going to die.

Russell had come very close to being killed. The Highlander who saved him was Sergeant William Forbes-Mitchell. It was an extraordinary coincidence. They had known each other in the Crimea. The sergeant's report of the attack reads:

> Several of the enemy were dodging through the camels to get him. We turned our rifles on them and I shot down the one nearest to Mr Russell ... in fact his tulwar [sabre] was actually lifted to swoop on Mr Russell's bare head when my bullet put a stop to him. I saw Mr Russell tumble from his saddle at the same instant as the Sowar fell and I got a rare fright, for I thought my bullet had struck them both.

There is many a correspondent who, having escaped death in such a way, would have written a very glossy and self-appraising account of it. That was not Russell's way. He made no mention whatever of it in his next Letter. But later, in his diary, he wrote a lament that is familiar to many a dispirited reporter far from home in a foreign field: 'Such are the chances of a special correspondent in the field that *The Times* seems to have very little feeling of what I go through, very little indeed.'

Russell might indeed have expected a little sympathy from the offices at Printing House Square. But, in the fashion of things, the management sent a rebuke. It had to do with the cost of telegrams. The telegraph was in full use throughout the Indian campaign. The line was run out wherever the army travelled and because Campbell was such a publicity-conscious commander, he allowed Russell to use the facility to speed his Letters via Calcutta or Bombay. Even then it took them up to four weeks to reach London.

However, as always when the story is nearing its end, the recriminations began. Russell was told that that his use of the telegraph had cost the newspaper over £5,000, an exorbitant sum then. And its cost-conscious accountants, insensitive as ever to a correspondent's labours and dangers, wrote to him that his telegrams 'never repaid the trouble and cost they had occasioned. Your private telegrams, as you know, sometimes lingered on the road.'

During the first weeks of the new year 1859, the last of the rebels had been pushed into an uncertain sanctuary in Nepal and Russell's mission was complete, his assignment over. In his final Letters, he repeated the warnings that had appeared in his very first from India. The need to win the trust and affection of all Indians if British rule was ever to prosper.

Let us not think our Empire in India is founded on rock. Compared with the dynasties which have rule here, our race is but the growth of yesterday. I believe we can never preserve India by brute force alone except at a cost that will swallow up all the wealth of the home country. Above all, let us beware how we rouse that silent, ever watchful irresistible power ... the hate of its subjects.

Russell's achievements in India were greater than he appreciated. He described a part of their empire that was all but unknown to his readers. Often he told them of things they might have preferred not to know, just as he had done from the Crimea. He wrote of India's barbarities, of its squalid poverty, of its perverse inequalities, of its caste system. But he also told them of its beauty, of its diverse religions, its ancient customs and cultures, of its vast landscapes and cities. He was unique in that he was able to create colourful, memorable word pictures and transmit them into the parlours and drawing rooms of Britain.

And in his final Letters, concerning matters of national policy and the obligations of an imperial power, he went way beyond the normal perimeters of reporting. They marked something radical and new in British journalism. It had come of age.

For the next two years, Russell kept his promise to Mary to not leave her again, and for a while she may even have believed it. He wrote a book on military tactics, holidayed in Switzerland, fished, played billiards at the Garrick Club and was content to be the principal leader writer of *The Times*, making magisterial pronouncements on foreign and colonial affairs.

In time though, he became restless with the disciplines of office routine. He was offered the editorship of a new weekly magazine that dealt entirely with military matters, the *Army and Navy Gazette*. But under the house rules of *The Times*, he was not allowed work for anyone else. It was agreed that he could contribute as a freelance and, should he decide to relinquish his editorship of the *Gazette*, he could return to his old position as and when he pleased. The call was not long in coming.

On the evening of 28 February 1861 Russell took his two sons, William and John, to dinner at Simpson's in the Strand. It was a special treat. He had something to tell them. They then made the short walk to the Garrick Club and there Thackeray proposed a toast to wish his friend good luck and Godspeed on his new assignment. Russell was off again, this time to cross the Atlantic to cover the American Civil War.

Abraham Lincoln had won the previous autumn's election convincingly, with the majority of his votes coming from the populous, industrial north. But the southern states, whose wealth came from the cotton plantations and the four million Negroes that worked on them, were suspicious of the President's declared intention not to abolish slavery in those states where it existed. That December, South Carolina declared that it was leaving the Union and soon after ten other southern states followed. Lincoln was adamant that no state could lawfully leave the Union and warned that he would do all his power to ensure none did. It would take four years and the slaughter of more than half a million Americans by Americans before that Presidential pledge was finally fulfilled.

Mary had given birth to her fifth child and was now weaker than ever. She had found it impossible to cope on her own and when Russell was away she and her children were looked after by friends. Even when he was at home, she lived in a state of constant anxiety. Now he was ready to depart once more. He arranged for her to lodge with friends in Bath and sent the children to boarding school.

Before he left, he went to Bath to kiss her goodbye. What he wrote in his diary afterwards are words that must be familiar to every foreign correspondent that has ever had to make those same farewells.

How sad are these partings, how frequent and what lessons they should teach us for the future. If we had prudence they need not be.

Never can I forget the look in those dear eyes and the poor fretted face and the melting lips so tender and so true. I went to the station in a storm of pain.

He sailed from Southampton on 2 March, on what was to be the most difficult assignment of his career. In the Crimea, as in India, there was only one side he could support; there was no latitude, no ambivalence on the tally of rights and wrongs. He had endlessly criticised the British military's conduct in both campaigns but he was a patriot and had never attacked its endeavours. But as Americans fought each other, he could not be seen to support either side. Impartiality must be his benchmark even if it did not suit him.

No man ever set foot on the soil of the United States with a stronger sincerer desire to ascertain and tell the truth … no theories to uphold, no prejudices to subserve, no interests to advance … a free agent … my own daily impressions without fear or favour.

Soon after his arrival in Washington and suffering a painful hangover after a night celebrating St Patrick's Day with his new hosts, he met Lincoln at the White House. Lincoln was anxious for British support and had been told, unwisely, that *The Times* would help.

There entered, with a shambling, loose, irregular, almost unsteady gait, a tall, lank, lean man considerably over six feet tall, with stooping shoulders, long pendulous arms terminating in hands of extraordinary dimensions. He said 'I am very glad to make your acquaintance Mr Russell and to see you in this country. The London *Times* is one of the greatest powers in the world … in fact I don't know of anything that has more power, except perhaps the Mississippi.'

Throughout March, Russell met many of the prominent activists,

Northerners and Southerners alike, and by the end of the month he was convinced that war was inevitable. Two weeks later, the first shots were fired when Confederate forces attacked the Federal garrison at Fort Sumner, which, after a thirty-six hour bombardment, surrendered with no casualties.

From Charleston he travelled via Savannah to the Confederate capital, Montgomery, Alabama. He arrived there on the very day that war was declared, 7 May 1861.

His opinions and predictions on the course of the war were formed during those first few months touring North and South and he was not to change them. In his Letters, he wrote of the Southerner's zeal and dedicated 'workmanlike' preparation for the battles to come in order to keep their slaves, so essential if they were to preserve their economies and way of life. But the Northerners, the 'Yankees', were equally entrenched, determined the Union should stay intact. Slavery did not concern them. Russell was convinced that the North's vast superiority in numbers, the wealth at its disposal and its command of the coastal waters would inevitably give it victory.

His views were echoed by the newspapers of the North, which wrote of an army of over one hundred thousand men 'in the highest state of efficiency'. But Russell was not impressed. From what he had seen, he estimated there were fewer than thirty thousand and most of those had no training and no discipline. Lincoln had called for volunteers to sign up and there was no shortage to rush to the colours. But they were only expected to enlist for three months and by the time they had been trained in the basics, they were ready to leave. Most of them were not American born at all but recent immigrants from Germany and Ireland.

The officers are dirty, the camps are dirty to excess and the men dressed in all kinds of uniforms. And it is with this rabble that the North propose not only to subdue the South but according to some of their papers, to humiliate Britain and conquer Canada afterwards.

Washington, 20 July, and General Irwin McDowell, commander of the North's Potomac Army, waited on the banks of the river, ready to cross it the next morning and invade Virginia. He had already invited his favourite correspondents to accompany him, including Russell, and had advised them, in all earnest, to wear white suits 'to indicate the purity of their character'.

Russell did nothing of the kind. That evening he laid out an old pair of boots from India, a Himalayan jacket, an old felt hat, a flask of brandy and a revolver. Then he went to bed.

McDowell's plan was to attack and overwhelm the smaller southern force, dug in at Manassas railway junction near a small river called Bull Run. He would have succeeded had it not been for the stubborn and bloody resistance of the Virginian brigade under the command of General Jackson, thereafter nicknamed 'Stonewall' Jackson. But Russell saw nothing of the battle. Bull Run was over thirty miles from Washington and he found the road clogged with wagonloads of people, including prominent Congressmen and their wives, hurrying expectantly to see the North's first victory. What they met on that road instead was McDowell's 'three month' army scurrying back in panic.

Russell forced his way forward against wave after wave of soldiers on the run.

'Turn back! Retreat!' shouted the men at the front. 'We're whipped, we're whipped.' They cursed and struggled with frenzy to get past. The teamsters of the advancing wagons now caught up the cry. 'Turn back, turn your horses,' and backing and plunging, rearing and kicking, the horses reversed and went off.

Sharp reports of some field pieces rattled through the wood ... at every shot a convulsion ... again the cry. 'What are you afraid of?' I asked a man running by the side of me. 'I'm not afraid of you,' replied the ruffian, levelling his piece at me and pulling the trigger. It was not loaded or the cap was not on, for it did not go off ... and I resolved to keep my counsel.

In his Letter to *The Times* and writing with the events fresh in his mind, he was unequivocal. It was a defeat, a rout and a monstrous disgrace. Never before, in all his experience of war, he thundered, had he witnessed such scandalous behaviour in an army. It was cowardice on a national scale. If the North is to win its war, he concluded, then it must be prepared to provide better leaders of better men or further encounters with the Southern armies would be more humiliating than Bull Run.

When his Letter was published in London, its contents were quickly relayed back to America. If the Southerners were, for the moment, delighted to read it, those north of the Potomac were livid. America at war was now divided into Confederates and Unionists, armies in grey and blue uniforms, but criticised and ridiculed by a representative of their former colonial governor, they became one again.

Immediately he became vilified as 'Bull Run Russell' and there was a fear that he would be lynched. His editor, Delane, wrote to him that delighted as he was with the vivid account, his fear was that 'the United States will not be able to bear the truth so plainly told'.

And he was right. For the next six months he had to endure public and personal abuse that might well have broken a lesser man. He was inundated with hate mail, he was threatened with the Bowie knife, the revolver and the hangman's noose. Yet the one person that might have hated him most offered some consolation. General McDowell had been demoted but told Russell:

I must confess I am much rejoiced to find you are as much abused as I have been. I hope you mind it as little as I did. Bull Run was an unfortunate affair but had I won it, you would have described the flying enemy and then you would have been the most popular writer in America and I would have been lauded as the greatest of generals.

But Russell could not be comforted so easily. He was in despair. A letter from his wife told him that the child she had borne him had died. He could not escape in Washington, he could not safely walk the streets and, except for allies in the British Embassy, he could enjoy no social life. He was refused all communication with the army and the politicians, including Lincoln, had turned their backs on him. The city had become a prison.

What he wrote in his diary then reveals the depth of his depression:

I am living in an air of danger and only the goodness of Providence saves me. Whilst I am expected to be jocose, enlightened, wise, witty and unflagging in spirits ... here are dark horrors of memory and pressing gloom around me ... the whole brain is shaken, the system becomes one vast repertoire of various disorders and the mind dwells on morbid images.

By mid-September he began to think seriously of returning home. There seemed no point in staying. He had not forgotten Delane's words as he had left England, that if he was exposed to any danger or outrage, he was to return at once. He was at his lowest ebb, fretting, writing long letters of complaint to his editor. His diary entries point, for the first time, to self-doubt, even self-pity.

His biographer Alan Hankinson writes:

He was a man who needed constant reassurances. Like many of those who give an impressive display of confidence and courage, he was sensitive and vulnerable and prone, when things went badly, to believe he was insufficiently appreciated, quick to suspect he was being exploited and sacrificed to the demands of his employer.

His employer was now running out of patience. Delane wanted him to stay, he was their only correspondent in America and they had no one of such stature to replace him. But Russell remained *persona non grata* with the army and more crucially Lincoln himself. He could not cover the war and there was little chance of him ever doing so. For the very first time in his long, loyal and illustrious career with *The Times*, he received its first and what would be its last rebuke.

> You must either go to the front or come home. You were charged with a mission which cannot be adequately discharged. It is your business to report the military proceedings of the Federal Army, to chronicle its exploits. Up to the beginning of the year you did well but since then you seem to have lost heart and have thrown us overboard. This cannot last. And so I repeat; go to the front or come home.

It was a devastating missive, unexpected and, given the circumstances, unpardonable. Its directness shocked Russell. But even as he read it, he had already made his decision. And so he abandoned his assignment even as the Civil War was gaining momentum and its slaughter multiplying. He left abruptly, knowing that his newspaper, the most powerful in the English-speaking world, was now unrepresented in a story of major importance. Not bothering even to cable his editor of his intentions, he booked himself a berth aboard the next ship sailing for England.

If there was criticism of him for what he did, it was muted. He was not forgiven, no newspaper man should have done what he did. But perhaps his peers took into account his state of mind, his despair at being barred from the war, the months of vilification and personal abuse he had suffered so long at the hands of insulted Americans.

There is no way of knowing what might have happened had he stayed put. Perhaps in time the Northern authorities would have relented. When their fortunes in the war improved they may well have thought it of great advantage to have the world's most famous war correspondent at their side to chronicle it.

Instead Russell returned to edit the *Army Gazette*, resumed a hearty social life at the Garrick and enjoyed his renewed close and comforting friendships with Thackeray and Dickens.

He was in great need of comfort. Mary, his wife, was now in an advanced state of senile dementia and confined to a nursing home in Henley. That September he had visited her on their twentieth wedding anniversary but she had not recognised him. 'God! What a wreck and ruin. Hours of cries, tears and bitter sorrow. The poor sad mind.'

Tolstoy wrote that all happy families resemble one another but that each unhappy family is unhappy in its own way. Russell, in those last months of Mary's life, tried to remember only the good times, those first few years of their marriage, when they were poor, the children were babies and there had been much happiness and love in the family. Just before Christmas, he visited her again and he knew it would be for the last time. 'She is going, my poor friend and wife, my only true friend who loved me as no one else can or will.'

Within three weeks she was dead.

Bull Run marked his nadir, the beginning of the end of his undisputed title as the world's premier war correspondent. He continued to dabble with war in a desultory way. In 1870 *The Times* sent him to cover the Franco-Prussian war and nine years later, sixty years old, he went on a one-off assignment for the *Daily Telegraph* to cover the war against the Zulus. It was his last campaign.

He had at long last dispensed with his correspondent's garb but he could not shed his wanderlust. He revisited a forgiving and peaceful America, returned briefly to India and then spent a long sojourn in Egypt. He retired in 1882. A year later, he fell in love.

He was now sixty-three, a commoner and a Protestant. She was thirty years younger, a Catholic and an aristocrat: the Countess Antoinette Mathilde Pia Alexandra Malvezzi. They had met at a shooting party in Scotland and it was an unlikely match. But their courtship was so rapid that within four months they were married. A year later he was knighted and on that occasion he proudly introduced her to Queen Victoria at Buckingham Palace. They toured Ireland together, made the fashionable Grand Tour of Europe and adventured in Chile, coming home via the new Panama Canal. She proved to be a caring wife, looking after him with practical devotion and providing the stability and dependability that had been so lacking in his life. Together they were feted by high society and to all they were a blissful couple, although she admitted in a letter to her sister that he could be difficult. 'He is very rampageous, sings songs at dinner and calls me a bloody fool when I object to his taking half a tumbler of whisky.'

Over a half a century of stressful, dangerous, arduous work and the many thousands of miles of travel were now beginning to take their toll. Russell began to suffer repeated bouts of bronchitis and was slowly crippled by arthritis, which would finally confine him to a wheelchair. But old age and public honours did nothing to moderate his caustic, unfashionable views. He remained a relentless critic of British imperialism.

Things rank and gross possess the world. Protestants and Papists are filling Uganda and the Prince of Wales has attacked me about my views on Egypt. The disgusting politicians care for nothing but gain, always clamouring for more land grabbing. What a maw the British Lion has to be sure. He will choke or die of indigestion. I see the worst side of the Saxon character, greed, selfishness, arrogance, conceit.

He never lost the love of his native Ireland and despaired of its destiny.

I read the Irish papers with much grief ... that revenge for wrongs long done is proving to be more powerful than reason. Hate masters every sense. I am really becoming a Fenian. The stupid ferocity of the British in dealing with the Irish question sickens and revolts me.

When he died on 10 February 1907, newspapers had their obituaries already written. They had been a long time waiting. He was buried in London's Brompton Cemetery, beside his first wife Mary and the two children who had died in their infancy. Among the pyramid of wreaths was one sent by King Edward and his Queen.

The eulogies from home and worldwide praised him for all he had done. One read: 'He elevated newspaper writing to the dignity of history and an agent of the daily press to that of a people's ambassador.'

But it was what he did not do that enabled him to ascend that difficult pinnacle to excellence. He did not go about his work with a mind already made up, content to pander to his own and his readers' prejudices or simply to please his editor and circulation manager. He was certainly not among those correspondents who were, in Rudyard Kipling's caustic words, 'sent out when a war begins to minister to the blind brutal British public's bestial thirst for blood'.

Nor did he ever attempt to glorify his role. Not once in his Letters did he ever refer to the very real dangers and hardships he suffered in all those years. Nor did he find it necessary, as so many others did, to embroider the facts to make a story more digestible, more enjoyable, more acceptable. To the last, he was true to his maxim: that a correspondent's only task is to see what is done and describe it to the best of his ability.

He was a paradox, a man of war but who, to his dying days, found no glory in it.

Two years after his death, a permanent memorial, a bronze bust, was placed in the crypt of St Paul's Cathedral. He is wearing a campaign cloak, notebook in hand, and beneath him is a list of his campaigns: the Crimea, India, America, France, South Africa. And below them the phrase that has yet to be challenged:

THE FIRST AND GREATEST OF WAR CORRESPONDENTS.

Sniping on the Road to Sidi Muza, 1909, by Frederic Villiers

FOUR

FREDERIC VILLIERS

1851–1922

E ccentric, flamboyant, Villiers remains to this day Britain's most decorated war artist-cum-correspondent and was the first to take a film camera to the battlefield.

He was the last of the great swashbuckling, adventurous, derring-do war correspondents, describing himself as a 'Soldier of the Pen'.

Known in Fleet Street as the 'War Eagle', he was used by Kipling as the model for Dick Heldar, the tragic hero of *The Light that Failed*.

He was the premier war artist of his generation. His sketches for the London-based *Graphic* and *Illustrated London News* were reprinted worldwide and inspired many other international artists, among them d'Haenen, Koekkoek, Michaels and Caton Woodville.

He variously arrived at the battlefronts on horseback, in a covered wagon and even on a bicycle. He appeared on lecture tours wearing full military uniform complete with campaign medals and, when on assignment, slept on his camp bed wearing his cavalry spurs 'to contribute to the military aspect'.

Over a fifty-year career, he was the guest and friend of emperors, sultans, khedives, brigands and gypsy kings. He exchanged pleasantries with Queen Victoria and once borrowed a hat from the Prince of Wales, so that, properly dressed, he could accompany him stalking.

During the Abyssinian campaign he rescued a small injured simian monkey which became his close companion.

He outdid Russell in the number of wars and campaigns he covered, twenty-one in all. He reported the Ottoman atrocities in Serbia, was with the Russians in their war against Turkey, rode with the Spanish in Morocco. He was with General Garnet Wolseley at Tel-el-Kebir, in Moscow for the coronation of Nicholas, the last Russian Tsar. He stood alongside Sir William Hewitt in the Abyssinian campaign, was with the expeditionary force in the relief of Khartoum and sailed with Kitchener up the Nile to Omdurman. He went to Burma, witnessed the Japanese army's invasion of Port Arthur, reported the Boer War alongside Winston Churchill. In 1911 he was with the Italian army in the invasion of Tripoli.

At the Battle of Mustapha Pasha in 1912, the King of Bulgaria turned to his Chief of Staff and, pointing to Villiers said, 'Observe that Englishman passing up with the artillery. He has seen more fighting than any soldier alive.'

He sketched his final war in the trenches of Flanders.

When Conan Doyle was preparing to write the death of Sherlock Holmes he thought of Villiers: 'A man like that must not die of a pin prick or influenza. It must be violent and intensely dramatic.'

※

He was born in London on 23 April 1851, which was an appropriate date befitting a future war correspondent, being the festive day of St George, the fighting patron saint of both England and Russia.

Aged ten he became a cadet in the Volunteer Corps and was taught not only to dress and drill like a soldier but pour the powder, bite the cartridge and ram the bullet down the barrel of a rifle.

Very little is known of his family or why he was sent to Guînes college in the Pas-de-Calais in northern France. His school uniform was dark blue with silver stars on the cuffs and collar and, arriving back in Dover for the summer holiday, he took great delight at being saluted by the Black Watch sentries outside the castle who mistook him for a Royal Navy midshipman.

Henry, his father, said the family were descendants of George Villiers, 1st Duke of Buckingham, a friend, adviser and possibly the lover of James I. It is said that just as soon as the young Frederic could grow a beard he kept it trimmed in the style of his alleged aristocratic forebear, copied from a portrait that hung in the Villiers's London home.

On his eighteenth birthday, he enrolled in art classes in South Kensington and the British Museum and within a year was admitted to the school of the Royal Academy of Art, no small feat for one so young. But his enthusiasm quickly evaporated. He found the classes boring and monotonous. There was no excitement, nothing challenging in the sedentary work, like drawing the skeleton of a giraffe or making a plaster-cast of a discobolus, painstakingly stippled. In his frequent reveries, he remembered how much more exciting it had been as a child painting toy soldiers and endlessly romancing their battles.

His third year in art classes was his last. A fellow student proposed that they should collaborate on a mural depicting a panorama of the Franco-Prussian war, now in its final days. Villiers was thrilled. He was to travel to Paris and sketch material for it. But he had no passport so it was arranged (there being no photographic identification then) that he would use his friend's and travel in his name. It was only when he had crossed the Channel as Edward Chevalier that he fully appreciated the danger of entering a country that was in the throes of a revolution. The French government was fighting the Communards. Challenged and arrested, he could have been shot as a spy. Yet he revelled at the prospect. Risk would forever spice his life and luck, that invaluable companion of every war correspondent, would never leave his side.

Paris was barely recognisable. The fighting had reduced much of the capital to rubble. It was the young Villiers's first sight of how thoroughly war destroys the familiar. The debris of the Communard emplacements had yet to be cleared away and the destruction of the buildings facing the Tuileries showed how they had stood against the massed fire of the Versailles infantry. Notre Dame, the Madeleine and the Avenue de l'Opéra were scenes of utter desolation and, in the Place Vendôme, Napoleon's statue lay scattered on the road in three pieces.

The cemetery of Père Lachaise had been the execution ground for hundreds of Communards and the earth and lime barely covered their bodies. The wall where they had stood before the firing squads was thick with dried blood and pitted by the lead of their executioners. Villiers saw it all in its ghastly detail. Yet he was able to return to England with his sketches, seemingly unaffected, except for a fierce hatred of the Germans. Bismarck had boasted that, having subdued the French, he would leave them to 'stew in their own juices'. Villiers wrote:

> This experience served to give me an insight into their brutal and merciless nature. After having raided and ravished the fair land of France from the Rhine to the Seine, they were now gloating over the internecine troubles in its capital around which they held a tight ring of steel.

He quoted the words from a French treatise he had picked up off the streets of Paris entitled *The Plebiscite*. Its authors warned the world of the threat that Bismarck's Germany represented and that England, by its indifference, would one day suffer the consequences. One paragraph was especially prophetic:

> The Germans, having terrified the world with their ambitions, will one day be made to rue their cruelty. In a hundred years they will be recognised as barbarians and their names inscribed on the rolls of the plagues of the human race.

Villiers, many years later, witnessing the slaughter of the First World War and sheltering from German artillery bombardment in the trenches of Flanders, would have good cause to remember those lines.

He was one of the many thousands who attended the grand London opening of Alexandra Palace and also one of the few volunteers who tried to put out the fire that eventually engulfed and destroyed that vast glass monument to Victorian engineering. Being an artist and moreover a man of impulse, able to turn a crisis into an opportunity, he hurriedly made sketches of the blazing building and sent them to the popular weekly *Graphic* magazine. They were published but, more importantly, it introduced him by proxy to the editor. It was an introduction that would dramatically change the direction of his life.

In the summer of 1876, he was suffering chronic indigestion and one afternoon, with little else to occupy him, he decided to walk it off. He had got as far as Holborn when he saw a crowd gathered around a newspaper seller's stand. He read the billboard headline. Serbia had declared war on Turkey. A tiny Christian kingdom had thrown down the gauntlet to Europe's most powerful Muslim neighbour, the Ottomans.

This was the age of romantic nationalism in the Balkans and what had begun as a local rebellion against Turkish rule in Herzegovina now threatened to develop into something far more dangerous and protracted. Russia, claiming to be the protector of all Orthodox Christians under Ottoman rule, sent three thousand 'volunteers' to help the Serbs and the combined army was put under the command of the Russian General Chernyaev.

Villiers saw his chance to escape the monotony of Kensington. It was a long shot. He quickly wrote a letter to the editor of *The Graphic* offering his services as a war artist and dropped it through the letterbox of the offices that evening. The following morning he was summoned by special telegram to present himself to William Thomas, the manager. The interview was short and very much to the point.

'Can you speak French or German?' he asked.

'I can get along with French.'

'That will do. When can you go?'

'At once.'

'Then please leave by this evening's train.'

Three hours later he left his mother in tears at Charing Cross station with twenty pounds in gold sovereigns in his pocket, a letter of introduction from his editor in his wallet and his heart full of expectation. He was twenty-four years old and on the way to his first war.

He arrived in the ancient Serbian city of Belgrade to the sounds of war being prepared: the blacksmith's hammer, grindstones sharpening knives and sabres, the roll of field guns over cobbles, the trot of horses and the tramp of marching soldiers. Villiers promptly kitted himself out in what he considered were the necessary accoutrements for a war correspondent. He bought riding boots and spurs, a felt hat, a water bottle, a waxed cape, binoculars and a 'Bulldog' revolver.

Other correspondents there were less concerned with such essentials. An Italian named Lazzaro wore a dark well-tailored linen suit with pocket handkerchief, lavender kid gloves and patent leather shoes with white spats. His only baggage was his monocle, a crocodile-skin satchel and a silver-mounted cane.

There was not a single saddle horse to be bought in the city so Villiers hired a mare and covered wagon from a company of troubadours. Satisfied that he was at last suitably equipped, he left Belgrade for the Serbian headquarters at Paratchin.

He travelled in his cart for three days through countryside that gave no hint of what was to come. He sketched its tranquillity, the slopes of ripening corn, picturesque villages, their cottages festooned with drying paprika, men in their traditional long white tunics and scarlet skull caps labouring in their fields, their women at spinning wheels on their verandas.

On the fourth morning, Villiers saw clouds of dust ahead of him and within an hour he knew the reason. A convoy of seventy or more wagons came towards him yoked by black buffalo and beneath the covers of grass matting and on litters of straw he saw wounded and dying soldiers, writhing and groaning in agony. The first casualties of his first war.

That evening he left his wagon at the town of Ivanitza and, riding the mare bare-back, climbed the summit of Mount Yavor to the Serbians' main camp.

I slept in my boots and spurs to be ready for the march at dawn. The Serbs were about to invade Turkish territory. It was a quiet night but for hours I could not close my eyes, for tomorrow I would see my first battle. What would it be like? How will I respond? Should I ever return home? The moon flooded the mountain and lit up the bayonets of the ever vigilant sentries. Tired out with watching them, I fell asleep at last.

He woke to the crack of rifle fire, followed by the yellow flashes and explosions of artillery. A tall pine above his tent disintegrated and covered him in splinters. The Turkish artillery were finding their range and as the Serb gunners looked for cover, shells landed in the middle of them.

I was in for it at last ... the ghastly realities of war ... poor fellows torn to fragments ... drenching the turf with blood. A faintness crept over me and for a moment, paralysis seemed to hold my limbs. Then straight in front of me, a few feet above the ground, little puffs of smoke and behind them ... like a poppy in a cornfield, flashed the red fez of a Turk. There was nothing between me and the enemy but a few boulders and a hundred yards of space. 'By Jove!' I thought. 'It's time to go.'

The Serbian army had been outflanked and the Turks now occupied the mountain's summit. All that night they continued shelling, the flashes from their guns mixing with the lightning of a violent thunderstorm. Hundreds of terrified cattle stampeded down the mountainside, tossing and goring everything in their way, trampling into the mire of mud the limping wounded and the already dead. For the newly anointed war correspondent it was a baptism of fire and water.

Villiers moved to safety in the town of Alexinatz and daily he filled his sketchbook with scenes of the defeat surrounding him. And he did what war correspondents today might not do. Every evening, he went to the school house that served as a field hospital and helped nurse the wounded and comfort the dying.

> I had been assisting the surgeons by passing the instruments from one room to another, holding a candle or pressing the hand of some poor creature under operation, until I became faint with it all and had to leave the room for fresh air. Outside, my leg was plucked by a poor wretch. His face, mere pulp, had been crushed by a shell fragment and was black with clotted gore. Slowly lifting his arm he pointed to the lower part of his face and then again and I understood. I knelt by his side and poured some brandy from my flask down his throat. He could not express his thanks but his eyelids trembled and he lifted his arm again, bringing his hand gradually to a salute. It will ever remain in my memory.

Villiers's first sketchbook was now full. It told the story of his first war in all its horror. There was a saying in those days, that where the hoof of a Turkish horse treads, no blade of grass will ever grow again and in the weeks following the rout, Villiers had no reason to doubt it. As the Turks moved forward, they destroyed all in their way, crops burnt, property fired and plundered, people whatever the age butchered. And nowhere did they do it more methodically, brutally and completely than in Bulgaria.

Bulgarian revolutionaries, encouraged by the Serbs' revolt, had decided it was their turn to break the Ottoman yoke. But they were disorganised and badly armed and did little in the way of preparation other than address public rallies and sing newly composed patriotic songs. The Turkish High Command, concentrating its regular army against the Serbs, sent in the bashi-bazouks, mercenary irregulars, to quell the stillborn revolution. The scale and thoroughness of their brutality outdid even the Turkish army.

Within months they had slaughtered an estimated fifteen thousand Bulgarians. When over a thousand women and children took refuge in a church at Batak, the bashi-bazouks barricaded the doors and set fire to it. All inside were burnt alive and their executioners danced to their screams.

The very worst of the atrocities were reported by the American correspondent whose unlikely name was Januarius Aloysius MacGahan and Villiers had used MacGahan's accounts, and what he had witnessed himself, to complete his sketchbook. The drawings were published in *The Graphic* and the engravers emphasised the bestiality and horror of the massacres with their own additions. The newspaper distributed the drawings throughout Europe and the Turkish High Command, absolving themselves of any responsibility for the irregulars' actions, was outraged. A bounty was placed on Villiers's head. Captured, he was to be summarily hanged.

※

'I must find the objects of which I am in search. Types of Bulgarian skulls I have promised to procure for my surgeon friend in old England.'

'Have no fear,' sighed my host. 'You will find in one hour enough to stock the surgical schools of Europe.'

If any one episode in the Villiers saga illustrates the cavalier way in which he and his fellow correspondents then viewed their profession, it is the story of the Bulgarian skulls.

Villiers had received a cable from his friend in London asking him to search for and send back three skulls for a specific lecture he was giving at a university college. For reasons he did not bother to disclose, they had to be Bulgarian, undamaged and the cranium of a specific size and shape. It was an odd request to make to someone in the midst of war but the task, eccentric as it was, appealed to Villiers.

It was winter, he was in Batak and in the aftermath of the Turkish slaughter there, frozen corpses still littered the streets. Villiers decided the snow was too deep for him to forage for skulls and so he let it be known that he would pay handsomely if specimens were brought to him.

Next morning, as he was on his way to the hospital, three old ladies were waiting for him holding out their aprons. Inside each was a selection of skulls.

> I was much shocked, even horrified, at the grimness of this. But I reflected that business was business and commenced negotiating with these ancient female ghouls by picking and choosing. At last I decided on three fine specimens and these ladies parted with the heads of their decapitated neighbours for two coins each. The nurses made me a sack in which the grim relics were packed.

The skulls were later sent to London, via Constantinople (Istanbul), addressed to the surgeon at King's College Hospital and labelled 'BULGARIAN ATROCITIES'.

Villiers had survived his first war and his reputation had prospered because of it. The year 1877 saw him as an established and increasingly respected war artist. He would end that year narrowly escaping death in the bloodiest of battles.

On 23 April the Russians declared war on Turkey and its army, under the command of the Grand Duke Nicholas, began their advance into Ottoman territory. Villiers, celebrating his twenty-sixth birthday, rode with him. It would take another five months and four battles to decide the victor and Plevna, a small Bulgarian town close to the Danube and with no obvious strategic value, was where both sides chose to fight it out.

The Turkish general Osman Pasha, having taken the town ahead of the Russians, fortified it with a ring of trenches and redoubts sixteen feet high. His army was considerably smaller than the Duke's but his firepower would more than compensate for that. His infantry was armed with the new American Winchester repeater rifle and the longer range Peabody-Martini and his artillery newly equipped with the German Krupp field guns. Yet so confident were the Russians of an easy victory that Tsar Alexander had ordered a platform to be built on the slopes overlooking Plevna, out of the line of fire, so he might have an unobstructed view of the slaughter of the Turks he so confidently expected.

On the morning of that first day of fighting, Villiers too might have persuaded himself that he would not have to wait long to enter the town; he was, after all, in the company of Russians accustomed to winning. In the next tent was an ex-cavalry officer who had re-enlisted, feeling it his duty to do something for his country in distress. He had interrupted his social season in Paris to do just that but he did not expect to stay long. As Villiers remembers it:

Reveille sounded, I lifted the tent flap to see a quaint, tall eccentric looking man in pink silk pyjamas with a monocle in his left eye, who was slowly stirring a steaming glass of tea with a silver spoon. He was gingerly standing in bare feet on a small mat of wet straw which his servant had collected from the stubble to prevent his master from soiling his feet with the thick clay which oozed around him. His monocled eye glanced on me.

'Take it, take it,' he drawled. 'There's plenty more my friend,' and his servant, who was tending the steaming samovar, at once brought another glass.

Villiers and fellow British correspondent Archibald Forbes, writing for the *Daily Chronicle*, watched the Russians' first advance towards the town. Under the first Russian infantry fusillade, the Turks began falling back from their trenches and retreating into the town. It looked a rout and a very quick and bloodless victory. Forbes later reported that the forward ranks of Russians, led by their officers, had nonchalantly walked into Plevna like tourists. But a bugle call was the signal for an ambush and from the roofs and windows of the houses, the Turks' Winchesters strafed the unsuspecting Russians at point blank range. Few survived. Over a thousand men were killed in just half an hour. The Turks reported twelve casualties.

As the Russians fled, fire from the Winchesters followed them and the line of retreat was ploughed by Turkish shells. Villiers could hear the Russians' returning fire, sporadic, hesitant, the rattle of their infantry 'like the pulse of a dying man, fitful and weak'. He was now caught in the panic of a mass of men and horses 'like a torrent of helpless fugitives, a tidal wave, carrying everything before them'.

Among them were remnants of the army band that had so confidently marched ahead of that first infantry column. Their instruments were now scattered behind them and the brass rim of a kettle drum, sticking above the mud, suddenly reflected the flare of a bursting shell and it frightened Villiers's horse. It reared and bolted with Villiers clinging to its mane. He reflected later that the kettle drum had probably saved his life because his horse had taken him away from what had soon become a massacre. The Turks overtook and overwhelmed the soldiers he had been with and slaughtered every one of them.

Osman Pasha might easily have concluded the war then and

there had he pursued the fleeing Russians across the Danube, but his masters in Constantinople ordered him to remain and entrench. It was the greatest mistake for it gave the Russians time to reinforce and try again.

A month later, they came back with 150,000 men and a promise to their Tsar that they would not return until General Osman Pasha and his army had been destroyed. But the town was not to fall for another one hundred and forty days of fighting and the surrounding fields would then be drenched with the blood of some seventy thousand casualties.

On 10 December, the Turks, with their general wounded, his army exhausted, its supply routes cut off and his men starving and dying from frostbite and gangrene, finally hoisted the white flag.

Villiers watched that surrender and filled his sketchbook with its misery and suffering. Each drawing was reinforced with his descriptions, as if he considered his sketches alone could not adequately portray the pathos of all he had witnessed.

The morning was bitterly cold, before us lay a vast plain of snow, dotted with stark corpses. The telegraph wires running along the roadside were encased in more than an inch of ice. Far off, breaking the horizon, a long dark line came slowly, caterpillar fashion, towards us. These were the Turks who had kept the Muscovites at bay for so long ... a ghastly line of living phantoms, half starved, almost dead with fatigue, many with fever burning in their eyes and rising from them, we sniffed the taint of smallpox and typhus.

Thousands of birds of prey whirled above, like sharks round a doomed ship. Half covered in the snow was the naked body of a dead Turk, stripped of his clothes by the living. Another lay nearby with his upturned face staring at heaven through the falling snow. Dogs and swine from the nearby village were quarrelling for their share of the ghastly feast.

Every page of his sketchbook and every caption written beneath every drawing told of the suffering.

> Presently out of the stifling fog came limping men with torn and bloody clothes. Here and there men carrying maimed comrades, two men carrying one of their own on a blanket stretched across their rifles. A dark liquid slowly dripped from the saturated blanket and marked a bloody trail down to the village behind the ridge to the first-aid station. As more casualties passed so that dark track grew ever wider.

Villiers spent those last December nights in a school house that served as a makeshift hospital. A Russian doctor tended Russians and their Turkish prisoners alike, refusing to discriminate one from the other. After his rounds in the filthy, vermin-infested rooms, he returned to his own and stripped in front of his stove as his servant sprayed him with Violette de Parme, an expensive French perfume, sponged his beard, and finally washed and combed his hair before a jewelled mirror he kept in a gold and turquoise dressing case, a gift, he said, from his Tsar.

In one of the rooms, prisoners huddled around a fire made from straw and rags taken from the bodies of the dead.

> One wretched Turk struggled for a place near the fire but was thrown back. He tried again and was beaten by those who would not let him in. The good doctor, who spoke fluent Turkish, demanded that the poor fellow be allowed some warmth. And so they did. The creature could not speak his thanks. Big tears stood in his eyes and rolled down his frost bitten cheeks as he crawled up to the doctor and out of gratitude, kissed his boots.

The moving ice on the Danube settled the week before Christmas and Villiers could at last cross the river on foot and begin his journey home. He was making for Constantinople and a ship to England and he might well have stumbled unknowingly into yet another war. The Russians, having agreed an armistice with Turkey, now threatened to break it and had begun their advance on the Turkish capital. But the British fleet, having passed the Dardanelles into the Sea of Marmara, had given notice that they would open fire on the Russians if they moved any closer. They did not.

The Russo-Turkish war was a war without purpose, without strategy, a war of sheer butchery. Seventy thousand killed and thousands more maimed. Yet such was the military High Command's casual dismissal of the cost in human lives that Duke Nicholas, on accepting General Osman's surrender, congratulated him on his stubborn resistance with the words 'This has been the most splendid exploit in this century's history.'

War correspondents can only find full-time employment in times of war and the in-between times can be frustrating, debilitating, depressing. The mood change from the daily and dangerously charged action to the plodding routine of what might be called a normal life is not easy to cope with. For many the worst moment in a war is the fear of not being sent to it. Some only find peace when at war. It is an addiction that few will admit to. Villiers solved it his own way. He would tour the world.

Britain in these intervening years had few foreign entanglements considered newsworthy enough for editors to dispatch their expensive correspondents. This lull in international belligerence was Villiers's opportunity to see a world untouched by war. He travelled first to Jerusalem and the holy places that surrounded that city and it was there he met the first and only love of his life. It was unrequited but, as all first loves are, overwhelming, wonderful and unforgettable.

I arrived in Judea full of fervour as a good pilgrim should be. But everything was wiped off the slate in the flutter of an eyelid one morning at breakfast … in the form of the most beautiful creature whom I have ever seen up to that date in my vagrant life. My heart went out to her as she trifled with a boiled egg. I will not attempt to describe her poise or beauty but simply say that she was a peach, but even more lovely that that tender, luscious fruit for she had eyes of blue and peaches don't run to the azure. Though I worshipped that lovely slender thread of humanity, I was too much enamoured ever to speak to her.

He never saw her again.

A year later he was in Bombay and from there he sailed to Australia to sketch and report for *The Graphic* the First International Exhibition in Sydney. Then on to New Zealand, Ceylon, Honolulu, San Francisco and finally New York.

There he was introduced to Thomas Edison.

The inventor had not been to bed for many nights but had dozed in his clothes on a couch in his laboratory to be always on the alert when these little lamps, which were strung across the workshops, showed any signs of change in the quality of their light. He looked puffy and unkempt like a man who had been watching beside a sick bed. He sat in deep thought, his strong and heavy face sunk on his shoulders. Now and again he would give a sigh of annoyance when a globe suddenly lost its glow and changed colour. I understood that it was a question of the carbon filament or the uncertainty of the vacuum within the bulb that puzzled the inventor. I was able to make a drawing of him, in Rembrandt effect, the light of his creation illuminating one side of his powerful face, the rest in deep shadow.

Villiers travelled for a year and found on his return, and much to his delight, that he was more of a celebrity than when he had left. He was invited to Scotland to shoot stags with the Prince of Wales and famously borrowed a hat from the future King Edward, who told him, in jest, that he was not suitably attired.

He sketched Queen Victoria and her children at play at Abergeldie Castle. She was interested in the technical details of transferring his pencil drawings, often hurriedly sketched under fire in the front line, to the elaborate engravings as they appeared in the *Illustrated London News*, for whom he was now working.

He told his Queen that his sketches were sometimes further embellished by artists in the magazine's London studios to create more dramatic scenes of individual heroics and sacrifice to thrill the readers in their insatiable appetite for second-hand adventures in far-off places. If these additional flourishes ever offended Villiers he never did comment.

With such royal connections he was the toast of high society on both sides of the border, and even William Russell at his prime could not equal Villiers's diary of social engagements.

But the lure of campaigning had become too strong for him to dally longer. In June 1882, *The Graphic* asked him to go to Egypt and within a week he was aboard a steamer bound for Alexandria. Riots had broken out in that city, Europeans had been killed and the Turkish Khedive, who ruled Egypt, was besieged in his Ras el-Tin Palace, along with his harem. If the rebellion spread, the Suez Canal, Britain's gateway to India, was at risk and with it substantial British investments. The Royal Navy was already on its way.

The revolt was led by a colonel in the Egyptian army, Ahmed Urabi. Gladstone's government feared the rebel's ambition might take him and his growing band of followers all the way to Cairo. The British Prime Minister also saw it as an opportunity, encouraged by the nation's jingoism, to give his Liberal Party a new lease of popularity and power.

Urabi had set up his guns in Fort Marabout overlooking the

harbour and when he failed to respond to the British ultimatum to surrender, the British gunboat *Condor* was ordered to open fire. Villiers was on deck to watch it.

Our muzzle loaders ran out all a port and blazed away. The smoke lay heavily about the decks. The flash of the cannonade lit up the faces of the men already begrimed with powder and steaming with exertion. The captain, with eye-glass in hand, watched anxiously the aim of his gunners and shouted:

'What was that my men?'

'Sixteen hundred yards sir.'

'Give them eighteen hundred this time and drop it in.'

'Aye, aye sir.'

And the shout from the men in the maintop told us the shot had hit its mark.

Our ship quaked again and again with the blast of her guns. And our men became dark as Negroes with the black powder and were dipping their heads in the sponge buckets to keep the grit from their eyes.

Urabi's emplacements inside the fort were very quickly destroyed and the shells that had overshot their target set much of the city ablaze. Within those few hours the British had established their authority and the rebel leader and his army fled the city, intending to retrench and fight again in Cairo. They would not get that far. General Wolseley and his army were already on their way to confront him in the Battle of Tel el-Kebir.

That evening, Villiers and his friend and fellow correspondent John Cameron decided to enter Alexandria to see the extent of the damage. They reached the Place of Mehmet Pasha, a famous tree-lined square of fine buildings and where the best European stores were located.

Never was a sight more appalling than this; a whole quadrangle of lurid flame. The trees, once the glory of the square, were shrivelling in the heat.

The rumble of the burning buildings as they flared and toppled to the ground, the hissing of the steam as the melting leaden pipes let loose jets of water into the burning debris and the screams of those we could not see and the howls of frightened animals, made the night hideous.

It was fraught with danger, but Cameron carried a repeating rifle and I had a six shooter and we agreed that if we were attacked he would kneel and I would stand up behind him and in this formation we would open fire and do our best.

Villiers's report of the *Condor* bombardment of Fort Marabout, the heavy casualties within it and the demolition of much of Alexandria would today be considered outrageous:

The episode of the *Condor* was one of the pleasantest I have ever taken part in. The famous historic city lay wreathed in smoke and the glare of the burning harem in the palace was the only outward sign that the great God of War had that day sailed in Egyptian waters.

There was no blood or hurt, at least not with us. This affair of ours was a water party with just sufficient black powder burned to create an appetizing thirst with a long drink, not necessarily a soft one, to quench it.

His words and sentiments would seem to be those of the cavalier, troubadour correspondent who sees his campaigns as a perpetual picnic interrupted by the occasional battle. Yet it is a contradiction, an emotional volte-face for a man who had sketched and written so compassionately, so movingly, a man who had wept openly at the suffering he was so often obliged to record. Was it a façade to disguise his feelings? Was it the mechanism used by many war reporters since, to enable them to bury recollections of recent horrors, to turn to a fresh page, to close the curtain?

General Garnet Wolseley, with forty British warships at his disposal, quickly and without casualties secured the Suez Canal. Now, with an army of twenty-four thousand British troops and seven thousand Indians, he pursued Urabi as he retreated south across the desert towards Cairo. The rebel leader decided to make his stand outside the city just north of the railway and the Sweetwater Canal at a place called Tel el-Kebir.

British reconnaissance parties had established that the rebels did not patrol their perimeters at night, so Wolseley decided to move his two infantry divisions silently forward between dawn and dusk. They would be led by the Highland Brigade. The desert before them was flat and unobstructed, like a vast parade ground, which gave Wolseley's troops clear access and Urabi's defenders no cover to protect themselves.

The order was whispered from to soldier to solider. Not a shot was to be fired. In the first attack at daybreak, all work must be done with cold steel.

At dawn on 12 September 1882, with the rim of the sun skimming the horizon and within three hundred yards of the Egyptian defences, bugles sounded the order to attack.

> Suddenly the shrill blast of the bugles and swiftly and silently the front line sped on. The terrible hail of musketry from the Arab trenches entangled the onrushing troops ... but only for a moment, for now our dogs of war gave tongue. With wild cheers and to the screech of the bagpipes, the Highlanders and the Royal Irish seemed to outdo each other to be the first to strike for the honour of their flag that morning. Then, mixing in deadly struggle with the foe, they commenced the bloody work of the bayonet.

The sun was barely full by the time it was over. Over a mile of trenches were crowded with Egyptian dead, the sand oozed pools of red. The silent bayonets had done their work.

It was not a battle but a massacre. Over two thousand of the Egyptian rebels were buried that day in the shallow mass graves of Tel el-Kebir. The British lost only fifty-seven of their own. Villiers helped count the dead.

I counted nine Highlanders, all resting in easy attitudes as if in deep slumber, all shot through the brain. One young officer of the Black Watch was dying by the side of his colour-sergeant who had just breathed his last. Standing by me was a little drummer boy and thinking I was about to sketch the painful scene, snatched a handker-chief from the breast of his dying officer and let it fall gently on his face. It was a graceful act I shall never forget.

That night, exhilarated in battle and exhausted by its aftermath, Villiers slept until dawn. When he woke he promptly vomited.

I had thrown my weary body on the sand. The atmosphere around me was sour enough but I was used to that and I slept peacefully until the aroma increased in intensity so that by the first peep of day I looked around to see if there were carrion around. I dare not describe the sight that greeted my eyes. I had been sleeping on the crushed and seeping body of a dead Arab.

Urabi was captured and sentenced to death. But fearing that his hanging as a martyr would re-ignite the rebellion, his sentence was later commuted to exile in Ceylon. The Khedive Tewfik was back on the throne and his harem reinstated in the palace. But it was the British who now governed Egypt, as they would for another half century.

Within two years, Villiers was back in north Africa, this time in the Sudan and again alongside his favourite Highlanders. In 1884, General Charles 'Chinese' Gordon was sent from London to organise the evacuation of Egyptian soldiers from the Sudan. They had suffered appalling losses in their extended war with the Islamic revolutionary known as the Mahdi. He and his army of fanatic followers, the Dervishes, were fighting to rid Sudan of foreign rule and recast the country in the most extreme tenets of Islam. They now held Khartoum, the last British outpost, under siege and General Wolseley was ordered to break it. It was known as the Gordon Relief Expedition and Villiers was hurriedly sent from London to join it.

As the expedition moved south from Cairo, it came under constant attack by the Dervishes. Villiers records how close he came to being killed in one skirmish:

Backward and forward our cavalry charged but still the enemy was not flurried but stood their ground and gave battle. Some rolled under the horses' bellies and cut and slashed with their two handed swords, hamstringing the animals and bringing their riders to the ground. Those of ours who fell never rose again. Nothing could stop these dare devil fanatics, not the Gatling gun nor even the cold steel. Unless a bullet smashed a skull or pierced a heart they came on furiously and even when the paralysis of death stole over them, in their last convulsions they would try to stab or even bite.

Dead bodies were heaped up and on one ghastly pile was an Arab lad, his head between his legs. I prepared to sketch two soldiers nearby picking up trophies of spears and shields, when suddenly the lad sprang into the air and flourishing a knife, bounded at me. Before I could draw my revolver, the boy came so close I could hear the rush of the knife in the air. Just as I felt the warm flush of his breath on my neck, the soldiers shot the lad dead before I could pull the trigger.

The fanatical glare was still in his eyes and the knife still clenched in his hand.

Wolseley decided the safest way was to take his army in boats up the Nile and he recruited a contingent of Canadian Indians, expert in manoeuvring craft in turbulent waters, to guide him. But progress was slow, the vast river's currents so shifting and the waters over the cataracts so violent that for days the flotilla had to be hauled by ropes from the shore.

When he received the final message from Gordon that he could not out hold much longer, the General sent his Camel Corps on the short cut, two hundred miles across the desert. Villiers hired a camel at Wadi Halfa and joined them. On the fourth day they were stalked and attacked by over five thousand of the Dervishes, some on foot, some on horseback. They knew that the corps, having ridden for so long in such heat, now desperately needed to replenish their water supplies and they could only do that by reaching the Nile, less than two miles away.

The Dervishes massed between the British and that river. The corps dismounted and Villiers, riding alongside his friend and fellow reporter, St Leger Herbert of the *Morning Post*, followed.

> The men were ordered to throw themselves down, for the scathing fire was already making many casualties. My friend had worn out his khaki coat and was wearing a red tunic he had borrowed from an officer.
>
> 'You are drawing fire with that infernal jacket,' I cried. 'Take it off.' Receiving no reply I looked round and poor Herbert was lying on his back with a bullet through his brain.

On the order, the corps stood up and formed the traditional British military square, each rifleman facing the Dervishes as they attacked in waves, described by Villiers as 'leaping, not running, dare-devil foes, tom-toms beating, brandishing weapons which mirrored shifting lines of light as the sun glinted from their balanced spearheads'.

Soon, there was not one soldier who was not by now splattered in gore. A bullet passed through Villiers's trouser leg, grazing his ankle but he went about the firing lines carrying boxes of cartridges and stuffing them into the riflemen's bandoliers. Such was the intensity of British fire, the Dervishes were lost from sight in the gun-smoke and when it finally cleared, there was a silence and the only Dervishes that remained were the dead and the dying. The rest had fled back over the Kereri Hills and into the safety of the desert beyond. The 'famous square' had repelled some five thousand of the enemy.

Eight British correspondents were there at the fighting that day and at the end of it Villiers helped bury four of them. Among them, St Leger Herbert and his friend John Cameron, who had been with him as Alexandria burned on the night of the *Condor* shelling.

> We now marched for water. The parched lips of the wounded were moistened with what was left of the dregs in the water skins, black as ink but precious all the same. The sun had dropped below the horizon but the faint light of the moon showed us a wide streak of silvery sheen. It was glorious water. 'The Nile ... the Nile' burst from every throat.
>
> The wounded were lifted from their litters to see the river they had so dearly fought for ... the precious liquid that would soften their caking wounds and quench their feverish thirst.

Villiers admired the discipline of the men. They stood patiently waiting for the order to go to the water by companies. Each soldier waiting his turn. They made the last miles to Khartoum without further attacks but they had come two days too late. The entire garrison had been massacred and Gordon's decapitated head was handed to the Mahdi as the prize of victory.

When the sun rose on our camp, so hushed was the little fallen fort that the reveille brought no wanted stir. From mouth to mouth was whispered 'Khartoum has fallen'. All our fighting, all our maddening thirst, all our waste of precious blood and weeks of misery had availed nought. Our advent on the Nile had been the signal for the sacking and Gordon's doom.

Kipling immortalised the siege in *The Light that Failed* and modelled his hero Dick Heldar on Villiers. Winston Churchill wrote of it dramatically in his book *The River War*. The campaign also served as a background for A. E. W. Mason's *The Four Feathers*, much filmed, and the siege and Gordon's death by a spear on the steps of his palace was made into the Hollywood sequel *Khartoum*. Charlton Heston played the part of Gordon and Laurence Olivier the Mahdi.

It would be another thirteen years before Villiers saw that city again. When the British eventually returned to Khartoum to revenge themselves, it would be an altogether different kind of war with an entirely new range of modern weapons brought up the Nile on gunboats in a campaign led by General Horatio Herbert Kitchener. Villiers would be there too and he would also bring with him something entirely new and revolutionary in the task of war reporting. His bulky cases of luggage would contain a film camera.

Villiers was only one among many war artists, the most prolific being Melton Priors and J. A. Crowe. Army officers with an artistic bent quite often provided sketches; Major John Crealock and Medical Officer John Sylvester supplemented their army pay as occasional freelancers.

But Villiers was the first to take a film camera to war. The year – 1898. The place – the Sudan. The Egyptians were determined to regain control of that vast country. Under Mahdist rule it had descended into anarchy and Britain, anxious that other colonial powers should not take advantage of the instability and claim it as their own, authorised a full-scale invasion, a combined Anglo-Egyptian force, under the command of General Kitchener. Like Wolseley before him, Kitchener took his army in gunboats up the Nile carrying the latest weaponry, including the formidable Maxim gun and light artillery.

There were many correspondents waiting in Cairo for permission to join Kitchener's river convoy but Villiers did not mix with them. A dominant feature of his personality was to keep apart, to scheme and work on his own, to share nothing. By his own admission, he was a poseur, flamboyant and extrovert in company other than that of his own profession. He saw his comrades as rivals and like him, each a law unto himself. He wrote, 'Birds of a feather flocked together, not out of affection for each other's society but to keep watch on one another and jump the news if they can.'

Nor was he ever anxious to acknowledge or praise his competitors. With the exception of his boyhood hero, Archibald Forbes of *The Chronicle*, who was something of his mentor in the early days, Villiers gives little mention of the many others who went to war with him. Despite living in the same era as William Russell and aware of his foreign exploits, nowhere in his reports or memoirs is the great man, the father of all war correspondents, mentioned even once.

He speaks of John Cameron as his close friend, yet when Cameron is shot through the lungs during the Gordon Expedition, Villiers hardly thinks it worth a mention. His wars and his part in them were self-possessing to the exclusion of all else. This must explain why, in all the many, many thousands of words he wrote of himself and his campaigns, he devotes less than a dozen to admit to a wife, a son, a daughter and the small mill house in Bedhampton, Hampshire, that they rented.

In Cairo, Villiers tried his best to keep his film camera a secret from the other correspondents but the equipment was too large to hide. He then discovered that two Italians had sent a courier to Cairo to buy one of their own. He was not in the least concerned.

Why they imagined they could get the necessary camera and spools simply by writing to Cairo as one would a packet of tea, I have no idea. The two who thought they could upset my plans looked upon me with some kind of pity thinking they would get in on the act. Presently, their box arrived and the look of triumph quickly died out of their faces when they found that instead of a camera, it contained a lantern projector and quite an amusing series of films of a racy terpsichorean nature to please an Egyptian audience.

As the military neared Omdurman, the Mahdist capital, that September for what would be the final battle, Villiers set up his tripod and bulky wood-encased camera on the foredeck of the gunboat *Melik*.

The Dervishes were now streaming towards us in great force, about ten thousand spearmen, just as I wanted them, in the face of the early sun and in the face of my camera. I had just commenced when our fore battery opened fire. The effect in my apparatus was instantaneous and astounding. With the blast of her guns, the deck planks opened up and snapped together and down went my tripod. The door of my camera flew open and my films were exposed. Camera, tripod and film then flew overboard and promptly sank into the Nile.

So he did as he had always done and recorded the battle in his sketchbook.

The fighting on the plains of Omdurman lasted less than five hours and the Maxim guns took their toll. When the gunners had finished, eleven thousand Dervishes lay dead. British and Egyptian losses were forty-eight.

Villiers now had a choice. He could return home to England and pay a rare visit to his family or accept an offer to cross the Sudan into Abyssinia. A British mission was there to persuade its ruler to allow Egyptian garrisons to be stationed along its frontier to hem in the marauding gangs of Mahdists. Villiers did not hesitate. Within days he was in the capital and there met William Ridley.

Villiers does not explain why a tiny simian monkey was so christened. He saw him limping and in pain, tied to a rope, and bleeding from his mouth. Villiers promptly paid the monkey's owners a dollar and discovered they had forced a stick between his teeth to stop him biting. Villiers extracted it, nursed him back to health and thereafter William Ridley never left his side.

> My monkey reeked with a pungent aroma and when he showed me any extra affection, by rubbing his little head on my cheek, I had perforce to pinch his tail in order to keep him at a respectful distance. He would then spring away chattering the rudest simian expletives.

On the train back to Alexandria the ticket collector demanded the full fare for the monkey. Villiers refused, saying that William was under age, really a babe in arms and should therefore travel free. When the irate official tried to capture William, he stood on the roof until the train had pulled away from the station, leaving the ticket collector cursing on the platform.

Villiers's recollections of his tiny companion are full of such goings on.

> Arriving back from dinner at my hotel room, William had disappeared but on the floor lay a smashed vase and debris all around. I saw at a glance what had happened. Being thirsty and smelling water, he had jumped on the wash-stand and dipping his head into it, had upset the jug onto the carpet. Then in his fright, he had leaped to the mantelshelf and discovering his replica in the looking glass and thinking it another monkey, had swept the shelf clean. He then made for the bed and I found him a shivering, chattering heap of mischief hiding under the sheets.

On another occasion, at the Hotel Continental in Paris, the chamber-maids, charmed by William, had brought him raw eggs. He did not eat them but stowed them away. One day Villiers returned to a commotion on the pavement. William was on the balcony throwing eggs at passers by ... 'One expensive silk top hat irredeemably damaged by a shattered and ancient egg.'

When Villiers finally returned to England, William Ridley was a favourite with the ladies in London's fashionable salons but the friendship was soon to end. Off on yet another assignment, this time to the Cape and the Boer War, Villiers left the monkey with friends who did not know monkey ways. The little simian found his way into a neighbour's garden and ate prize vegetables. The police promptly arrested him and he was sentenced to be caged in London Zoo. A month later he died there and when the news was cabled to far-off Villiers, he knew that William Ridley had died of a broken heart.

In the following years his war diary filled with more extraordinary journeys from one world battle zone to another: the Greco-Turkish war in 1897; then with fellow correspondent Lieutenant Winston Churchill in the Boer War. At the Kimberley diamond mines he met and interviewed Cecil Rhodes. He reported the Russian–Japanese war in 1904, the Spanish Expeditionary Force to Morocco in 1909 and the Italian invasion of Tripoli in 1911.

After Villiers's watery experience in the Sudan, losing his first camera in the Nile, he resolved to wait until they were less bulky and more reliable. In 1912, he took a newly designed one to the Balkan War, this time filming for the first time in Kinemacolor, developed by the American Charles Urban.

The First World War, 'the war to end all wars', was Villiers's last. He was sixty-three and to prepare for it he spent many hours on horseback, galloping around Hyde Park to satisfy himself that he was fit enough to go. His sketches from the front lines are now considered classics of their time. Few wars since have been reported in such depth by British war artists.

But this would be like no other war, for the soldiers as well as for those like Villiers, who followed them. His generation of correspondents were the last who could wander from war to war, despite military and political cunning aimed at smothering the truth.

> The delight I felt ... when correspondents had free rein and could go everywhere ... to be riding from some great battle knowing I had in my valise something that would thrill all Europe from the lowest in the street to the highest in the land.

How the new generation of correspondents, like Philip Gibbs of the *Daily Chronicle* and *Daily Telegraph*, envied him:

> In talking to him as I often did over a bottle of wine, I heard the inside of the world's history for half a century; anecdotes as strange as the Arabian Nights, tales of terrible, fantastic things, of wild passions, of crimes and massacres, of heroism and gallantry and human love; the hotchpotch which men and women make of life. He was a handsome, eccentric, romantic figure, dependent on his own resources, initiative, daring and audacity. He pitched his tent in strange places and made his way by bribes and threats unsupported by British armies.

Villiers was treated badly by the British military and for the first time in his long career, having freely moved among so many foreign armies, he was introduced to a word new to him – censorship.

He arrived in Paris and within a few days had received a permit to be with the French forces, signed by General Joffre himself. Villiers's delight was short lived. The very next day he was summoned to the British Embassy to be told that the War Office had forbidden British correspondents to go with the French. The veto was to last months. He wrote scathingly about the sour relations between the War Office and British correspondents. Censorship was complicated and time-consuming. Every sketch and every written report had first to be examined in London, then sent out to the British military attachment in St Omer for their comments and then returned to the War Office for the final vetting. He had submitted an innocuous drawing of a British soldier watering a patch of daffodils near his trench in Flanders with a perforated jam tin. Villiers was astonished that even that had to be sent to St Omer for vetting. He protested but the official was adamant.

> I saw that further talk was useless or I might have told him that if the jam pot was a give-away to the enemy, I could easily disguise it as a beer mug.
>
> The utterly illogical attitude was beyond comprehension. I resented being treated so scurvily by my own folk when throughout forty years of British warfare, I had been persona grata with generals. Time and again I called at the War Office to ask for an explanation but with a shrug, an official told me there was none. So I became a tramp, a refugee and saw more of the fighting in those first few months than if I had been properly accredited. At first it was an irksome business dodging those gentlemen in khaki with red tabs on their caps and collars. But at last it became a joy to circumvent them.

He wrote that it had been as hard to dodge obstructive British staff officers as it was German bullets. He was subject to arrest, imprisonment and insult and yet he succeeded in getting to both the British and French fronts, when all his other rivals had failed.

In time censorship was relaxed and his drawings provided the

British public with the pictorial commentary of the war. He did not hide its horrors and his editor of the *Illustrated London News* had the courage to defy the government and publish them. His catalogue is full of titles like 'Identifying the dead', 'Over the top', 'The first poison gas cloud', 'Within fifteen yards of the Hun', 'Time for prayers', 'Cutting barbed wire under fire' and 'The Hell of La Boiselle'.

The British government and military were denying that trench warfare existed. But Villiers sketched the trenches in all their squalor. The faces of his soldiers told of their despair and wretchedness as no written dispatch could ever do. His pen and pencil imprinted on the public psyche the slaughter, the desolation and the futility of the battlefields.

Philip Gibbs, who was with him during much of the war, wrote that the war Villiers drew in black and white contained a vivid and visible truth, something Gibbs would take a thousand words to describe.

His sketches are valuable historical documents. They reveal details of our methods of attack and defences and of scenes and places before the intensity of gun-fire altered the landscape forever.

In one he gives a vivid picture of the way our rifles were linked together and fired together in trench warfare so as to act as machine guns at a time when we were grievously weak in that weapon. In another, a French officer is setting off trench mortars by touching them with the burning end of his cigarette.

Then there was that first Christmas day of war when out of the slimy trenches of Flanders, British soldiers and German soldiers met in No Man's land and said, with the ironical laughter of men living in the same hell, 'Merry Christmas'.

On some of the French positions on the Western Front he noticed a clever idea to more easily identify the hastily buried. Letters or small articles found in their pockets were stuffed into empty beer or wine bottles, corked up and stuck in the mud of the graves.

And then there is his sketch and description of the famous bath house:

> Armentières, the town that marks the border line between France and Flanders, will probably be remembered by the British soldier more than any other town on the Western Front. For it has within it an institution which was much cherished by the trench worn Tommy. Tired, foul and lice covered soldiers limped daily into this institution and in a few hours came out changed men, fresh, clean and as bright as pins.
>
> It took place in a disused jute factory, whose bleaching vats were night and day steaming with hot water, in which platoons of soldiers squatted, washed and scrubbed themselves to their heart's content, while their foul outer garments were sterilised in a fumigation room nearby. Fresh under-linen was given to each man on leaving his tub and in the twinkling of an eye, he was a new man, body and soul. Nothing during the war gave me greater satisfaction.

Gibbs praised Villiers as 'a very perfect gentle knight of old renown. And I can vouch for the truth of Villiers' pictures, for I was there.'

Villiers wrote as graphically as he sketched. Many of the illustrations he sent back to London were accompanied by written reports which were published in full. This, near the British Front headquarters at St Omer:

> In the wooded sector of the battle front, an ingenious device was used to guide men after dark to their dug outs. To avoid carrying even the dimmest lantern, served to troops in the trenches which would sometimes give out a tell tale glow and bring at once a bullet from an enemy sharpshooter, empty wine and beer bottles were strung on a cord attached to the limbs of trees. Thus belated soldiers, by keeping in touch with the bottles, could find their way home in safety.

In another, he wrote of the night he was almost shot. It was only a week away from the November Armistice. Sheltering in an empty house in Epernay, he was woken by shouts and banging on his door:

> The scene at the head of the stairs was truly dramatic and pictur-
> esque. The guard stood in front of me with a levelled revolver in his
> hand. The light from the candle held aloft by another guard was glint-
> ing along the barrel of the gun. It looked so Rembrandt, a wonderful
> study in black and white and I was just about to say, 'Don't move
> please. Keep like that while I get my sketchbook', when the revolver
> was suddenly thrust at my right temple.
>
> With a fury that startled me in its intensity they cried, 'You are a
> German spy.'
>
> I was beginning to feel uncomfortable. Three German spies had
> been summarily shot that morning in Epernay.

At the last minute, Villiers was saved by the mayor. He had, by chance, drunk coffee with him the previous day.

❦

After two and a half years on the Western Front, Villiers could face its horrors no more. Instead he travelled through Egypt and Mesopotamia, then to India and on the North West Frontier cover-ing tribal insurrections.

When he finally retired from war reporting he went on his second tour of the world, visiting the Great Wall of China, made five trips to Australia and finally achieved his lasting ambition to meet Charlie Chaplin in his studios in Hollywood. In his absence, the British government awarded him an annual state pension of £100. He had the temerity to ask 'For what service did I render it?'

In Canada, he was taken ill, the first time in his sixty-plus years. It was a prolonged and painful illness and he was treated at the Montreal General Hospital. The dedication in his two-volume autobiography, published in 1922, was to the doctors and nursing staff who looked after him.

And always the man to have the last word, he wrote in the foreword of his autobiography *Villiers: His Five Decades of Adventure*:

> To those who happen to pick up this volume and do me the honour of reading it, I wish to state that they will find no fiction in its pages. Every incident I have set down can be corroborated by comrades who have shared my vicissitudes. There is nothing in this book, as the old adage goes, 'to make the dead turn in their graves'.

He returned to England, to his rented mill cottage in Bedhampton, and having survived a lifetime of dangerous adventures, died peacefully in his sleep on 5 April 1922 aged seventy.

At his request, he was buried with his spurs on.

Henry Nevinson

FIVE

HENRY NEVINSON

1856–1941

He was christened the 'King of Correspondents'.

A man of letters who, by his own admission, could only find peace when he was at war.

A very English gentleman of great humanity and melancholy humour and of such distinguished bearing he was nicknamed 'The Duke'; a man 'of physical perfection' who loved many women as many women loved him.

He was the champion Edwardian crusader, a born rebel. He founded 'The Men's League for Women's Suffrage', rode a white charger at the head of suffragette marches and married one of its leaders. He campaigned tirelessly for the poor and destitute.

He was a prolific writer and published over thirty books, their subjects ranging from classic Greek architecture to the history of democracy. Thomas Hardy and John Masefield praised his prose, John Galsworthy fictionalised him in his novel *The Patrician* and T. E. Lawrence (of Arabia) was just one of many famous admirers.

He wrote pro-revolutionary articles from Russia, pro-nationalist pieces from India and his support for the Irish Republicans won him the praise of Michael Collins.

He won an exhaustive battle to expose slavery in the cocoa plantations of Portuguese Angola.

He was a living contradiction: a rebel who had respect for tradition; a literary man who loathed war, calling it murder sanctioned by the state, and yet was fascinated by it. The lure of action and the coupling of the pen and the sword proved irresistible. For his motto, he reversed Shakespeare's epithet to read 'The better part of discretion is valour'.

He did not begin his career as a war correspondent until he was forty and has since been recognised as the first 'subjective' war reporter 'writing not just what I see but what I feel'. Respected as a scrupulous journalist, he enjoyed that extra talent of always being in the right place at the right time.

His first assignment was the Greco-Turkish war in 1897, but it was his dispatches from the Boer War that first made him famous. His fellow traveller Winston Churchill wrote highly of him.

At the outbreak of the First World War, Prime Minister Asquith, at the request of Lord Kitchener, refused Nevinson accreditation. His liberalism made him suspect. The veto was eventually lifted and he was with the British fleet off the Dardanelles and was wounded in Gallipoli.

His dispatches were concise and, like Russell's, fearlessly critical of inept military strategy. On the Western Front in 1916 he despaired at the relentless slaughter of 'lions led by donkeys' and was one of the few British correspondents who later admitted to being disgusted with himself at the subservient role he played, doing the military's bidding.

When he died in 1941, those who attended the funeral service reflected the range of his lifelong passions, among them representatives from the Poetry Society, the Labour Party, the English Folk Dance and Song Society, West Indian Students in Great Britain, the Society of Authors and many from the BBC. Messages came from Moscow, Athens, Prague and Rome.

Such was his fame and the respect he earned over a lifetime.

❧

Henry Nevinson was born in Leicester of devout, evangelical parents. Shakespeare was declared immoral and banned; children's fairy tales were forbidden because they were not true. Readings out loud from the Bible began and ended the child Nevinson's day, the little boy constantly being reprimanded and warned that the slightest misdemeanour would invite God's wrath. He later wrote that 'the flames of hell could almost be felt licking our feet'.

When he was fourteen he was sent to board at Christ's College in north London, which, according to him, was modelled on a prison. Boys were referred to by numbers not names and 'strenuously underfed'. It was there, under the classics master Willie Hutchinson, a rugby international, that the young Nevinson learnt to love Greek and Latin verse. It was a brutal curriculum. Every morning he had to learn forty lines of verse or prose and translate them with scrupulous accuracy by the afternoon.

At nineteen he was admitted to Christ Church, Oxford. He remembers it as two initial miserable years followed by two of great abandonment and enjoyment. He rowed, skated, played the violin, attended lectures in philosophy at Balliol and flirted in the bars around Paradise Street. All of which might explain why he only managed a second-class degree. It surprised and irritated him. He would thereafter often refer to 'the Oxford man' as 'self centred, superior, contemptuous of the actual men around him and maddeningly given to lecture and put others to right'.

He was nevertheless proud to have been a product of the place and was never shy at reminding people of it. He was history lecturer at the Bedford College for Women and through his friendships there became involved in the suffragette movement. At twenty-seven, after the briefest of courtships, he married one of their leaders, Margaret Wynne Jones. He had known Margaret since childhood and as a pacifist and academic, she and Henry would seem to have had much in common. But it quickly proved to be a disastrous marriage and, with the birth of a daughter four and a half months after their wedding, it was assumed that Henry had done the proper thing to right an improper one. He wrote in his diary that it had all been a mistake and that their honeymoon in Germany had been a disaster.

His entries also reveal his long periods of depression and evaporating self-confidence: 'This half-hearted life, without grandeur, without concentrated aim. It is worse than death and I am sinking down to hell with no one to help me.'

He and Margaret lived for a while in a tenement block in London's East End slums to gather material for his book on the living conditions of the poor, ten interlinked short stories under the title *Neighbours like Ours*. It was not well received.

He diverted his energy instead to forming a cadet force among the young eastenders. He called it 'St. George's in the East Company' and it was the first of its kind in London. It was remarkably successful and his diaries at the time are full of complimentary references to the boys' drill, parades and their camp life. A year later he published a second volume on the Black Country, which had only marginal success. He despaired of ever becoming a writer.

For nearly twenty years I have been trying to learn how to write but I perceive that I shall never succeed in learning the great art in this life. For what others do so easily day by day, still costs me endless distress. My spirits nearer suicide than ever.

But within the space of a month his life would be turned around and, at the age of forty, he would be launched into a new career that would bring him fame and the grandeur he longed for.

On 14 March 1897, on his first visit to the National Liberal Club in London's Whitehall, he was introduced to H. W. Massingham, editor of the *Daily Chronicle,* a newspaper with a Liberal bias but also known, surprisingly, as the British military's favourite read. The two men talked for less than a minute but, within those sixty seconds, Massingham offered Henry a job. Three days later, this failing, brooding author, suffocated for so long in a dismal, unhappy marriage and the boredom of his nondescript life, was on his way to Athens. He was the newspaper's newest correspondent and his first assignment was to cover the Greco-Turkish war. For the next forty years, with the exception of Villiers, he would travel further and cover more wars than any of his generation and earn the unchallenged title 'King of Correspondents'.

The war of the Greeks against the Turks lasted only thirty days. It was described by some as the 'comic' war, by others as the 'unfortunate war'. It began on the island of Crete, then under the rule of the Ottomans. The island had suffered years of violent and sometimes murderous clashes between the Greek and Muslim communities. That January, Greek irregulars had landed on the island to support their brethren and the Cretans had raised the blue and white Greek flag, demanding independence. Istanbul quickly responded and reinforced its garrisons there.

But when war was officially declared, the battlefields were not to be on Crete but across the Aegean Sea and on the mainland. On 18 April the Greek army crossed the border into Ottoman Macedonia, a rag-tag army of unprepared, untrained and ill-disciplined men and no match for the Turks.

In the Greek capital Henry was given his marching orders. He was to travel over the mountains to Arta, close to the Turkish border. He recruited an interpreter named Scaramangar and, travelling light, carrying only a canvas rucksack, a rug and a mackintosh, the two began their trek.

In the village of Baltino the war had come early. Young Greek irregulars had attacked a Turkish encampment and some hundred and thirty Turks had only managed to escape a massacre under the cover of a snowstorm that night. Henry telegraphed his story to his newspaper and it was something of a scoop; it had only been a skirmish but his was the first reported eyewitness account of the beginning of hostilities.

Yet Henry was confused. As an academic, a writer of history, accuracy had always been paramount. Sources were checked and re-checked, there was no room for presumptions or bias. Yet he had just sent his 200-word story to London which within days would be read by thousands. How could he be certain that the stories told to him by the young and excitable Greeks, puffed up with excited hyperbole, were accurate? He admitted to a doubt that plagues every correspondent trying to make order out of chaos: 'The truth of the event was undiscoverable by me. I could hardly put down a single sentence and be sure it was really true.' It was the first lesson in his apprenticeship and one he would never forget. Scrupulous accuracy in reporting became his trademark.

Henry received a telegram from his editor. He was to cross the Pindus mountains and cover the war along the Epirus frontier. It was not an easy journey. Climbing those snow-covered mountains has been described as like climbing a perpendicular ladder. Scaramangar refused to accompany him on what he considered was a suicidal journey, so Henry hired two ponies and paid two local men to guide him.

The tracks up the peak were so narrow they had to hold the ponies by their manes and tails to prevent them falling and in the drifts; the snow almost covered them. In one hollow the path was blocked and they built a raft out of fallen pines to cross a river that he learnt later was known as 'The Sewer of Sorrow'.

Henry slept for two nights in the open, drenched by the snow and rain until he was offered shelter in a house. There he collapsed, crippled with stomach pains. The old lady of the house laid him out on a plank and then pounded his stomach with her fists. She placed a poultice of warm bread with four lighted candles on it and finally balanced a glass tumbler in the middle. Within an hour, the pain had gone. She told him it was the 'Venduses' to draw out the evil humours and, grateful, he did not doubt it.

It took them three days and nights to reach the border and as he entered the Janina Pass he came under fire for the first time. The Turks were less than four hundred yards away. He later wrote of that moment, of how beautiful the mountains were, how plentiful and colourful their flowers, even naming the anemones and lavender and how vivid it all was in the sunshine. He reminded himself just how urgent it was to stay alive. Indelible recollections experienced in moments of great danger; exhilaration and fear mixed. And how familiar that sensation is to those who have similarly crouched low under gunfire. The proximity of death magnifies everything.

Henry joined the Greek forces along the edge of the summit and helped them build defences from the loose rock. But it would not stop the Turks and in one final assault the Greeks abandoned their line and ran. 'They came rushing down the mountainside, with black figures waving red flags and firing down upon us. There was no attempt at defence. Officers and men just walked out of their trenches and disappeared.'

The Greeks returned to fight again in the Battle of Gribovo and Henry was witness to their defeat yet again. He saw, for the first time, men shot dead close to him and he helped bury some of them. The Greeks had fought stubbornly against overwhelming odds yet there were correspondents who, in their reports, called them cowards.

125

Henry would have none of it. His sympathies were for the Greeks. They had lost to the Turks but he wrote that their greatest pain was the loss of their pride and prestige.

It is very easy for comfortable Englishmen, whose greatest risks have been to run a football match, to sneer. But when I hear them, there rises in my mind a picture of a thin blue line going into action against impregnable entrenchments at Gribovo for a cause they knew to be hopeless.

There were murmurings among correspondents that Henry's reports were overly partisan, emphasising Greek bravery, downplaying the Turks, successes. One wrote that Henry had reported as if he regarded the war as a modern Greek tragedy. Henry promptly replied that he thought exactly that.

Greece is still what she was of old, the one barrier against Oriental darkness and oppression. She alone had the courage to strike another blow against the barbarian despotism which still holds many of her race in bondage.

Such partisanship did not appear in his reports, kept for the book he wrote on the war a year later. He returned to England but, to his relief, he was not asked to suffer domesticity and a fretful wife for long. He was sent to Ireland, the first of his many visits, and soon after, in 1898, to Spain.

Cuba was demanding independence from Spanish rule and to Madrid's anger the Americans tacitly supported them. When the American battleship *Maine* was blown up in Havana harbour with the deaths of many hundreds of American sailors, it was presumed to be the work of Spanish divers and war was declared. Cuba beckoned but instead a reluctant Henry was sent to Madrid to assess the government's resolve. There were rumours that Spanish warships were about to sail from Cadiz and Henry, as was his manner, bluffed his way past sentries and entered the military zone. There he brazenly took photographs and was promptly arrested as a spy. By lucky coincidence, the British Governor of Gibraltar was in Cadiz and on hearing of the arrest of an Englishman on such a serious charge investigated further. Days later Henry was released, promptly deported and returned home in mild disgrace.

The altercation over Cuba - it could hardly be called a war - lasted ten days and the outcome was never in doubt. Cuba became independent under Washington's protection and Spain lost the valuable colony it had owned for over four hundred years.

In November 1899 Henry came as close to dying as at any time in his long career. He was under siege, enclosed by disease, starvation and death. The place was Ladysmith in Natal, South Africa, and the Boer War was his reason for being there.

Ten years earlier, the British had fought the Boers, the Afrikaner name for farmers, who were determined to resist what they saw as the expansion of British imperialism into land they had always considered theirs. They were fierce, competent fighters and their guerrilla tactics coupled with their superior marksmanship caused heavy British losses at battles such as Laing's Nek and Majuba. It had ended in an uneasy truce and needed only the slightest spark to ignite the conflict again.

That came in October 1899. The British had for some time attempted to force the Boers to accept their demand that immigrants, mostly from Britain, should be given the vote. The Boers saw this as a cunning move to change the demography of South Africa, which would make them the minority. They also suspected that the dispatch of large numbers of troops from Britain signalled the government's determination to seize control of both the Boer republics, the Transvaal and Orange Free State. Their President, Paul

Kruger, issued the British government an ultimatum: arbitration and the withdrawal of British troops from their borders. When the ultimatum was ignored, war was declared and the civilian army of farmers was now prepared to fight the world's most powerful nation.

It was one of the most expensive and protracted conflicts Britain had ever embarked on. Not since Henry V's reign had Britain sent such a large army abroad.

It was also to become the most reported war in British history, only superseded by the Great War fourteen years later.

In this first 'Media War' over two hundred correspondents, almost entirely from Britain and the Empire, flooded into Cape Town, including Winston Churchill, Edgar Wallace, Arthur Conan Doyle and Rudyard Kipling. The Reuters news agency recruited over a hundred freelancers and film cameras recorded the arrival of the British troopships as they docked in Cape Town.

Henry landed there in the last week of September, hired horses and a young Zulu servant and began his trek northwards to Natal. On his forty-third birthday he entered the small town of Ladysmith. That same day, 11 October, the war began.

The Boers made early gains in the first five months, laying siege to Kimberley and Mafeking in the Cape Colony and Ladysmith in Natal. But the sheer size and firepower of General Roberts's army slowly overwhelmed them. Kimberley was retaken and later Mafeking, its commander, Baden-Powell, acclaimed a national hero.

But Ladysmith remained isolated and at the mercy of the Boers and their artillery. Over fifteen thousand civilians and soldiers were trapped inside the town and would remain there for another hundred and eighteen days. On the first day, Henry's diary records heavy shelling from all points of the compass. The two British commanders, Major General French and his Chief of Staff, Major Haig, both destined to become overlords in the Great War, escaped on the last train, their carriage riddled with bullets. Henry could have escaped with them, as some correspondents did, but he remained. 'To stay was not a question of courage but simply of common behaviour. I am in the very front line and for a war correspondent that is the choice of all the positions in the world.'

But to remain only made sense if, as a correspondent, he could get his reports out. Telegraph lines had been cut. So Africans were paid to run through the Boer lines carrying the reports. More were killed than ever managed the journey. The courier carrying one of Henry's longest and most dramatic reports (about the fighting on Wagon Hill) was shot dead only half a mile from the town. When finally the siege ended, the Boer who had shot him handed Henry's report back to him.

The Boers' shelling from the thirty-three heavy guns surrounding the town was relentless. Two hundred and fifty shells landed in Ladysmith daily, the guns only silent on Sundays and at temporary ceasefires, to allow both sides to bury their dead.

Henry wrote this on Christmas Eve 1899 in melancholy humour.

The Boer guns gave us an early Christmas carol and at intervals all day, their shells joined in the religious and social festivities. Our north end of the town suffered most and we beguiled the peaceful hours in digging out the shells that had nearly killed us. They have a marketable value. One perfect specimen of a 96-pounder fell into a soft flower bed but did not burst or receive a scratch. A brother to it pitched into a boarding house close by us, blew the whole place sky high, including all those resident in it. But little contretemps such as shells did not in the least interfere with the revels. About 250 children are still left in the town or in the river caves, where one or two have recently been born and it was determined they should not be deprived of their Christmas. So four enormous trees were brought in by Colonel Rhodes and Major Davis with toys ransacked from every remaining shop and Father Christmas stalked about with a snowy cap. It was 103 degrees outside.

To add to the festivities that evening, the Boers, showing an uncharacteristic sense of humour, fired a shell charged with plum pudding into the town square.

By now, six weeks into the siege, medicines were in scarce supply. Nurses were using carbolic toothpowder as an antiseptic on wounds. Henry suffered from suspected typhoid fever and spent two weeks in the makeshift hospital in the chapel. The disease was rampant and over five hundred would die of it, twice the number lost to the shelling. Henry records that if the Boers had attacked on foot, the soldiers protecting the perimeter of the town would not have had the strength to resist.

It would be a good thing if the army could be marched through London's Regent Street as they looked this morning. It would teach people more about war than pictures of plumed horsemen and the dashing charge. The smudgy khaki uniforms soaked through, the draggled greatcoats heavy with rain and thick with mud, the blackened battered faces, unwashed, unshaved and the peculiar smell. There is not much of a brass band and glory about us.

In another, later, report he describes how a column of British soldiers, sometimes called a 'flying column' because of their speed and surprise, were ordered out. He does not romanticise.

Every few hundred yards one fell down or dragged himself on all fours into the rocks. From every side arose the stupefying smell of horses, dead from starvation. Doubled together with dysentery, twisted with rheumatism, green with hunger, so the flying column crawled out to intercept the enemy.

To the misery of typhoid fever and dysentery was added starvation. Food rationing had been abandoned, there was so little to distribute. Horses were slaughtered, butchered and made into a stew. It was called 'Chevril' – the horse meat equivalent of Bovril, the popular beef extract. It was flavoured with almond hair oil and Henry wrote of it as 'smelling like a vulgar woman's hair and neighs in the throat'. Nevertheless, twenty-eight horses were slaughtered daily for Chevril soup and the final butcher's bill was over two thousand.

The trapped garrison became indifferent to the shells and the suffering. There were caves by the river where the women and children would run to when the artillery opened fire but now few bothered to move, as if they cared little for their survival, accepting death as an inevitability.

George Steevens of the *Daily Mail*, Henry's closest friend throughout the siege, wrote:

> Beyond is the world of war and love. You are of it but not in it, clean out of this world. To your world and to yourself you are every bit as good as dead, except that dead men have no time to fill in. I know how a monk without a vocation feels. I know how a fly in a beer bottle feels. I know how it tastes too.

Soon after writing that, Steevens died of enteric fever, a form of typhoid.

By the New Year, the British commander General Redvers Buller now had over twenty thousand troops in Natal fighting fewer than five thousand of the enemy. The Boers began to retreat on all fronts; the siege at Kimberley had been lifted.

In February, preparing to attack the Boers overlooking Ladysmith, British troops built a pontoon bridge across the Tugela River and, unseen, quickly outflanked the Boer positions. Retreat was their only option. On 28 February shouts and singing woke Henry. Crowds were moving to the edge of the town and he followed. From there, less than a mile away, he watched the long convoy of Boer wagons and artillery pieces moving away from the Tugela Heights. Soon after, Lord Dundonald led a column of his troops into the town and alongside him rode a young officer who was also serving as a journalist, Winston Churchill. The 118-day siege of Ladysmith was ended.

Henry had been fiercely critical of Buller, calling him a donkey leading lions, and he shattered the myth that the general was the hero of the campaign. He catalogued his blunders from Colenso to Spion Kop and said it was utter nonsense for British newspapers to report that the general had been the first to liberate Ladysmith. He had, in fact, arrived after Dundonald a day later when the fake pictures of his entry had been taken.

Henry travelled to Durban to convalesce and enjoy the luxuries of hot baths, clean sheets and enormous breakfasts. The relief of Ladysmith did not excite the British public as much as he had expected. This was partly because the siege of Kimberley had been lifted only two weeks before and the siege of Mafeking was still ongoing. It had also started a month earlier and Baden-Powell was commanding it and correspondents there had made a hero of him.

Henry had expected to be sent by his newspaper to join British troops as they advanced on Pretoria, the Transvaal's capital. He was disappointed. Instead he was ordered to return to Ladysmith to write his final article. Sadly and reluctantly he entered the town: 'In this city of the dead I am like a ghost who has escaped for a week and now returns to his former tomb. On almost every rock there sits a ghost who nods his head and speaks quietly to me as I pass.'

In June, he joined the Grenadier Guards as they entered victoriously into Pretoria to mark the ending of the three years of war. He watched the Union flag raised and sang the National Anthem but he wrote that his oddest pleasure that day was to hear, coming from a Boer's home, a gramophone playing Beethoven's 'Waldstein' sonata.

In later articles, he analysed the lessons the British military could learn from this war. He stressed the need for long-range and mobile artillery, he praised the Boers' tactics, their marksmanship and above all their courage. And something new entered the military vocabulary: guerrilla warfare. The Boers, as farmers, knew their land well, knew its hiding spots and the best places for ambush. In their dark brown and tan clothes they were comfortably camouflaged unlike the British redcoats. They moved in small numbers, avoiding pitched battles, and, because they were on horseback and mobile, gave the impression they had greater numbers. They could pick the fight where they wanted it and at a time that best suited them.

He pointed to the absurdity of anarchic, individual acts on the battlefield, done in the name of duty and heroism. It was no longer necessary, he said, for British officers in bright red coats and plumed hats to strut around under fire waving their swords. He ended with a plea for the role of the war correspondent to be reconsidered by both government and military. They should be treated as valuable members of any operation, given access to those in command and above all given respect and consideration by officers and the censors alike.

Much of the British press, in keeping with the national mood of triumphant jingoism, continued to depict the Boers as enemies. Henry was not among them. To him they had been simply a nation of farmers fighting for their land. Britain, on the other hand, he wrote, only wanted South Africa's gold and diamonds and, in Cape Town, a vital port on the route to India.

Then details became public of the British military's scorched-earth policy in the Boers' lands and the deaths and misery of the British detention centres, later known as concentration camps. The Hobhouse Report revealed that to separate the Boer fighters from their only source of food and succour over a hundred thousand Afrikaners, mostly families, had been held prisoner in thirty-three camps. Of those, some twenty-seven thousand, mostly women and children, had died from disease and malnutrition.

Henry could not hide his outrage. He became a very public sympathiser and attended many pro-Boer public rallies. In one, he was so viciously attacked by an angry crowd he escaped only with the help of the police and arrived at his newspaper office bleeding and with his clothes half torn off him.

Henry's Greco-Turkish war had lasted only thirty days. The Boer War lasted thirty months and it was the making of him. He was no longer a fledgling. On the last day of May 1902, on the day the war was officially over, his final dispatch radiates the optimism he felt.

Pile up the arms in stacks, fold up the tents, cut away the barbed wire. Let this trampled earth rest and nature begin her ancient task of healing. Call in the sentries so that sons of stout hearted people may meet us as better friends. The long bitter war is done.

Henry now entered a period of his life that changed as his whims and moods changed and they were many and unpredictable. He was journalist, campaigner, adventurer and, in between these pursuits, something of a lothario. He was a passionate and sensual romantic involved in multiple relationships and behaved as if he was not married at all. He talked about home as a foreign country, alien and hateful, and complained of his wife's ceaseless nagging and ill temper. He would not even refer to her by her name but only by her initial M. 'I waste my life in loneliness and futility and commonplace because I married wrongly and too soon. I am treated with contempt at home and she speaks evil of me.'

Margaret could be forgiven. Her life was more wretched than his could ever be and she was more alone. He had married her because he had made her pregnant and he blamed her for it more than himself. He had fathered her two children, Philippa, conceived four months before their marriage, and five years later Richard. His daughter might not have existed at all he so seldom mentions her, and Richard was sent early to boarding school at Uppingham. He summed up his children as 'a quiver of arrows to the heart'.

War correspondents must live in two very distinct worlds, the contaminated world of war and the relatively docile and mundane one to which they return. The journey back is never easy and few manage it without some distress. Henry found inaction intolerable. 'How frightful is it to have to get up in the morning like any ordinary man?'

Maybe it helps explain, if not excuse, his reckless affairs of the heart.

He recorded many of them in his diary, giving the impression that hardly a week went by when he was not in love. There was no moral conflict in adultery, despite his strict religious upbringing. His conquests were invariably ardent politically minded feminists and, as an active campaigner for the suffragette movement, it is not surprising that his young ladies were recruited from its ranks. Potentially the most dangerous liaison – and by far his most passionate – was with the young, vivacious and volatile Dubliner Mrs Nannie Dryhurst. She was an anarchist, a dedicated member of Sinn Féin and a professed communist. She was also on the surveillance list of Scotland Yard's newly formed Special Branch.

None of which seemed to have mattered to Henry. He trod a thin line between his respectable, often sanctimonious public image and his private amours, yet no risk was too great to satisfy his powerful libido. He was infatuated with Nannie and describes her as his inspiration. His frequent visits to Ireland and his often covert support for Irish nationalism seem entirely due to her influence. He writes of her in unabashed sexual innuendo:

> She is magnificent in wrath, longing to drink hot blood, slitting into me with scorn and irony and hatred ... urging any and every weapon like a noble lion in the chase. Every day has to be conquered afresh, like an enemy.

Attracted as he was to women, so were they to him, a tall, strong and handsome man of such distinguished, aristocratic bearing that his friends nicknamed him 'The Grand Duke'. He was courteous, cultured, debonair, not overbearing, and he could, when the moment demanded it, affect shyness. He was also a poet and much of his wooing began with a loving couplet. But he had also mastered that most appealing and winning asset to women: he was a good listener.

In 1901 he met Evelyn Sharp at a skating rink in Knightsbridge and fell in love with her boyish figure and expressive brown eyes. She was an active Liberal, a suffragette campaigner and the sister of Cecil Sharp, founder of the English Folk Dance and Song Society. It was a relationship that would last another thirty-two years.

Finally, and to add to the ménage, Henry flirted with the wife of his best friend and fellow reporter Noel Brailsford. Jane was still in her twenties, Scottish and an early Fabian. Henry was attracted to beautiful, intelligent and independently minded feminists and she was all these things. She would not wear her wedding ring because, she said, it was a mark of bondage. But for Henry, the magnet was her unavailability.

In a letter to him early in their odd relationship, she wrote:

I am not an iceberg but a wild animal ... yes but with a brain. A mere body I will not be for anyone and you must find in me something more than physical excitement. Having once before been regarded like that by a man I took it as proof of his inferiority.

She secretly admitted her love for him but her real pleasure was in teasing him, mocking him, pretending to scold him for his advances, bringing him on and then pushing him away. And like a besotted teenager, he came back for more.

In one scene that might well have been written by his favourite playwright, Oscar Wilde, Henry was descending the stairs of a London theatre arm in arm with Jane, when coming up towards them were Nannie and Evelyn. It could have been an explosive moment but alas there is nothing in Henry's diaries to tell us what happened next.

Only the lure of a foreign assignment could interrupt these liaisons. His newspaper sent him to pre-revolutionary Russia, then to an India already aspiring to independence. He attended peace conferences in The Hague and Finland, raised funds for the relief of Macedonia, continued to march with the suffragettes through London and founded the Men's League for Women's Suffrage. He reported the Spanish conflicts in Barcelona and Morocco and the wars in Bulgaria and Albania. Then, in 1905, he went on an expedition to 'The Islands of Hell'.

São Tomé and Príncipe are two tiny equatorial islands off the coast of west Africa, colonies of the Portuguese for over three hundred years. In 1904, the prestigious American *Harper's New Monthly Magazine* commissioned Henry, for a fee of £1,000, to investigate reports of slavery in the island's cocoa plantations. He agreed to go without hesitation. Given his evangelical roots, his passionate sympathy for the underdog, a wife he could barely speak to and his teenage fascination with Livingstone's 3,000-mile journey into the heart of darkness, it was not an offer he could possibly refuse.

Slavery in the Portuguese dominions had been officially abolished in the 1870s but the islands' plantation owners continued it under a different guise. The four thousand natives who were shipped in from Angola every year came as 'contract workers'. But those who arrived never returned home. São Tomé, the largest island, was known as 'Okalungo' ... the Abyss of Hell.

Henry sailed from Liverpool and four weeks later, with stops in Nigeria, the Ivory Coast and Cabinda, arrived in Luanda, the Angolan capital, on Christmas Day. On New Year's Eve he boarded a mail boat steaming south to Benguela, which had been Angola's main slave port for over three hundred years. Here Henry began his journey into the hinterland to trace the old slave-trading route.

He left in a wagon pulled by twenty-four oxen for a journey of some five hundred miles that would take an estimated six weeks. His driver was an Englishman who said he had come to Angola years before to collect insects for the British Museum and had not returned home. He never felt obliged to explain why.

They rumbled over barren rock and up to a high forest plateau, the watershed of the Congo and Zambezi rivers. In five days they had to ford five rivers, firing at crocodiles to keep them from attacking the oxen's legs. They passed fortified villages built inside stockades to keep out lion and leopard. At a mission station at Chisamba, Henry rested for three weeks with ulcerated feet. Then he had to abandon his oxen because of the dense jungle and travelled on by foot accompanied by sixteen native bearers. He had now entered what was called the 'Hungry Country'. The Portuguese had another name for it – *A Terra do fim do Mundo* (The Land at the End of the Earth).

Along a path well trodden by centuries of slave traffic and scattered with bones, he found shackles hanging from the trees and the remains of skeletons at the base of the trunks, captured Angolans who had died from disease, exhaustion and starvation. They had been hung up by the traders to feed the jackals and hyenas.

The slave ships left Benguela every fortnight, their holds crammed with men and women with tin discs tied around their necks stamped with their number and the name of the agent who had sold them. A slave delivered in good condition would fetch over £30. The voyage took a week and once ashore, the slaves were divided into gangs. São Tomé had over two hundred plantations and each employed up to a thousand slaves. Yet the Portuguese planters denied it was slavery, arguing that as the worldwide demand for cocoa had increased, so had the demand for labour and that was the price Europeans had to pay for the comforting drink of which they were so fond.

Henry, suffering from malaria and recurring bouts of rheumatism, returned home in July and his article, lavishly illustrated and headlined 'The New Slave Trade', appeared in *Harper's* the following month. He waited for the public's response which he assumed would be overwhelming and condemning. He expected the British Quaker temperance cocoa giants, Cadbury, Fry and Rowntree, who purchased two thirds of Angola's crop, to impose an immediate boycott of the trade. He waited in vain. The three companies collectively smeared him, insinuating that he had never been to Angola. One newspaper even suggested that he was acting on behalf of international property speculators and deliberately spreading rumours to bring down the price of plantation land. Henry described the accusation as 'a vomit of poison'.

The Foreign Office eventually and reluctantly responded to Henry's repeated demands for official condemnation: 'We have repeatedly called the attention of the Portuguese government to these abuses, though it has not recently been thought polite to press the matter unduly.'

Edward Grey, the British Foreign Secretary, granting Henry an interview, was offensive:

> He looked agitated and asked me, 'Do you want us to reduce these wealthy islands to a wilderness?' Then, with rising indignation, he demanded, 'Would you have England police the world where ever there is slavery?' Imitating the official manner, I replied in the affirmative, saying that was what I thought England was all about! Where ended the interview in courteous animosity.

When he wrote in his newspaper that the God-fearing trio, Cadbury, Fry and Rowntree, were deliberately blocking reform to protect their profits, they threatened to sue and the newspaper issued an apology. Cadbury then forwarded a letter they had received from their own agent on the plantations, George Burtt:

> It would seem that Mr Nevinson does not speak Portuguese and therefore cannot appreciate the situation as it exists here. Nor should he be so affronted. The Angolan natives have been enslaved

for so many generations, the child drinks it at its mother's breast. Submission flows in the blood.

Henry had naïvely expected to achieve so much but he had hardly rippled the surface of concern. His failure to rouse a nation's conscience, his defeat by the commercial giants and apathy from a government whose predecessors, such as Wilberforce, had fought so hard to abolish slavery, depressed him.

But in time, international charitable institutions did eventually take up the baton and years later, the Portuguese planters were obliged to abandon their enslaved labour, even though it was principally because of changing commercial interests. Those who were transported in the slave ships to the 'Abyss of Hell' were finally repatriated and Henry lived to see it.

> When I come to die, my deep regret at leaving this world may perhaps be tempered by the vision of thousands of little black men and women dancing around my bed to the sounds of drums, crying in grateful ecstasy … 'He sent us home … he sent us home!'

In that summer of 1905, Henry had been suffering malaria in the sweltering heat of equatorial Africa. That winter he was in Russia, knee deep in snow. In June that year, Russian sailors aboard the battleship *Potemkin* protested at being ordered to eat rotten meat. The captain ordered the mutineers to be shot. The firing squad refused to carry out the execution and instead threw their officers overboard. The '*Potemkin* Mutiny' spread throughout the navy and to units in the army. Factories closed and over two million workers from all over Russia went on strike; the nation's entire railway system was paralysed. Leon Trotsky founded his St Petersburg Soviet and within a month, fifty of these soviets had been established across the country.

In October, Henry was sent to Moscow to cover the revolution for the *Daily Chronicle*. He was thrilled at the prospect of being present at what he believed, indeed what he hoped, was the beginning of the end of Tsarist Russia. He wrote of the 'passionate excitement' he felt at being among the revolutionaries that would bring it about, the Bolsheviks and Mensheviks. For the next six months he would travel some eight thousand miles across a wintry Russia by train and by horse and sledge to Moscow, St Petersburg, Odessa and Vilna, from the Baltic to the Caucasus; he would interview, among others, Trotsky and Tolstoy. Once again he would witness and contribute to yet another first draft of history.

When striking workers had gathered in front of Tsar Nicholas's Winter Palace in St Petersburg to present him with 'a most humble and loyal address' requesting, not demanding, reforms, the Tsar's response was to order their massacre.

In Moscow and other cities, factory workers were now being taught how to fight by disaffected soldiers who supplied them with arms, ammunition and explosives. Barricades were erected in the streets to disrupt cavalry charges and, when Henry photographed them, a revolver was pressed to his forehead and he was obliged to hand over his film.

From the balcony of his hotel he saw people shot in the streets below and when the chef of the hotel went out to see what was happening, he fell with a bullet through the heart. Henry watched a boy in school uniform run for cover then fall in the snow, 'his mouth a dark red hole'. He wrapped the boy in a hotel tablecloth and carried him inside but he was already dead.

Officers began murdering in the name of their Tsar as the first barricades were built across the streets. The air crashed and whined with bullets and shells and the snow was reddened with blood. I saw a pitiful row of dead lying on the stones and between the stones, for the first time, I saw men's blood trickling as in a gutter. The feeling of disaster grows and I fear the highest moment of revolutionary success lies behind us.

The Tsar's feared and hated Semenouski Regiment was ordered to attack the area of Moscow where vast numbers of the striking workers lived. Their heavy artillery bombardment killed thousands in their homes and entire districts were reduced to rubble. The survivors surrendered and, within three months, over fourteen thousand of them were executed and another estimated eighty thousand sent to the gulags. At such a cost, the Tsar's authority had been restored.

The months of bloodshed drained Henry's idealism and his revolutionary passion. He was emotionally and physically exhausted. He watched as Russians returned to their streets, to their factories, to their railways and offices. The appearance of normality, so rapidly accomplished after such mayhem, surprised him. And yet:

> Think of our own City men if suddenly the morning train which for years they had caught successfully, stopped running and shells rained. With what common sense would they welcome the restoration of any tyranny and with what scorn, decry the fallen sentimentalists who had cared for freedom. So in Moscow, law and order met with a greasy smile.

The Tsar and his autocracy had survived because the revolts had not happened simultaneously. They not been co-ordinated, the country was too vast for the communication of one rebellion to be transmitted quickly enough to others. But Russians had glimpsed what they recognised as liberty, something indelible.

The coming of the longer-lasting revolution would have to wait another twelve years and, when it happened, Henry welcomed it, if hesitantly. On 17 March 1917, celebrating the Revolution, he addressed a packed meeting in London's Albert Hall and asked the ten thousand there to stand in silence in memory of those who had been sacrificed in the struggle. It was the first time this custom, now a familiar one to honour the dead, was introduced in Britain.

Henry was in the wrong place at the wrong time when 'the war to end all wars' began, which was most unlike him. Had it not been for the German police he might not have survived to report it. On 4 August 1914, the day that Britain went to war, he was in Berlin. Crowds weaved between the trees on the Unter den Linden singing patriotic songs and shouting praises of their Kaiser.

Henry was staying at the Hotel Bristol but even as he watched the Anglicised sign over its front door torn down, he still did not appreciate the danger around him. Then his room was ransacked and outside he heard a crowd shouting, demanding that he and any other British reporters be brought out into the street. Henry, in the tradition of an Englishman under siege, sat alone in the dining room finishing his soup. The police then arrived and, with two revolvers pressed to his head, he was dragged out into the back yard, forced into a van and driven to the police station. For his own safety he was kept in a cell until he could return to the hotel and prepare to leave. The Kaiser ordered the entire British Embassy staff to leave Germany and that night Henry joined them on the last train to cross the border into Holland. The following day he was safely back in England.

He left the *Daily Chronicle* and joined the *Daily News* where his name was on the list of correspondents to accompany the British Expeditionary Force once they left for France. He was told that he and eleven other reporters would go with only minimal luggage but they would be given a servant and a horse and the honorary status of captain. They would wear an officer's uniform with a green armband to identify them as correspondents. It was all very encouraging but it did not happen.

Lord Kitchener, now Secretary of State for War, had loathed journalists ever since his Khartoum campaign, considering them 'thorns in the flesh of the military'. He issued orders that the conduct of the war *and* the reporting of it were the sole responsibility of the military and nobody else. A press bureau, the initiative of Winston Churchill, was established in the War Office and known, friendly and compliant reporters were recruited to staff it. Lieutenant Colonel Sir Edward Swinton was nominated the official War Office correspondent, appointed to 'feed news to the newspapers'.

In another more sinister development, and one kept secret at the time, an official register was kept by the War Office of reporters 'whose patriotism was in no doubt, were on the military's side and could be trusted to comply with regulations and not betray military information to the enemy either by accident or design'.

To make censorship complete, Asquith's government, in emergency legislation, now controlled all telegraph, cable and wireless communication. Henry spoke for all his colleagues when he wrote of his frustration.

> It is absolutely impossible to imagine men of our experience and quality giving away our country or making dangerous revelations or mistakes, even if we stood under no regulations at all. We would die rather. Everything is ready and yet we are kept chafing here while a war for the destiny of the world is being fought within a day's journey.

Although the bureau issued information and directives to newspaper editors, they were not obliged to print them. But with the embargo on free reporting and with newspapers anxious for any news of the war, what the bureau said was what most newspapers published. So Henry and correspondents like Frederic Villiers were obliged to go secretly across the Channel to find the truth themselves at the risk of being caught and imprisoned by the British military or caught and shot as spies by the Germans.

On 20 October the Allies launched their first Ypres Offensive. It lasted a month and ended in a stalemate with enormous British casualties. Henry went by ambulance to Nieuwpoort where he described it as 'strewn with bodies and by day and night the thunder of imminent destruction never ceased'. He helped take the wounded to the hospital and he wrote of what he had seen. But his report was never published because his editor thought his account 'was too horrible for readers to bear'.

Henry's son Richard was now twenty-five and an established artist with works in many London galleries. But it was his experiences in France that would make him one of, if not *the*, premier British war artist of his generation. His painting *The Machinegun* of 1915 established him as both the modern painter of war and the painter of modern war.

A limp, caused by rheumatic fever, disqualified him from military service. Instead, he completed a short course in motor engineering and in mid-November father and son joined a Quaker ambulance unit and went as orderlies to France. At Dunkirk they found over three thousand wounded, and together helped stretcher them to the waiting hospital ships. German prisoners lay on beds of straw with stinking gangrenous wounds but the French and Belgian doctors refused to attend to them. Henry comforted them with his few words of German and Richard later joined the Royal Army Medical Corps as chief nursing orderly at a hospital at Malo-les-Bains.

In Ypres, they drove their ambulance into the town to collect British wounded. It was in ruins and they saw only remnants of what, a month earlier, had been an entire British division. The Germans suddenly began their shelling again and, in the midst of it,

A random battalion came marching through the south end of the square singing 'Tipperary' as they came. I went with them beyond the ancient walls and moat ... until we came to the [German] batteries trying to conceal themselves among the trees. That confused little body of Englishmen advanced, straight towards the line of smoke and fire and death. It was the saddest sight I have ever known.

Henry had to wait eight months after the war had started before the War Office finally accredited him as a war correspondent. He was immediately invited by the army to accompany units and tour the battlefields, but it was not what he expected. He was obliged to attend lectures on military discipline and watch drilling at a cadet school. He was told how the army was fed and transported, how it was organised into companies, battalions, brigades, regiments. He was told nothing he did not already know. He could hear the sound of distant guns but he was not allowed to see them. He was told of British advances but not given the opportunity to verify the claims himself. The excuse was that their small motor convoy would hamper essential military traffic. It was nonsense.

He fought his battle at home and abroad against what he saw as the duel dictatorship of government and military. He called it 'The New Despotism' and demanded to know why so many of the nation's civil liberties were being surrendered under the guise of patriotism and the war effort. He objected to the way conscientious objectors were treated as criminals and he attended the funeral of a Durham miner who had refused to serve on moral grounds and died in prison of maltreatment and pneumonia. Henry and son Richard were publicly abused, accused of being conscientious objectors themselves.

To silence those who attacked him, he published his reply and wrote the most powerful description of his own personal experience as a man of war:

The noise, the confusion, the surprise of death, the terror and courage, the grandeur and appalling littleness, the doom and chance, the shouting, curses, stink and agony ... the air full of the shriek and boom of bullets and shells, the hammering of machine guns, the shouting of captains, the crash of cannon ... the deadly microbes crawling in the suppurating wounds, devouring the flesh ... the pestilence that walks in darkness at work in the midst of gigantic turmoil. That is the very essence of war.

Written in anger, it is one of the greatest and saddest of all of war's epitaphs.

'A remarkable tough old egg ... hard as nails.' Such was the summing up of Henry Nevinson, aged sixty, as he prepared for his penultimate war as correspondent for the *Manchester Guardian*. It was the opinion of two correspondents who were about to sail with him to the Dardanelles in April 1915; two much younger men who, despite their praise, thought him far too old for the hazardous journey ahead. In the event, the two fell sick and returned back to England. Henry stayed the course and reported the Gallipoli Campaign to its disastrous finale.

The Dardanelles is a narrow thirty-mile passage that links the Aegean Sea to the Sea of Marmara. Gallipoli is on the European side and part of the Ottoman Empire, which had just allied to Germany; he who held Gallipoli controlled the sea route to the Russian ports. That spring the Allies, which included armies from Australia and New Zealand, were determined to capture it in a sea-borne invasion.

From the outset, Henry was convinced an attack from the sea would fail. On board a Royal Navy cruiser that first morning, he began his report:

Orders for washing and cleaning clothes (to avoid septic wounds) were issued and in clear and calm weather, 'General Quarters' was sounded. The firing began at eight. Our squadron drew their fire at extreme range of 12,500 yards.

Churchill, who had helped plan the campaign, had been confident the Royal Navy's twelve-inch guns would 'blow the Turks sky high'. But they did not, on that first day or any day thereafter, as Henry reported:

> Our guns continued shelling throughout the morning but the evidence was that the effect of long range bombardment is slight. The big naval shells threw up stones and earth on the forts as from volcanoes and caused great alarm. But it was temporary. The effect of long range bombardment by direct fire on modern earthwork forts is slight. Mr Churchill's expectation of crushing the Dardanelles' defences by the guns of *Queen Elizabeth* and *Inflexible* is frustrated.

Five divisions, some fifteen thousand men, landed on 25 April at Cape Helles with covering fire from those guns. The Turks were well prepared, waiting on the cliffs above, their heavy machine guns trained on the beaches. As the troops of the Mediterranean Expeditionary Force touched the sand, they were mown down. There was nowhere to hide and the surf turned crimson.

Some accounts reaching London reported that the initial attack had been successful and that the Turks were in retreat. Henry's dispatch, scrupulously accurate, reported otherwise: 'The next day landing parties of Marines were put ashore but were driven back with some loss. The story that Marines had tea at Krithia and had climbed Achi-Baba for the view is mythical.'

During ten days of repeated and unsuccessful assaults on the Turkish positions, the Australian and New Zealand battalions, thereafter known as ANZACS, lost nearly ten thousand men, a thousand a day. There were other casualties. The Commander-in-Chief, General Sir Ian Hamilton, would eventually be relieved of his duties, Lord Fisher, the First Sea Lord resigned and Winston Churchill at the Admiralty was sacked.

Henry wrote in detail of 'the black chaos of slaughter', but as has been the custom to this day, the military censors blanked out all references to casualties. Instead correspondents were encouraged to stress the heroism of the troops and to profile individual companies. He sent this to the *Manchester Guardian* in July about the East Lancashire Regiment, with the censor's blessing:

> Here at the front of the firing line, just forty yards from the Turkish sandbags, is a wilderness of mounds and pits and trenches. There are heaped up stores and rows of horses, tarpaulins, dressing stations and carts and wagons continually on the move. Clouds of dust pervade everything and flies multiply. Trenches have Lancashire names and a long communication trench captured from the Turks is called Wigan Road. Former miners, weavers and spinners are almost naked in the blazing midday sun, picking lice from their clothes and cooking on little wood fires as shells fly over their heads.

In August one final attempt was made to dislodge the Turks at Suvla Bay. Again it failed with over six thousand casualties and Henry was one of them. The Turks were pounding the Allied positions with their heavy artillery as British troops in the front trenches prepared to advance, bayonets fixed. A shell exploded close by:

> I fell like a slaughtered ox and I heard a machine gun officer say 'Are you hit?'. I put my hand to my head and blood dripped from my fingers. 'I suppose I am,' I said. I saw my brown shirt running with blood and the warmth of it was like hot water against my skin. I wondered that a man could have so much blood.

He was taken to a dug-out and an orderly bandaged him. Within an hour he returned, a trifle pale, back to his position to witness the last actions of the failed campaign. He later joked that the shrapnel had hit his skull but rebounded, 'finding it impervious to all but reason'. Those who had thought him too old for the job were charitable enough to reverse their opinion.

But an incident at Gallipoli threatened to tarnish his reputation. Ellis Ashmead-Bartlett, the *Daily Telegraph* veteran correspondent, had from the start been highly critical of the campaign and especially of General Ian Hamilton. He compiled a letter, addressed to Prime Minister Asquith and the Australian High Commissioner in London, detailing the expedition's failures and, in a scathing condemnation, blamed Hamilton personally for the dreadful loss of life. Coming from a respected correspondent of such long standing, his criticisms would have been taken seriously. He could not, of course, send it via the usual military courier, so he persuaded a young Australian correspondent, Keith Murdoch (father of Rupert), who was leaving for England to hand-carry the letter to London for him.

But Murdoch was arrested at Marseilles, the letter confiscated and the finger pointed at Henry Nevinson for alerting Hamilton and betraying a colleague. His only response was that Ashmead-Bartlett had breached the accepted rules of censorship, a lame excuse considering his own detestation of them. Others suggested the motive was simpler. In journalistic parlance, the *Daily Telegraph* correspondent had the scoop of the campaign and his competitor had done his best to sabotage it. In fact, much later, General Hamilton confided to Henry that the culprit had been a Royal Navy photographer, although there is no second source to confirm it.

It was a minor incident but, in the opinion of the British military and the government, it showed that war reporters were dangerous meddlers and it was a mistake ever to have imagined otherwise. And it proved that, with some cunning, rigorous censorship could be bypassed.

In 1917 Henry took his army officer's khaki greatcoat and had it dyed black. It was a symbolic gesture. He was sixty-one, had been seriously ill from blood poisoning and continued to suffer from chronic rheumatism. He assumed that Gallipoli was his last campaign and twenty years of adventurous, dangerous wanderings were at an end. It was premature. Months later, and to his surprise and delight, he was summoned to the offices of his old newspaper, the *Daily Chronicle*, and asked to go back to France to report the final chapters of the war.

When he arrived to join other correspondents at the British Somme headquarters, he found that the relationship between the press and the military had changed in the most surprising way. The bullying animosity had gone and another more subtle strategy to control the media had been introduced. The army courted the reporters and, in turn, made them wholly dependent. Today we would call it 'embedding'. He would be in a small minority when he later confessed to the unease he had felt at the subservient relation-ship with the military:

> We live chirping together like little birds in a nest, wholly dependent on the military to feed us. Food appears, falling like manna from heaven without any stir by servants, like slaves from the *Arabian Nights*. The Staff motor is at our door at exactly the appointed time and a friendly Staff officer accompanies us to whatever part of the line or advance I wish to visit.

But then the war was almost over, there was talk of an armistice and relationships needed to be repaired, reputations reinstated. The army needed a 'good press'. Senior officers such as Montgomery and Vivian were prepared to talk to correspondents and even share a confidence or two. They were told that General Haig, Commander-in-Chief, was planning a final push across the Somme battlefields and they should prepare themselves. Accompanied by an army press officer, Henry left for Amiens. They walked along a ridge in thick mist and as it lifted, entire companies of Germans came walking towards them, prisoners of the British troops that surrounded them.

On 9 November 1918 at a military post in the small town of Orchies, he was told that the Armistice would be signed at eleven o'clock on the morning of the 11th. With his press officer, he drove at speed to Mons and the clock struck the hour as they entered into the Grand'Place. Crowds surrounded the arch and there was silence as the terms of the peace agreement with Germany were read out. National anthems were sung, the bells rang a semblance of 'Tipperary' and there was much weeping and laughter. Low overhead, an aeroplane dropped brilliant white stars. The war had ended where it had begun.

Henry sat alone in the dining room of the Dom Hotel in Cologne but ate very little of his Christmas dinner. He was in no mood to celebrate. On his table was a tiny Union Jack on a stick but he was not inclined to wave it. General Haig, before his hero's return to England, had presented a flag to the war correspondents he had so publicly loathed. Perhaps he had expected them to wave him good-bye, like children at a party. It was such an absurd gesture that Henry suspected that he did, after all, have a sense of humour.

Many of the war correspondents were later offered a knighthood. Some accepted but Henry did not. He saw it as a bribe to keep silent about all he had witnessed, all he had been forbidden to report.

He remained in Germany when all his colleagues had gone home. He knew that the war against the German people had not ended with the Armistice, their suffering would now compound itself and, always the humanitarian, he was duty bound to report it. On Boxing Day, he left Cologne and began his tour of the broken nation.

The Peace Treaty of Versailles dictated the amount and terms of war reparation Germany must pay the Allies. But simple arithmetic confirmed that the instalments far exceeded Germany's ability to pay. From Berlin and Leipzig he wrote of the total collapse of the currency and a destitute middle class; in the Ruhr, he saw starvation among the miners' families in the coalfields, the simmering revolt on the railways and in the ports, and the sixty thousand jobless workers at the Krupp factories who were dependent on soup kitchens.

He was outraged by the vengeance of the French and condemned their plan to further weaken Germany by confiscating the Rhineland territories of the Palatinate and Saarland, turning them into client French states. In the Ruhr, its army had commandeered schools as barracks and hundreds of teachers lost their jobs and 130,000 children their classrooms. At a children's hospital in Lindenburg he saw babies dying from starvation, their mothers' breasts dry. The French army had taken herds of cattle to supply milk to their troops. Henry's report damned them for it and appealed for milk bottle teats. The cows were soon released and within a week, a million teats had arrived from his readers in England.

Prophetically, he issued this warning:

> We have a choice before us. It is easily in our power to reduce Central Europe to a desert. Yet world peace will not be insured by the destruction of a great and laborious people or by implanting in them the poisonous seeds of revenge.

Yet the plight of the Germans, for so long the detested enemy, was hardly likely to raise much sympathy beyond that of the suffering of the children. So much of France and Belgium had been reduced to rubble, vast areas of their landscape were now a moonscape. An entire generation of three nations' young men had been lost or scarred. British newspapers, especially the Northcliffe press, continued to vilify the 'Hun', one of its newspapers even sending a directive to its reporters stating: 'Under no circumstances must news testifying to the plight of the German that is likely to arouse sympathy in England be telegraphed home.'

There was a conspiracy of silence in the British press regarding the suffering throughout Germany. Henry was the first to break it.

When a war correspondent reaches the end of his or her career, it comes as a surprise to many. Some can rise one morning and say to the mirror on the wall ... it is all over, no more, enough is enough. For others, perhaps for most, redundancy creeps forward slowly. The telephone does not ring so often, calls are not returned, the expected assignment goes to another and then another. The blurred signals come gradually into focus; it is all over and the decision was not of your making. No longer does the heart beat faster at news of a coup in the Middle East or new fighting somewhere in Africa. There is envy in reading of a younger rival's exploits, a little something dies inside and you grapple with the unfairness of it, the ingratitude. There is a void, but how to fill it? The future appears more threatening than any field of battle.

Henry embarked on his journey into retirement with no such misgivings. He did not have the time.

Sixty-two years old, already a legend in his profession and crowned by his peers, Henry wrote how he hoped to retire to a 'peaceful and contemplative life in preparation for my latter end'. That was not, one suspects, ever his intention. He successfully made the transition from war to peace and for another ten years travelled the world, writing mostly for the *Manchester Guardian* and the *Baltimore Sun*, but insisting it would not be as a news reporter, rushing to meet daily deadlines, but as a features correspondent writing descriptive pieces.

In 1920 he went to America for the first time. He marvelled at the morale and enthusiasm of the world's newest superpower, the confidence of its people, the unfamiliar consumerism, the height of its skyscrapers, the frightening modernity:

Central heating, and radiators, fit symbols for the hearts they warm ...
elegant bathrooms and copious meals, the land of ham and eggs and

violent tea ... the long stream of limousines and the signal lights upon Fifth Avenue ... the land of split infinitives and cross-bred words, where strangers say 'glad to meet you' and really seem glad.

He went there on a lecture tour billed as 'The Dean of the English War Correspondents' and was invited to New York, Chicago and Cornell University. He attended the first Disarmament Conference in Washington and went to the White House. He returned to America many times, the last with Ramsay MacDonald, the first visit by a British Prime Minister to an American President.

He toured the Middle East, his first stop Jerusalem in what was then British Mandated Palestine, to report on the arrival of the first Jewish immigrants. Amundsen, conqueror of the South Pole, asked him to join him on the race to be the first to fly over the North Pole but Henry declined, pleading old age.

When Amundsen disappeared, presumed dead, Henry mused over the style and content of his own obituary had he gone down with the explorer. 'I would appreciate the distinction, the flattery, the fine form of death and of course, the burial!'

Three weeks later Amundsen emerged unscathed from the snows of Alaska, which caused Henry to regret his decision. Ever the man to court publicity, he cited a triumphant and heroic return from the dead as an opportunity lost.

Soon after, in 1932, Margaret, his wife for nearly half a century, died. Henry married Evelyn Sharp, the girl he had met at the Knightsbridge skating rink thirty-two years before. The bride wore black.

In 1940, war came suddenly to him, the man who had spent so much of his life searching for it. He and Evelyn were living in Hampstead, north London and in his diary that September he records over thirty air raids; three bombs had demolished streets nearby, neighbours were killed. It was the beginning of the Luftwaffe's Blitz on the capital. Two weeks later the house next door took a direct hit. They lived in a makeshift shelter inside the house; there was no gas, electricity or water. A new entry in his diary reads: 'At home in a beleaguered city, exposed to bomb fire day and night. Day and night merge. We miss the sunshine for many windows are boarded up and we live like things forbid.'

In November they left for the peace and safety of the Cotswolds and the bomb-free sanctuary of Chipping Campden. He was angry that the war had removed him so far away from the city that had been home all his life. He had called it 'the centre of the living earth'.

He missed the company and conversation of its intelligentsia and he did not want to die so far away from it. He was now nearing his eighty-fifth birthday and, preparing himself for death, he began writing farewell letters to his closest friends. He signed them 'In Exile'.

His last diary entry is dated 20 October 1941 and he notes that the Russian army was holding firm against the Germans only five hundred miles from Moscow. War correspondent to the last.

On 8 November, Armistice Sunday, Evelyn woke to find him barely conscious. She sat on the bed by his side and, to stir him, read him passages from his favourite poem, *The Rime of the Ancient Mariner*. She deliberately misquoted 'Sleep is a *blessed* thing'. He opened his eyes and whispered her the correction: 'gentle'. It was his last word.

Martha Gellhorn, Ernest Hemingway and Chinese officers, Chunking, 1941

SIX

MARTHA GELLHORN

1908–1998

She was a legend in her own lifetime, the first woman to break the monopoly of men reporting from the front line of war.

She was fearless, generous, unpredictable and, like most successful correspondents, ruthless.

One of America's top magazines described her thus: 'Blonde, tall, dashing, she comes pretty close to Hollywood's idea of what a big league woman reporter should be.'

She was beautiful and unashamedly exchanged sex for military favours, flirting and sleeping with men, and coaxing them to do her bidding if the story so demanded.

Her motto was simple and self-destructing: 'You can do anything you like if you are willing to pay the full price for it.'

Her career tracked flashpoints of the twentieth century: the Spanish Civil War, the German invasion of Czechoslovakia, the Normandy landings on D-Day when she smuggled herself aboard a ship.

She was with the French and the Polish at Monte Cassino, with the British at Arnhem, with the US Infantry at the Battle of the Bulge.

She witnessed the liberation of the Dachau concentration camp and reported the Nazi trials at Nuremberg.

She covered wars in Israel, Vietnam, Cambodia and Central America and landed in Finland the day the Russians invaded. She reported from Hong Kong, Burma and Singapore. At the age of eighty-one, she reported the American invasion of Panama. It was only in the Balkans in 1992 that she finally conceded she was too old to cover it. She was then eighty-four.

Her enemies described her as a woman who 'drank, smoked, travelled and loved with abandon, wearing expensive designer slacks while reporting the horrors of war'.

Her friends, who included Eleanor Roosevelt, Leonard Bernstein and Robert Capa, thought otherwise: 'She was guided by a deep-hearted, deep-seated concern for justice, for the dispossessed, the oppressed, the neglected. She just happened to be beautiful.'

Her private life was messy and volcanic. In 1940, she married Ernest Hemingway and divorced him four contentious years later saying she did not want to be a footnote in somebody else's life. He called her 'a career bulldozer, a phoney and pretentious bitch'.

She described the war in Vietnam as her worst because 'I felt personally responsible. It was my country doing this abomination to the people we had supposedly come to save. It remains with me as a source of grief, anger and shame.'

She was a committed leftist all her life, often flirting at the edge of communism. As an atheist, she famously described all religions as 'horrible, cannibalistic, voodoo of the ugliest sort'.

※

George Gellhorn, a young German doctor, arrived in St Louis, Missouri in 1900 to join the hundred thousand Germans already settled there. He was the son of a cigar maker from Breslau and, having spent years travelling the world as a ship's doctor, he decided he would not return home. He had two reasons: he hated the Kaiser's rising militarism and, being half Jewish, was aware of the anti-Semitism that was creeping into Germany.

He opened a practice in St Louis with a fellow German, Dr Washington Fischel, also half Jewish, and, soon after, married his daughter Edna. Their first child was named after her father, their second was named Walter and, on 8 November 1908, Martha was born.

The Gellhorns were a close, happy and popular family who lived well in a spacious leafy suburb of the city. They held tennis parties, enjoyed Sunday excursions to a log cabin on the Merrimac River and picnicked on the Creve Coeur Lake. St Louis' conservative middle-class society thought the doctor disturbingly unconventional. He was obsessed with fresh air and fitness and often made his children sleep out on the porch even in winter, despite their protests. He ate hot dogs and potato salad in his box at the opera. His wife was considered a dangerous radical because she was a prominent suffragette and would regularly be at the head of seven thousand women as they marched through the city centre.

An uncompromising and unconventional father; an ardent feminist, campaigning mother. Such was Martha's pedigree.

In 1926, on her eighteenth birthday, she was enrolled at the girls-only Bryn Mawr College in Philadelphia, but it was not a success. She objected to being obliged to study for a degree that qualified her for a job she knew she would never want to have. Because by then she knew what she did want. She wanted to travel and to write.

Her first article, published by the *New Republic*, was a mocking parody on the teenage American heart-throb crooner Rudy Vallee. It earned her $5 and small praise but shortly after her twenty-first birthday she was taken on as a cub reporter for the *Albany Times Union*. She did the rounds that none of the regulars wanted: the tedious court cases, Women's Institute meetings, the police beat and the bureau of missing persons, most of whom she would later meet on slabs in the city morgue. She endured the smoke, foul language and sexual advances in an all-male newsroom where she was nicknamed 'The Blonde Peril'. But it was there that she learnt the essentials of writing:

> Rework what you write ... hack it to pieces ... cut and change ... writing is a self-conducted apprenticeship. The great temptation is to do fine writing, the beautiful mellow phrases and carefully chosen words. That I must avoid like the plague. Only simple clear words, only the straight clear sentences. I want to be a faultless carpenter.

She was now determined to leave the mundane and slowly suffocating life of St Louis. That Christmas, with money lent her by her mother for the one-way train ticket, she left for New York. When she kissed her mother goodbye at the station she had expected to cry but she could not. She had expected to feel afraid but she did not. She was barely into her twenties and at the very beginning of an adventure. It was to last for more than another half century.

> I was getting back to something that had roots in me and was part of me. I knew that now I was free. This was my show ... my show. I had a theory that you can do anything you like if you are willing to pay the full price for it.

In the spring of 1930 Martha arrived in Paris with a suitcase, a portable typewriter and seventy-five dollars. Like many young middle-class Americans at the time, she had been drawn to the French capital by a best-selling novel, *The Sun Also Rises*, written by Ernest Hemingway. Here the young could immerse themselves in French culture and find inspiration in the fashionable world of Chanel or Molyneux for the novels they were all determined to write. St Germain was the home of the largest American colony in Europe and there was much to keep them occupied. Scott Fitzgerald had long gone but Gertrude Stein was sometimes seen drinking at Les Deux Magots and at Le Casino, where Josephine Baker, the black ebony statue, nightly wowed her audience wearing only a single pink flamingo feather.

Martha rented a room in a brothel, although she was not aware of it at the time, found herself a job as a receptionist at a beauty salon and was sacked within a fortnight. Then she was fired almost as quickly by United Press, where she had worked as a copy taker-cum-coffee maker. She never did explain why.

She fell hopelessly in love, as a pretty young American in such a place was bound to do, with Bertrand de Jouvenal, a minor aristocrat who told her he had lost his virginity to Colette on his fifteenth birthday. His father was a politician and editor of *Le Matin,* one of France's most influential newspapers. Cupid had chosen wisely.

It was still possible, even then, to believe in the League of Nations as it strived to maintain world peace by peaceful means. Bertrand wrote articles for *Le Matin* supporting its ideals and he promptly recruited Martha to the noble cause. Bertrand also belonged to a group of young liberal-pacifists who preached détente with Germany and condemned the Versailles Treaty, which had impoverished that country. Their rationale was simple – as long as the two countries remained friends there could never be another European war.

One year before Hitler became Chancellor, the pacifists, including Martha and Bertrand, were invited to Berlin to meet young Germans of similar ideals. Or so they thought. They were met at the *Bahnhof* by young men in immaculate uniforms who introduced themselves as the *Hitler-Jugend* and taken in a fleet of limousines to a luxury hotel. Their hosts were charming and disciplined and welcomed their French guests by singing 'La Marseillaise' in French and giving a speech that began by quoting the French dramatist Romain Rolland:

'Germany and France are the two wings of the West. Whoever breaks one of them impedes the flight of the other.'

That evening they were entertained to a play in which a blond member of the *Hitler-Jugend* rescues a similarly blonde maiden from the clutches of a mob of obvious Jewish origin. The evening ended with a speech on the separation of races.

Martha returned to Paris sickened by the visit and refused to listen to any more talk of rapprochement. She had seen National Socialism for the first time and the experience was important, although she could hardly have known it then. Years later, the memory of it would help propel her into her first war.

But this was 1934 and letters from her mother told her of suffering on the home front. She described scenes of poverty and disease, even starvation, in an America descending into the social and economic mire of the Great Depression. She told of children swarming over refuse dumps, picking for scraps of food, of the thousands of dispossessed living in shacks made of cardboard and of the many thousands more roaming from state to state desperately searching for work.

Paris was suddenly insignificant and Bertrand unwanted. Martha sailed for home, but when the ship berthed in New York she did not travel to St Louis but to Washington and a new job.

Franklin Roosevelt had been in the White House for nineteen months and had appointed a young social worker called Harold Hopkins to oversee his programme of federal investment, his remedy if the slide into chaos was to be halted. Hopkins knew the scale of the problem but not the detail nor the depth. So he set about recruiting a team of investigators to tour the country coast to coast, from the Rocky Mountains to Mexico: journalists, novelists, dramatists, anyone who could ask the right questions and listen to the answers. Their brief was vast but simple: dig deep, talk to everyone, write it all down and send it back to Washington. The pay was $35 a week. Some went by car, most by bus. Martha, at twenty-five and the youngest in the team, was dispatched south to the Carolinas and north to New England.

She discovered another America, another world and one she could not, in her worst nightmare, have ever thought existed. In the textile mill towns of North Carolina she interviewed five families a day, sometimes more, each of their stories meticulously written into her notebook, each a story of despair, desperation and, worse, resignation. The more she travelled, the worse it became and the greater her shame and indignation.

In Providence, Rhode Island, she collapsed in a state of physical and mental distress.

> Thank God I have no children and want none ... this mess is unworthy of new life. It is ugly, horribly ugly, raw and unkempt, nasty, littered, the trees don't grow tall enough and the land is torn ... and over it are spread the haphazard homes of shifting, unrooted, grey people ... too few faces with warmth.

Towards the end of her months of touring she was in a small town in Idaho where she met men who were being exploited by a crooked contractor. The authorities had turned a deaf ear so she told them to do something dramatic to grab attention. The next morning they smashed the windows of the local relief agency and said they had done it on Martha's advice. She was accused by the FBI of being a communist sympathiser and promptly sacked. When the President's wife Eleanor heard of it she suggested Martha write a book about all she had seen. It was published as a series of short stories in 1936 as *The Trouble I've Seen*. Eleanor and Martha remained friends for life.

Martha first saw Ernest Hemingway in Key West, in a bar called Sloppy Joe's. He was drunk. He looked scruffy in dirty shorts and vest and she was disappointed. In her college days, she had pinned photographs of him on her bedroom wall, bought all his books and cut out and filed magazine articles about his macho safari exploits in Africa, killing lion and leopard.

Martha's father had died and she had come to the Keys to be away from St Louis and a family in mourning. Hemingway showed her around the island and his house in Whitehead Street and they talked about books, about politics and finally about the war in Spain. He told her he was planning to go there; he also told a friend that he would bed her within three days. He did not. He would have to wait some months before they made love for the first time and it would be in Madrid, to the sound of shells and small arms fire.

Spain in 1936 was a country of two parts. A general election had been held but it was inconclusive. There were dozens of political parties whose names changed from place to place and whose manifestos were just as changeable. A Republican government was in power but only just. Anarchy spread across the country that summer; riots erupted in the cities, there were communist-led strikes among the miners, attacks against the landowners, churches were burnt and clergy violated, the Catalans and the Basques demanded autonomy.

The Spanish divided themselves into two camps, the Republicans and the Nationalists, led by young officer Francisco Franco. It was a war of many titles, a war of opposites: fascists against democrats, atheists against believers, communists against capitalists, the rich against the poor. And they were not all Spaniards. During the three years of fighting some forty thousand foreigners from fifty nationalities joined the International Brigade to fight the Republican cause. But many, perhaps the greater number, came to join in the greater battle; to kill the canker of fascism that now threatened to envelop Europe from its heartlands in Hitler's Germany and Mussolini's Italy. Unhindered, both dictators were ready to ignite another European war that might extend well beyond its mainland.

If the politicians were prepared to procrastinate in the name of appeasement, the intelligentsia were not and they were the bulk of the volunteers. To fight in Spain was, to them, a moral duty, a struggle of 'the light against the night'; a privilege to be there at the birth of a new social order. The English poet Louis MacNeice wrote: 'Our spirit would find its frontier on the Spanish Front, its body in a rag-tag army.'

For Cecil Day Lewis, the fight against fascism was made 'in the image of simple men who have no taste for carnage. But sooner kill and are killed than see the image betrayed.'

How seductive it must have been to the young. What allure to go into battle with such compatriots in such a cause in such a country. The only thing holding Martha back was the cost of a boat ticket to Europe. It did not delay her long. She quickly responded to an advertisement asking for volunteers to be guinea pigs for a new experimental face cream that claimed to get rid of wrinkles. It ruined her skin but it paid for the ticket. As she boarded the liner bound for France, she wrote a quick note to a family friend in St Louis, 'Me, I'm going to Spain with the boys. I don't know who the boys are but I'm going with them.'

The cafés along the Left Bank in Paris were the assembly points, the waiting stops, for those wishing to go south. Martha decided to go it alone. She caught the train to Andorra and, avoiding the border posts, simply walked across into Spain. She carried a change of clothes in a knapsack, a duffel bag full of tinned food and $50 in her pocket. She then boarded a train for Barcelona. Two days later she hitched a lift in an ammunition truck leaving for Valencia, another took her on to Madrid. That evening, with the boom of distant guns and occasional shudder of explosions nearby, she ate her first meal with the collected press corps in the basement of the Hotel Gran Via. She had found 'the boys'.

She also found Hemingway. He considered himself the grand doyen of the international correspondents and acted out the part, for some too riotously. He lived in a two-room suite in the Hotel Florida, both rooms conveniently out of the line of fire of the Nationalist artillery on the surrounding hills. He had a manservant who cooked him ham and eggs, his own chambermaid and two cars with plentiful fuel given by the local military. Such was his reputation. When he invited Martha to join him and share his luxuries, she considered it an offer she could hardly refuse. He made love to her for the first time in room 109 but it was not of her wishing; it seemed the wisest thing to do. She was there to see a war and he knew it better than most. And as she was the only attractive blonde around, she thought it better, for safety's sake, to belong to someone.

> If I practised sex out of moral conviction that was one thing. But to enjoy it seemed a defeat. I accompanied men in action in the extro-vert part of life. I plunged into that. But not sex. That seemed to be their delight and all I got was the pleasure of being wanted and the tenderness (not nearly enough) that a man gives when he is satisfied.
> I daresay I was the worst bed partner in five continents.

Madrid, sitting on a plateau with the Guadarrama Mountains to its north, was now in its fifth month of daily bombardment. Food was scarce, salami, rice, oranges and sausages made of mule meat was the staple diet of most. But the correspondents, as has always been their way, elevated themselves above the common hardships and enjoyed better things. When there was a lull in the fighting, Hemingway took his rifle into the hills to shoot partridge and rabbit and there would be a communal feast. There were many parties and there seemed to exist a constant mood of celebration. They drank fine wines ransacked from King Alfonso's cellars, the best whiskies purloined from abandoned haciendas and, in the intervals between the shelling, they listened to recordings of Beethoven and Mahler on the portable gramo-phone. Among their many visitors were returning fighters begging a hot bath: W. H. Auden, Errol Flynn, Sean O'Casey, J. B. Priestley, George Orwell, the British scientist Professor J. B. S. Haldane. Such was the company that sometimes Madrid was more like Bloomsbury.

In such an atmosphere, it was not considered bizarre to go the cinema and watch Fred Astaire in *The Gay Divorcee*. Nor was it unusual for journalists, with the front line only two miles away, to catch a tram and walk the last few hundred yards through a honeycomb of trenches. This was not what Martha had come to see. It was surreal, it was cruel and, what irritated her most, it was *boring*!

It was during a particularly intensive bombardment that Hemingway said she should write about it. She said she knew nothing about war, nothing about the size of shells and the range of the guns. She said she was militarily defunct and had only ever written about peoples' daily lives. He took her to the window and pointed to the people below going about their daily lives as best they could. She watched for a while, then sat and wrote her first war report. It ended:

Shells have been falling on the square, roaring as they hit the granite cobblestones. Then for a moment it stops. An old woman with a shawl over her shoulders, holding a terrified thin little boy by the hand, runs out into the square. You know what she is thinking, she must get the child home, you are always safer in your own place, with the things you know. Somehow you do not believe you can get killed when you are sitting in your own parlour, you never think that.

She is in the middle of the square when the next one comes.

A small piece of twisted steel, hot and very sharp, sprays off the shell. It takes the little boy in the throat. The old lady stands there, holding the hand of the dead child, looking at him stupidly, not saying anything and men run out toward her to carry the child. At their left, at the side of the square, is a huge brilliant sign which says 'GET OUT OF MADRID.'

She sent the article to *Collier's* magazine and it was published under her name. She sent a second piece and they printed that too. Then came a substantial offer from the *New Yorker*. She had arrived, one of the boys. She was a war correspondent.

But it was a war her side was losing. Franco's forces now controlled two thirds of the country. Hitler's Heinkel and Dornier bombers had devastated Republican-held towns, thousands had died in the ruins of Guernica, Mussolini's submarines in the Mediterranean were attacking ships bringing in desperately needed supplies. This was altogether a new kind of war, a modern war that for the first time brought the battlefield to the people.

By autumn both sides were suffering from hunger. Troops from Franco's Moorish brigade had fought their way into the medical research laboratories at the university and died of typhoid having eaten the monkeys and guinea pigs kept for experiments. In Madrid death carts now trundled the streets at night collecting the bodies of those who had been killed by the shells or had simply starved to death.

And yet, surrounded by this misery, seeing it daily and reporting it fully, Martha managed to celebrate her twenty-ninth birthday in the grandest style. She was presented with a large basket of flowers and sat down to a meal of caviar, *pâté en croûte*, *marrons glacés*, ham and Christmas pudding. Hemingway produced a bottle of champagne and the evening's entertainment was complete.

Nobody there that evening thought their carousal callous and uncaring. Perhaps they considered it was simply a matter of equilibrium; time on, time off. Martha believed that for people to stay half sane in war it was necessary for them to suspend a large part of their reasoning, lose most of their sensitivity and laugh when they got the smallest chance. War comes in intervals and like the people of Madrid, she squeezed normality in between. Their fatalism was infectious.

You could only wait. You waited for the shelling to start and for it to end and for it to start again. I saw people standing in doorways, just standing there patiently and suddenly a shell landed and there was a fountain of granite cobblestones flying into the air and silver smoke floated off softly.

You see people examining the new shell holes with curiosity and wonder. Otherwise they went on with the routine of their lives, as if they had been interrupted by a heavy rainstorm and nothing more.

Women are standing in line, quiet women dressed in black with market baskets on their arms, waiting to buy food. A shell falls across the square, they turn their heads and move a little closer, but no one leaves her place in the queue.

By early 1938, Franco's armies had reached the Mediterranean, splitting Barcelona from Valencia and Madrid. The Italians had captured Tortosa and the Luftwaffe intensified their bombing of the last remaining Republican strongholds. In March they attacked Barcelona and it suffered the most sustained bombing of the entire war. During two nights, the Heinkels carried out eighteen raids concentrating on the most densely populated parts of the city. One reporter wrote that he had seen things 'which Dante could not have imagined. Blood flowed down the gutters as deep as a man's clenched fist.'

Martha arrived in a city that was burning. But in the way that had now become her trademark, she left the trauma and tragedy, the death and destruction, for others to report. As always, her story would be about the survivors.

She found a munitions factory and, uninvited, walked into a large barn where women were working at long tables filling shells with high explosive. She expected to be turned around but the woman charge-hand came forward smiling, welcoming, like a salesgirl in a showroom.

In the centre of the building the new shells were stacked in squares and oblongs and pyramids, painted black and yellow. There were 75mms looking neat and not very harmful at all. And the tall shells, the 155mms that frighten one more when they're coming in. We admired the shells and at this moment, like a dream or a nightmare or a joke, the siren whined out. The howling, whining whistle rises and screams and wails over the city and almost at once you hear, somewhere, the deep boom of the bombs. I looked at my companion and smiled ... thinking foolishly, never forget your manners, walk don't run ... and we sauntered out of doors.

The planes now showed themselves clear and silver, the sky dotted with a few small white smoke bubbles from anti-aircraft shells. The men came out of the factory and leaned against the wall so they could get a better view and smoked. Some played an innocent game, pitching a coin. The women sat down in the sunshine and started knitting. They did not bother to look up.

They all liked working in the munitions factory because they get an extra two bread rolls a day as a bonus.

That evening she went to the hospital, huge and ornate. It was suppertime and she found her way to the children's ward. The small beds were lined against the wall and it was very cold.

The children looked like toys until you came closer, tiny white figures propped up with pillows, swathed in bandages, little pale faces showing, great black eyes staring ... small hands playing over the sheets. A little boy named Paco sat up in his bed with great dignity. He was four and very beautiful and had a bad head wound. He had gone through his pain very quietly, the nurse said. He had been very patient with it and he had grown solemner and more elderly every day. Sometimes he cried to himself but without making a sound and if someone noticed he would stop. We stood by his bed and he watched us gravely but he did not want to talk.

Thousands of refugees were now flooding the city. Martha sent a cable to *Collier's* offering a story on the dying Republic, which she likened to the last days of Pompeii. The magazine editor replied with two one-liners: 'Not interested in Barcelona story stop. Stale by the time we publish.'

The war was no longer interesting. For Americans it was as good as over. *Collier's* instead offered Martha assignments in France and England and perhaps Czechoslovakia; was there another, bigger, longer, bloodier war on the way? Martha hesitated; she was exhausted. But the magazine then offered the additional bait of $1,000 a story, three times what she had been earning. She could hardly refuse.

Within months, the Republicans were defeated and Franco would rule all of Spain as dictator for another thirty-six years. Mussolini was about to extend his African empire and Hitler had launched his ambitious thousand-year Reich. The free world, as it liked to be called, waited, hesitant and fearful.

Martha left by train for Paris. Two years before she had come to Spain the young idealist full of Republican fervour, convinced that to defeat fascism, war and killing were justified. She had abandoned the journalistic edicts of neutrality and objectivity. For her, there could be none. Bias had to be on the side of the good. She had written with her heart as well as her mind and 'objectivity was shit!'

Which is why, like so many with her, she had preferred not to report the atrocities committed by the Republicans, the persecutions, the torture and summary executions, what Hemingway would much later confirm as 'the carnival of treachery'. He admitted knowing of a French commander in the International Brigade who had personally ordered the execution of five hundred Spaniards he regarded as Franco's spies.

Nor did correspondents bother to mention how Moscow had sent Russians to join the Republicans as volunteers but who were in fact Soviet officers whose one objective was to recruit and create a Soviet army within Spain. Martha, Hemingway and the rest had chosen not to write what they knew to be happening with the excuse that it was for the greater good. They had taken sides.

She left Spain in tears. She had loved the land and the stoicism of its people, the first to suffer the relentless totality of modern warfare. Of it and of them she wrote:

> There will be millions like me who will never know what to believe in again or what to do for their beliefs. Maybe history is a stinking mess and a big injustice done and victory is always wrong. But one thing is sure. Good men are as absolute as mountains and as fine, and as long as there are any good men then it is worthwhile to live and be with them. One cannot feel utterly hopeless about the future knowing that such people exist, whether they win or not.

For the next twelve months she zigzagged across Europe to gauge its mood. She reported that fear of imminent war was everywhere. She went to Prague as the Czechs were building their frontier defences in expectation of a Nazi invasion into the Sudetenland. To France, already defeatist, bankrupt in weapons and equipment and reliant on its impotent Maginot Line defences. And finally to Britain where she despaired of what she called the cowardice and dishonesty of Chamberlain's government. War, she wrote, was now certain and she doubted whether European democracy would survive it. She wrote her last story for *Collier's* and went home.

When you try to recall a great or tragic historical event, the memory strains to pinpoint where you were at that moment and what you were doing: Kennedy's death, Armstrong on the moon, the fall of the Berlin Wall, the birth of a child. In her memoirs, Martha remembers nothing in particular when war was declared that September day in 1939. But then she had been expecting it and it was just about on schedule.

In October, the magazine asked her to go to Finland. There was talk of a Russian invasion. She said she would let them know; she had first to find it on the map. Since her return to America she had holidayed in Cuba and Sun Valley, Idaho and the prospect of an assignment in the frozen north did not appeal. But she reminded herself that she was, after all, a reporter and anyway she needed the money. Two weeks later and cancelling a dinner at the White House with Eleanor Roosevelt, she boarded a grain ship bound for Belgium. It entered British waters ten days later at night and had to drop anchor until daylight because the English Channel was heavily mined. The previous day a Dutch ship with six hundred passengers had been blown up with the loss of all lives. In the morning, Martha saw the mines and the bodies.

That November, Stalin decided that he must take Finland before the Nazis. Using an attack on a Soviet border post, orchestrated by the Soviets themselves, as a *casus belli*, he declared war on the Finns. Martha had been travelling for two weeks but she arrived in Helsinki only one hour before its first bombing raid.

No siren gave the alarm. Only the swift breath-taking roar of the bombs. The Russian planes flew high and unseen and the raid only lasted one minute. It was the longest minute anyone in Helsinki had ever lived through. Firemen worked fast putting out the fires. They could dig out the bodies later.

A curious migration started that afternoon and went on all night. Lost children, whose parents were gone in the burning buildings, straggled out alone or in twos and threes, taking any road that led away from what they had seen. They went on evacuating children in hearses and cattle carts, anything that would run on wheels. The florists sent flowers to the hospital and made wreaths and little processions of unweeping people followed the pretty coffins to the cemetery.

The Finns were vastly outnumbered. The Soviets had three times the number of troops, thirty times the number of aircraft and a hundred times the number of tanks. But the Soviet troops were poorly trained and badly equipped for fighting in an Arctic winter. They were also badly led; in his Great Purge three years earlier Stalin had executed or imprisoned the top layers of his military command. So the odds appeared even. In the first week of December, Martha was taken to the Karelian Front, close to the Russian border. Leningrad was only a hundred miles away.

This was the Finns' first big night operation. The Russians were only half a mile ahead and all that day they had been manoeuvred into a trap. The colonel in command said an entire Russian division was caught in the pocket. I hear the same story about the Russian infantry. They attack en masse in line and the Finns, hidden and dispersed, just mow them down with machine-gun fire. They are being outfought and here, as everywhere else, I hear soldiers talk sadly that these men should not die stupidly like slaughtered animals.

At Vyborg, she was taken to a prison holding captured Russians.

The chief warden was a spare grey man with pince-nez and a stammer and the gentle manner of a professor. He was talking to a Russian flyer who said pilots only had ten hours of combat experience. They had been told the Finns had no anti-aircraft guns and no fighter planes. The Finns have both and splendidly manned. The flyer had a sad, tired face and stood as straight as fatigue would let him and answered questions in a soft humble voice. I asked if he had family. He did not move and his voice did not change but tears rolled down his cheeks and his jailers looked away, they did not want to look. The flier said in the same soft voice that he had two children, one so high and one so high and his wife was expecting another. He simply stated these facts, not asking for pity. But his loneliness was terrible to see.

He was not lonely for long. After four months of fighting the Finns exchanged territory for a peace treaty and the Russians, having extended their border, retreated and the prisoners of war returned home. It was a short war and a prelude of what was to come. The Finns had comfortably held their own against Moscow's military machine but the Russian Bear had shown just how weak it was. The importance of that was not lost on the ever-watchful Hitler.

Like the war itself, interest in it was short. The *Collier's* contract was ended prematurely and Martha, in her words, 'bolted from Europe'. Two weeks later she married Hemingway in the dining car of the Union Pacific Railroad at Cheyenne, Wyoming. One newspaper headlined it 'The Pairing of Flint and Steel'.

Throughout 1940, Martha followed Hitler's march across Europe from the radio news bulletins in Sun Valley, Idaho. She called it her daily funeral bell and she fumed and ranted against the shame and ugly, selfish expediencies that had allowed the Nazis to goose-step unhindered all the way into Paris. Yet nowhere does she write that she was yearning to cross the Atlantic again. Two cheers for democracy were all she could manage.

Then, in September 1941, Japan joined the Axis powers, a menace in the Pacific that threatened both British and American interests. In the spring of 1941, *Collier's* asked Martha to fly to Asia to assess British defences in Singapore and Hong Kong. She then went on to China and Burma to report the land war against Japan. The magazine editor did not, however, include in her itinerary a visit to Pearl

Harbor in Hawaii, nor did Martha suggest one. It was an omission both would regret.

She completed her Asian assignment in six weeks. Then she returned home and that December she and Hemingway motored south for yet another holiday.

> We were drinking daiquiris in a mingy little bar on the Mexican border when a tattered Indian child came in clutching some newspapers and said, *Con la Guerra ... la Guerra*. No one noticed him the first time round. Then the word caught on and we called the boy and he sold us a newspaper, damp with his own sweat. Smeary type announced Pearl Harbor and America's declaration of war.

Despite the dramatic news, the Hemingways continued with their vacation and sailed for Cuba. It was a contradiction and Martha does her best to excuse it. *Collier's* wanted a series of stories from her about American involvement in the war but she refused. The military, she said, were so opposed to the idea of women war correspondents that she would get nothing worthwhile. The magazine then suggested she tour the Caribbean on the improbable likelihood, as it seemed then, that it could be a killing ground for German submarines. It was suggested she might also like to investigate the rumours of anti-American and pro-Axis Falangists in Havana planning to sabotage American installations. She thought the entire proposal a fantasy but the prospect delighted her; it would end months of boredom. She treated it as a well-paid holiday and bought four cool white dresses and a copy of Proust to take with her. A war correspondent she was not.

The trip was a disaster and what she wrote of her little adventures was treated as a joke by her editor. Only many years later did she discover that during the summer of 1942, U-boats had indeed been active along America's eastern seaboard and had sunk seventy-one ships in sixty-one days.

There followed two years of indolence, years trying to write a novel, years of self-indulgence and self-pity and an accelerating sense of failure. But it was her growing dislike of her husband that finally decided her. She objected to his drunkenness, his grubbiness, his bullying and braggadocio and above all his success. In November 1943 she boarded a Pan Am clipper bound for London. She was on her way to join 'the boys' again.

She found an England very different from the one she had chastised so vehemently and publicly five years before. 'It is a new country, the home of a new people. Nothing becomes them like catastrophe. Their negative qualities turn positive in a glorious somersault … complacency changes into endurance, a refusal to panic.'

She booked into the Dorchester Hotel in Park Lane, fastidious as ever about style and comfort. It would be some time before the accountants at *Collier's* were aware of the cost of a room there but by then she was indispensable. The city was crowded with correspondents, many already exhausted veterans after four years of reporting the war – Ernie Pyle, Chester Wilmot, Alan Moorehead, Richard Dimbleby and Ed Murrow. On the second day she went shopping, first to a bespoke tailor in fashionable Savile Row to be fitted out for a khaki uniform with the capital letter C for correspondent on its left tunic pocket, and then she took a taxi to Whitehall to collect her papers of military accreditation.

She was reminded that all stories were subject to censorship, a breach of which would result in accreditation being immediately withdrawn. Articles criticising military operations might have the same effect. As if to underline official distrust of all correspondents, she was told she was expected to support the war effort and galvanise public morale.

Most reporters, whatever their nationality or sex, did precisely that because they wanted to.

But to Martha, fresh to it all, this was anathema. She was by nature arrogant, combative and dismissive of authority; not one to be directed. She might, by her cunning and good looks, manage to dodge regulations here and there but there was one obstacle she could not bypass – the ban on women reporters from the front line. Until she could find a way around that, she must settle for stories on the home front.

Hearing that Ed Murrow had flown in a bombing raid over Berlin, she wrote her first dispatch from a bomber station in Lincolnshire.

The moon was skimmed over with cloud and the great black Lancasters waited. The crews stood together near their planes. They were very young, kind, polite and far away. Talk was nonsense now. The big black planes wheeled out … a green light blinked and the first was gone into the blackness … the tail light lifting and presently the thirteen planes floated against the sky as if the sky was water. Then they changed into distant, slow moving stars. That was that. The chaps were off. They would be gone all night … going south to bomb.

No one who flies could make detailed plans but each man thinks of that not so distant, almost incredible past, when the day was quite long and there was an amazing number of agreeable ways to spend it. They want that again. They want a future that is as good as they now imagine the past to have been. It is a long night when you are waiting for the planes from Europe to come back.

Other stories followed fast, each one painting emotive word pictures about the impact of the war on ordinary people. She was where she wanted to be and once again in love with the human race. She wrote about Polish refugees who told her of Jews being forced into cattle trucks and taken who knows where. She learnt in grotesque detail about life and death in the Warsaw ghetto. She visited Archibald McIndoe's burns unit in Sussex where he was re-moulding the faces of young flyers.

By the end of January 1944 she had written six articles for *Collier's* but was now mockingly referred to as 'The Dorchester Correspondent'. The news bulletins were reporting that the Allied forces had been brought to a halt just below Monte Cassino. On impulse she left for Italy.

When they had landed at Salerno the previous autumn the Allies, including a large French contingent, met ferocious German resistance. By the end of the year they were still only halfway up the Italian peninsula. Martha sailed to Naples from Algiers and hitched a lift with a French transport officer. They joined an endless slow-moving convoy of ammunition trucks, jeeps and field guns ploughing the mud. It was a journey of desolation made worse by the constant rain. Every building had been destroyed, first by Allied shelling and then by the Germans as they retreated. The countryside was littered with destroyed vehicles and equipment, burnt-out lorries, dead horses, pigs and goats and upturned rifles dug into the earth, a helmet on the butt. They passed Sardinian soldiers carrying supplies of food and water up the mountainside to the forward troops, and others coming down, bringing back the dead, tied to the backs of mules.

An ambulance was parked by the first aid station. A dead girl driver was lying on a bed with her hands crossed on a sad bunch of flowers, her hair very neat and blonde and her face simply asleep. She had been killed on the road below San Elia and her friends, the other girls who drove the ambulances, were coming to pay their last respects. They were tired and awkward in their bulky, muddy clothes. They passed slowly before the dead girl and looked at her with pity and great quietness at her face. Then went back to their ambulances.

Down a dark stony passageway was the room where the doctor worked. A soldier lay on the improvised operating table. Under the blanket you could see he only had one leg. Another sat quite silent nearby. The two had been repairing a telephone line when a shell landed. It blinded one in his left eye and almost severed the leg of the other. The blinded man made a tourniquet of telephone wire to stop his friend's haemorrhage and then, because the leg was only hanging by its skin and tendons, cut it off with his clasp knife. 'I love my friend,' said the soldier on the table in his soft old-fashioned French. 'But he shouldn't have cut off my leg.'

Within the month, Martha had returned to the clean starched sheets and room service of the Dorchester and to the unwelcome news that Hemingway had decided to taste the war for himself. He was already on his way. Out of cussedness that bordered on cruelty, he had offered his services to *Collier's*, the magazine that had long employed Martha. She knew that she was now the junior of the two. Their marriage was nearing its end and out of spite he knew this was the neatest way to wound. But there were no tears. Not now. Not with D-Day imminent.

The Allies had been preparing their invasion for over two years and by that summer two and a half million men were standing by for the order to cross the English Channel. Waiting to go with them aboard the landing craft were over five hundred journalists and photographers. There was not a woman among them; they were resigned to write from the home front. All, that is, except Martha.

That evening of the fifth of June, she caught a train to Southampton docks. She was stopped at the gates by military police and in the way that made her many favours, she explained she was going aboard the hospital ship to interview nurses for her magazine. She was waved through. When she came close to the gangplank she helped carry the stacks of stretchers aboard as one of the nurses. Once aboard, she locked herself in a lavatory. She was surprised at her own audacity and astonished at how easy it had been. That night the white ship with the red crosses painted on its side steamed for France.

At dawn, she was on deck as the ship moved slowly through the mine-swept lane and joined the Allied armada. 'A seascape filled with ships, the greatest naval traffic jam in history, so enormous, so awesome, that it felt more like an act of nature than anything man-made.'

The hospital ship anchored off Omaha Red, the American sector. Bulldozers on the beach were detonating mines, she watched shells from the warships hitting German emplacements on top of the Normandy cliffs. And bobbing up and down along the bows were bloated grey sacks: the dead, men who had jumped into the water from their landing craft too soon and had drowned under the weight of their equipment.

Casualties were already being winched aboard in what looked like open wooden coffins. Martha found her way to the surgery and spent that first day fetching for the hungry and thirsty and comforting those who were conscious.

> It will be hard to tell you about the wounded. There are so many of them. They had to be fed, most had not eaten for two days. Shoes and clothing had to be cut off, plasma bottles fetched, cigarettes to be lighted and held to those who could not use their hands. It seemed to take hours to pour hot coffee via the spout of a teapot into the mouth that just showed through bandages.
>
> We knew them by their faces and their wounds, not their names. Men smiled who were in such pain when all they wanted to do was turn their heads and cry. They made jokes when they needed all their strength to survive.

That night she went ashore with the stretcher bearers, wading waist high to help collect casualties. She was deafened by the shelling, red flares lit up a scene of mechanised mayhem. She followed a path across the beach, a narrow avenue of white tape, a path cleared of mines. Then she

> smelt the sweet smell of summer grass, the smell of cattle and peace and the sun that had warmed the earth some other time, when summer was real … and all the people who had holidayed on this same beach had swum in this sea.

By dawn, the hospital ship's casualty bunks were full. It weighed anchor and turned for England.

A ship carrying a load of pain, with everyone waiting for daylight, everyone longing for England. It was that but it was something else too; we were together and we counted on each other, from the British captain to the pink-cheeked little London mess boy. The ship moved steadily across the Channel and we could feel England coming closer. The air of England flowed down through the wards and the wounded seemed to feel it, the sound of their voices brightened and sharpened.

Martha was arrested by the military police soon after she stepped ashore and as a punishment sent to a training camp for American nurses just outside London. It did not delay her long. One night, soon after she had arrived, she crawled under the camp's perimeter fence and hitched a ride to the Dorchester. But she was now without military accreditation, without travel papers, without even a ration book to buy food. If found, she could face internment.

For the remaining year of the war, she would need to be constantly on the move, sometimes risking it in her uniform, sometimes not, ducking and dodging, using her cocky charm and physical attractiveness to coax and cajole her way from front to front, to have men do her bidding.

She went to places others were denied and she did not pretend there was no price to pay. But then it was no secret that the very best women reporters were now prepared to do exactly that and the prettier they were, the greater access they got. The story was all that mattered.

She smuggled herself back into Italy and joined up with the Carpathian Lancers, the Polish cavalry regiment that had escaped over the Carpathian mountains and became the heroes of Monte Cassino. She was with the British in Florence and wandered the Boboli Gardens, where the dead were stacked naked in open pits, and the Pitti Palace, which had become a centre for refugees who cooked and slept among the masterpieces of da Vinci and Michelangelo. She hitched a lift on a military aircraft to Paris the day after it was liberated in late August and visited the Gestapo torture chambers in the Avenue Foch. The walls and floors were dark brown with dried blood and a prisoner had scratched on the wall 'Revenge me!' She was with the troops as they entered Brussels and again at Antwerp, where the zoo was emptied of its lions and German prisoners and their women collaborators were put into their cages. By late September she was following British forces waiting to link up with the airborne divisions dropping on Arnhem.

In the winter of 1944, she joined the American 82nd Division, which was encamped three miles from Rheims, waiting for the final long push to Berlin. It was bitterly cold, so cold that men died in their foxholes and plasma for the blood transfusions froze solid. They had fought the Battle of the Bulge in the Ardennes Forest, where four American divisions had been trapped in a German counter-offensive. Martha met and began an affair with General James Gavin, at thirty-six the youngest divisional commander in the American army. He took her to the town of Bastogne, which had been entirely demolished by the American air force.

I drove up to Bastogne on a secondary road through breathtaking scenery. The Thunderbolts had created this scenery. You can say the words 'death and destruction' and they don't mean anything. But they are awful words when you are looking at what they mean. The road passed through a curtain of pine forests and came out on a flat, rolling snowfield. In this field, sprawled and bunched bodies of Germans lay thick, like some dark, shapeless vegetables. You have seen Bastogne and a thousand others in the newsreels. It is a job of death and destruction and it was beautifully thorough.

Martha's bravado, her derring-do, had made her the war's premier woman correspondent, an undisputed title after she wangled her way aboard a C47 aircraft for a flight over Berlin, the first woman correspondent to do so. But what distinguished her was the quality of her writing and the impact it had on her readers. It was direct and uncomplicated by opinion or analysis; she wasted no space on arguments about military strategy. She wrote not only what she had seen but what she felt. More compelling was the way she managed to convey, in the simplest, most honest way, the thoughts and anxieties of those she wrote about. There was no pretence. As a battle-weary veteran she confessed she remained confused by war. There were no lessons to be learnt however long you survived it. War was always worse than she knew how to describe it.

> A battle is a jigsaw puzzle of fighting men, bewildered, terrified civilians, noise, smells, jokes, pain, fear, unfinished conversations and high explosives. You cannot note everything that happens during a battle and often you cannot understand it. Suddenly you see antlike figures of infantry outlined against the sky … then they disappear and you do not know what became of them. Tanks roll serenely across the crest of a hill, then the formation breaks … and then in what was a quiet valley you unexpectedly see other tanks firing from behind trees. On the road that is quiet, empty and therefore dangerous nothing is more suspect at the front line than the silent places. And when you think you have found a nice restful place to camp, German shells start landing.

She had followed the war all the way from Normandy and wherever she could reach it. Finally, it led her to Dachau.

Towards the end of the war, correspondents were hearing stories from refugees about German death camps, stories so grotesque as to be barely believable. Martha met a young French Jew who claimed to have escaped from one of the camps where, he said, thousands were gassed and their bodies burnt in giant incinerators.

The Russians had already liberated Treblinka and Auschwitz but the Germans had quickly destroyed the camps to hide evidence of their atrocities. It was only when the British discovered Bergen-Belsen that the full horror of the Nazis' Final Solution became known to the world.

A report by the BBC's correspondent Richard Dimbleby was held up for twenty-four hours because nobody in Broadcasting House could believe his account of what he had witnessed. The American Ed Murrow, reporting for CBS, said at the end of his broadcast: 'I have reported what I saw and heard. But only part of it. For most of it I have no words.'

Two weeks later, the US Seventh Army reached Dachau, Hitler's model SS camp built as early as 1933 to hold people in 'protective custody'. Martha entered it a week later.

She was taken to the crematorium, where the victims' clothes had been stacked in neat piles and the naked bodies dumped like garbage to rot in the sun. She stood as a witness to it but she did not open her notebook; like Murrow, she did not have the words. They came later.

Behind the wire and electric fence the skeletons sat and scratched themselves for lice. They have no age and no faces; they all look alike and like nothing you will ever see if you are lucky. Prisoners rushed to the fence and were electrocuted. Others died cheering because that effort of happiness was more than their bodies could endure. There were those who died because now they had food and they ate before they could be stopped and it killed them.

In the hospital sat more skeletons and from them came the smell of disease and death. They watched us but did not move; no expression shows on a face that is only yellowish, stubbly skin stretched across bone.

Down the hall, a surgeon got out a record book for data on operations performed by the Nazi's SS doctors; castrations and sterilisations on Jews, gypsies and slave labourers and the most terrible, terrible experiments.

At the end of the grey unheated ward, a little boy was talking to a man. He sat at the foot of an old iron cot and they were talking seriously and amiably as befits old friends. They had known each other for almost six years and had been to five different concentration camps. The man had been wounded but his leg had never healed. He had a white suffering face and cheeks that looked as if the skin had been roughly stitched together in deep hunger seams. The little boy was fifteen though his body was that of a child. Between his eyes there were four lines, the marks of such misery as children should never feel.

If you want to rest from one horror you go to see another. A woman alone in a cell screamed for a long time on one terrible note, was silent for a minute and then she screamed again. She had gone mad in the last few days. We had come too late for her.

We had been told the war was over and Dachau seemed to me the most suitable place to be to hear the news of victory. For surely this war was made to abolish Dachau and all the other places like Dachau and abolish them forever. And we are not entirely guiltless, we the allies, because it has taken us twelve years to open the gates of Dachau.

That day changed everything for her. She had seen vast open pits of decaying bodies and she knew them to be Jews and she was half Jewish. She became a lifelong champion of Israel and a hostile antagonist of post-war Germany.

The adults of Germany, who knew Nazism, and in their millions cheered and adored Hitler until he started losing, have performed a nationwide act of amnesia. No one individually had anything to do with the regime and its horrors. The young realise this yet each one explains how guiltless his father was.

Santayana observed that if a man denies his past, he is condemned to relive it. The Germans, trained in obedience and moral white-washing are not a new people, nor are they reliable partners for anyone else.

She left the concentration camp in shame and revulsion and abandoned her preciously held certainty that justice and kindness would always prevail in this world. Entering Dachau, she said, was like falling over a cliff and suffering a lifelong concussion.

That day, 4 May, on Lüneburg Heath, General Montgomery took the German surrender and the war in Europe was over. There was a pause as the world waited hesitantly for the next.

Martha spent VE day in Paris celebrating with friends, drinking champagne and dancing arm-in-arm along the Champs-Élyseés. Then she motored to Berlin to continue her passionate affair with General Gavin, who was now commanding the Allied sector of the city. When she finally returned to London she had made two important decisions. She would not marry her General, despite being in love with him. And she would divorce Hemingway.

Over the next years she covered the Nuremberg Trials and the Paris Peace Conference. Beyond that the future was a void and it frightened her. War had made her internationally famous but her career prospects in the peace were scary. She was thirty-seven, alone and with nowhere to go except home to mother. And she vowed never to go to war again.

I had seen enough dead bodies, enough refugees and enough destroyed villages and could not bear to see any more. It was useless to go on telling people what war was like since they obediently went on accepting it. If you can do nothing to change events, you are free to live your own life.

During the next four years she wrote two more books and travel articles for *Atlantic Monthly*. When the infant state of Israel was attacked in 1949 she went there, not as a war reporter but as a feature writer. It was the briefest of wars and her article was never published; the editor complained that it had been written with too much unrestrained enthusiasm.

While she was living in Mexico she heard of the outbreak of the Korean War in the summer of 1950. Once again nations had embarked on large-scale killing and once again American troops were in the middle of it. But it could not lure her away from retirement. By now she had even given up reading newspapers and topical magazines, only listened to music on her radio, played a great deal of solitaire and drank too much wine. She had declared her own separate private peace, determined to live only in the present and not sink into nostalgic gloom.

She remained in that state of leisurely limbo until the day she heard that a monk had set fire to himself in a city called Saigon in a country called Vietnam. She could not find the country because her atlas was so old it was still called Cochin-China. It was small and far away and unimportant. But then it was reported the monk had committed self-immolation in protest at the brutality of a dictator who had been installed by her own government and sanctioned by her own President.

When the French were finally humiliated at Điện Biên Phủ and left Vietnam in 1954, the international peace brokers agreed there should be national elections. But the winner would most certainly be the dedicated communist Hồ Chí Minh and the Americans could not allow that. They believed in the 'domino theory': if one country were to fall to communism, others throughout the Orient and Asia would follow. They had failed to prevent Korea becoming a communist state and reluctantly agreed to a compromise; Korea was split in two, a communist north and a quasi-democratic south. So the

Americans divided Vietnam at the 17th parallel, thereafter known as the Demilitarised Zone, and without any local democratic consent President Eisenhower nominated Ngô Đình Diệm as President of South Vietnam. He also privately pledged America's military to protect him. South Vietnam was now the puppet state of Uncle Sam. Except that Hồ had waited long to rule an independent country and was now betrayed. War was never declared but a war began and it was to last another quarter of a century.

For ten years the CIA had covertly sanctioned and supported Diệm's brutal regime and American military advisers had been secretly training his army. But it was no match for Hồ's Vietcong guerrillas who had so completely infiltrated every corner of the South. It was only a matter of time before American combat troops would have to come to Diệm's assistance. In March 1965 the first divisions came ashore on the beaches of Đà Nẵng. That day Martha came out of retirement.

> We were suddenly enormously involved in a war without any expla-
> nation that made any sense to me. Instead of reason and fact we got
> exhortation and propaganda. All the war reports sounded inhuman,
> like describing a deadly football game between a team of heroes
> and a team of devils, chalking up 'body counts' and 'kill ratios'. The
> American dead were mourned but the Vietnamese dead were forgot-
> ten. Yet they were being freed from aggression … mercilessly.
>
> I want to write only about the Vietnamese people … I want to try
> humbly to give them faces so we know who we are destroying.

She would go to Saigon but it would not be easy. She was now in her late fifties and it was twenty years since she had heard the sound of gunfire. She assumed she could pick up an assignment with one telephone call but she was wrong. A new generation had taken over in the newsrooms and she had been out of circulation far too long. There is a saying that a reporter is only as good as his last story and Martha's sat somewhere deep in the press cuttings archive, long forgotten. It did not help when she publicly attacked the American invasion; such hostility that early in the war was not sellable copy. Eventually *The Guardian* offered her a contract, six articles if she paid her own expenses. It was not what she had expected but it gave her press credentials for the necessary military accreditation.

When she arrived in Saigon early in August 1966, America already had over a quarter of a million troops in the country at a cost of $2 billion a month. They had come to stand and fight but what they found was not what they expected. They had been trained in Texas and Virginia, Florida and California but it had been nothing like this. They were infantrymen, ready for set-piece battles behind tanks, covered by artillery, a war of attrition, the kind of war they had fought in Germany and Korea, the only way they knew how. But it was not the way of their enemy. This war was going to be fought on their terms and where they chose to fight it.

The enemy would be invisible, hiding in jungles, hiding in tunnels. They would be the killer shadows, ghosting at dawn and dusk, a foe by night, a smiling farmer planting rice by day, a child hiding a grenade. Vietnam would be an endless hallucination. The Americans would discover to their dismay their enemy's genius for surprise and unique ability to defeat expectations.

But this was not Martha's brief. She had not come to report how the war was being fought, the napalming of villages, the defoliation of forests, the body counts, the daily roll call of Killed in Action and Missing in Action, the search-and-destroy missions, the 'hearts and minds' charades. There were already more than enough correspondents in Saigon to do that and for many it would prove to be the best move of their career. She had no need to go looking for the front line because there was none. It was all around her. What unsettled her was that although she was carrying American military press accreditation and an American passport, she knew she was with the wrong side.

She stayed in Saigon for only a month but it was enough time to fill five notebooks for the six lengthy articles she intended to write. She dined with no generals, attended no military briefings, joined no platoons, ate no C rations, flew in no helicopter sorties and made no friends with soldiers whatever their rank. At Mỹ Tho in the Mekong delta she described a typical infantry officer who had come to kill 'gooks'.

My host was a big balding major who looked like everyone's idea of a New York cop. A certain chill had already fallen on the major and me because I asked disagreeable questions about some Polaroid snapshots. He was delighted with them and expected praise. They were coloured photos of Vietnamese corpses; the major and his men had just killed them. They were allegedly Vietcong but I doubted the proof and I suggested that instead of displaying these bloody bodies in the market place ... *pour encourager les autres* ... he might stick their heads on poles. We were not getting on well together.

She wandered at will, visiting hospitals and refugee camps. In an article headlined 'Suffer Little Children', she wrote of a visit to an orphanage full of more and more children parentless because of the shelling and bombing of villages and hamlets:

We love our children, we are famous for loving our children.

And every month of this war, two thousand children become orphans here. We cannot give back life to the dead children, we cannot now fail to help wounded children as we would help our own. But more and more dead and wounded children will cry out to the conscience of the world, unless the bombing of Vietnamese hamlets is stopped.

She interviewed doctors, nuns, aid workers and teachers, anyone who felt it was safe to talk to her. She learnt the terrible meaning of napalm and saw the effects of phosphrous shells, the white powder that gnaws into the flesh like rat's teeth until it reaches the bone. She hitched lifts with other correspondents to outlying villages.

> In theory, the peasants are warned in advance of an air attack but in what the military call their Free Fire Zones, or some such jargon, there is no warning and people are bombed at will day and night. Sometimes they are warned to leave by loudspeakers at night but no one moves readily in the dark in Vietnam and, in their haste and fear, how could they take all their possessions which they value so fiercely because they have so few.

In one hamlet she was introduced to a young woman called Phuong who said she would rather live with the threat of American bombers than leave her home, her family and their rice paddies.

> Still some cling to this fearsome, hopeless life in their hamlets. I asked Miss Phuong if she was not afraid of the Vietcong. For an answer she wept. Tears for her own family, hatred of both sides, terror of our weapons, a longing for peace.
>
> In time it should be possible to drive all the peasants from the land. It would also starve out the nation. But they cannot survive our bombs.

She had hoped her articles in *The Guardian* would be published in America. But they were not what Americans that early in the war wanted to read; after all, their generals and politicians were telling them the war was being won. Martha, even after such a short and glancing visit, was certain they were wrong. Her final article reads like a lengthy prophecy, written when the war was barely two years old.

It is a small war and maybe our ultimate chance to learn that we can no longer afford even small wars. We pay for our weapons first and pay for our real needs with the cash left over. Every year we economise on money for life to spend more on weapons and still our weapons are futile. Our B-52 bombers, each carrying thirty tons of bombs, do not crush the Vietnamese who carry little home-made bombs on bicycles. We are not maniacs and monsters but our planes range the sky all day and all night and our artillery is lavish. This is indeed a new kind of war and we had better find a new way to fight it.

This is not a war of unparalleled brutality as we have been told. One day in Auschwitz was far more brutal than anything the Vietcong has done or anything they could possibly do. But unless we crave the propaganda of fear we have to keep a grip on reality. Refugees are proof of fear but how many have fled from the Vietcong and how many more from our bombs and artillery?

We are uprooting these people from their lovely land and the uprooted are given not bread but stone. Is this an honourable way for a great nation to fight a war, ten thousand miles from its safe homeland?

Martha did not return to Vietnam. They would not let her. She had written the truth and as the war was being lost to the communists and American casualties increased, so too did bitterness towards those, who like Martha, had warned it would happen that way. When she appealed, the South Vietnamese said it was an American decision, the Americans said the reverse. She tried to obtain a visa to visit Hanoi and tour the north but that too was refused. She wanted to write a book about all she had seen and experienced but she did not. Instead she had to be content to write from a great distance about Vietnam and the Vietnamese, fired by the memories of those four short weeks. Of all the nine wars she had covered, Vietnam, she said, caused her the most grief.

I hated Vietnam the most because I felt personally responsible. It was my country doing this abomination to the people whom we supposedly had come to save. I am seeing napalmed children in hospital, seeing old women with a piece of white sulphur burning away their insides, seeing the destroyed villages and people dying in the streets. My complete horror remains with me as a source of grief and anger and shame that surpasses all the others.

She did not go to war again although her passion for reporting it never left her. She remained the insolent, irreverent, angry hack and there was always a newspaper or magazine in the Western world carrying one of her articles. She continued writing books, ten in all, some of them well reviewed; one, on her lifetime travels, became a best-seller. To stave off boredom she travelled extensively whenever her health and budget allowed. She went three times to Russia after the break-up of the Soviet Union title, many times back to Spain, to Italy, to Malta, Belize, Tanzania, Kenya, South Africa, and even steamed up the Nile. She paid for her own flight to Brazil to write an article about the killing of the street children. In 1989, aged eighty-one, she wrote articles about the American invasion of Panama.

What she could not cope with, what she admitted had always been her worst fear, was growing old. She did her best to deny old age, fought it, tried not to recognise it, paid exorbitant sums for a face lift and operations to tighten up her body. She bought a cottage in Wales, hiked across the mountains and installed an expensive indoor heated swimming pool so she could swim twice a day. She visited a gym every week and dressed as she always had, chic, elegant, attractive. At the age of eighty-two she boasted she would swim in three separate seas in one week: the Mediterranean, the Aegean and the Red Sea – and she did.

But her body was already worn out and she was furious she could do nothing about it. She began a course of morphine to dull the pain of osteoporosis in her back, and cataracts had almost blinded her. She walked with a stick and at times she was overcome with helplessness and deep depression. 'There are two things the matter with me. One, my body is too old and I can no longer do what I want. I am as close to sedentary as I can get without being actually tied to a chair. The second is that I am bored.'

In some of her last lines she wrote of the two main regrets in her life. She had never written a great book or had a close and lasting relationship with a man like the one her mother had with her father.

One Saturday in February 1998, when she was eighty-nine, Martha decided it was time for her to die. She could cram no more into her life and she was exhausted. It takes courage and desperation to commit suicide and she had both. Late that afternoon in her London flat in Cadogan Square she tidied up her living room, rearranged the vases of flowers, stuck labels to furniture as presents to friends and put rubbish in a little plastic bag outside her front door. Then she put on her favourite cream silk nightgown, lay on her bed and took the pills.

She was cremated a few days later and her closest friends took a launch down the Thames and scattered her ashes into the outgoing tide. She had asked it to be done 'for my last travels'.

James Cameron

SEVEN

JAMES CAMERON

1911–1985

He was the quintessential war reporter. The most respected journalist in post-war Britain.

The son of an unsuccessful lawyer, he began his apprenticeship as an office boy for a Scottish Sunday newspaper.

Acknowledged as one of the world's most defining journalists, his career reads like a chronology of the twentieth century's global conflicts. He covered the Berlin Airlift in 1948, reported Eva Perón's Argentina and went ashore with the US Marines in Korea.

He was there during the Algerian War, the Six-Day Israeli–Egyptian war, the Mau Mau rebellion in Kenya and the Hungarian uprising against the Soviets, he reported the Suez crisis and was in Beijing in the days of the 'Bamboo Curtain' and the 'Gang of Four'. He was at the trials of Mandela, Eichmann and Kenyatta and crossed swords with Nikita Khrushchev in the Kremlin. He shared a train compartment with Mahatma Gandhi travelling across India and became a friend and admirer of India's first Prime Minister, Pandit Nehru.

He once wrote that it was against the rules to have a war without him. Vietnam was his last and he was one of the very few international correspondents allowed into Hanoi. He was the only Western reporter privileged to dine with Hồ Chí Minh.

He was a cantankerous, compassionate, fearless, abrasive, chain-smoking, hard-drinking, workaholic nomad and an unashamed philanderer. He was also the establishment's most persistent dissenting voice. He was in his own words: 'A professional pain in the neck with a built-in bullshit detector.'

No other correspondent of his or any other age had such infallible irony, wit, cynicism and world-weary wisdom. In his characteristic way he wrote that journalists 'splash in the shallows, only occasionally applauded to the rare heights of mediocrity'.

Like Nevinson and Gellhorn he wrote not only what he saw but what he felt and he was never short of opinions. 'I have never been too good at the basic principle of reporting, which is total objectivity. I imagine I have been subjective about everything I have ever done.'

A socialist and a pacifist, he witnessed America's twin experimental atom bomb explosions at Bikini Atoll and became a founder member of the Campaign for Nuclear Disarmament.

He was a relentless critic of American foreign policy, never shy to shred that nation's icons. Of his experiences in Vietnam he wrote: 'Nothing in my life has been as lowering as this brutal and muddled war. I hated it then, I hate it now.'

※

The son of a Scot from a never-ending line of Scots, baby Cameron was born in Battersea, just across the Thames from Chelsea on 17 June 1911, some five hundred miles from his ancestral homeland. His father was an unsuccessful lawyer who, late in life, discovered he could write and under the pseudonym Mark Allerton published novels of shadowed marriages, horrific unsolved crimes, venal judges and star-crossed love. When the time came to name his child, he chose Mark. Nevertheless, the son was thereafter called James by his mother, an Englishwoman. Her husband lovingly described her as a cross between Queen Victoria and the popular queen of the music halls, Marie Lloyd.

Despite a small income from father's novels, the Camerons were poor, verging on the desperate and James remembers times of mad improvisation when father and mother dressed for a dinner of boiled eggs. At the outbreak of war in 1914, his father failed the medical examination for active service and became a clerk in the War Office. It was boring work and those around him were also so indifferent that he found he could continue to write his novels in office hours without anyone noticing.

When the war ended in 1918, father Cameron, for reasons that were never adequately explained to his son, cashed his small savings and moved the family to France and a small seaside villa in Brittany. James was sent to a series of village schools which meant his education was sketchy and erratic. History lessons dwelt almost entirely on France's global conflicts and he was beaten by classmates when his teacher accused him of being party to the burning of Joan of Arc. He was taught basic arithmetic with chalk and slate but only learnt the simplest multiplication in his teens.

> I sat in a cloud of incomprehension, scratching on my slate, wondering what on earth I was doing there, listening to the drone of Monsieur intoning the Napoleonic dates or the mysteries of dividing eight by two and praying to God to bring a thunderbolt down upon us so that dramatic death could relieve us all of the charade.

His teacher was the first man to bring the brutality of war to the attention of young James. He had served in the Great War and was vehemently anti-German, a hatred that both frightened and fascinated his class. He would diverge from whatever subject he was teaching and rant about '*les sales Boches ... qui m'ont fait*'. His voice grew hoarse, his face turned bluish-red and his eyes narrowed.

And then he did a thing that has stayed in my memory most vividly ever since. He seized his left arm by his right hand and pulled it out by its roots. For a moment he stood brandishing it like a club and brought it down on my desk with a crash. I almost fainted. Never before had I witnessed an argument brought to such a ferocious and even magical climax. It was also the first time I had ever seen an artificial arm.

Monsieur would then leave the classroom to re-attach his limb and return to carry on with the lesson as if nothing had happened.

His entire education seems to have come from newspapers. Having come to France to rid himself of England, his father was hungry for news of it and arranged for every British newspaper to be sent to him across the Channel on a daily basis.

Newspapers abounded. Even as a child I was fed with small paragraphs with the morning coffee. My father actually showed a perverse pride in proclaiming that he was hooked on his daily news and my mother, who was a sweet and wholesome woman in every other way, would move furtively off after breakfast with her share of the Satanic mischief from Fleet Street. In no time at all, a paragraph grew into a complete news item and soon I was ingesting a whole editorial and could absorb two whole *Telegraph* leaders before nine in the morning.

But father Cameron grew tired of France as he was getting tired of life, and the family returned to England and to Wendover in Buckinghamshire. There, as James recalls, the family 'disintegrated'. His mother died a slow death from severe anaemia; she was only forty-two. James would see a lot of death in the years to come, mostly sudden, cruel and ugly. But hers was the first and it was peaceful.

For months she had looked sixty but that morning she was suddenly like a bride; death had left her with a smile of private contentment on her face and I realised that she had been very pretty. Even as I cried and protested, I knew I had lost what I had barely known.

Without wife and mother, father and son became welded in a relationship that was tender and yet perverse. Unable to cope with the complexities of life on his own, the father became dependent on his son and for his remaining years James became a father to his father. In later years he wrote: 'It was a relationship difficult to define, so close it became so poignant and dependent that its echoes are still meaningful to me thirty years after his death.'

He entered journalism by the back door. It was 1928 and he had just turned seventeen. It was to be a long, meagre and dispiriting apprenticeship; in those days there were no evening classes in media studies or degree courses in journalism. His first job was with D. C. Thomson, a Dundee-based company, strictly non-union, that published everything from schoolboy magazines like the *Hotspur* to children's comics like the *Beano*. The pride of the company was the moralistic, suitable-for-the-family Scottish *Sunday Post*. He made tea, filled the paste pots and ink wells; the general factotum, the dogsbody, the fetch-and-carry office boy on call to all demands. For this he was paid fifteen shillings a week. He moved into lodgings. The landlady had three daughters and he fell in love with the youngest; Elma was sixteen, an art student.

He progressed slowly up the Thomson ladder and on his twentieth birthday he was assigned to work on the *Red Star Weekly*, a mawkish magazine which catered entirely for Scotland's working-class girls.

Their tastes verged on the sadistic, so heavily were our pages soaked in gore. The memorable quality of these pages was their purity. The most frightful things happened; stranglings, knifings, disembowellings, suffocations, torments rich and varied. But at no point was there permitted even the hint of sexual impropriety. No matter what ferocious indignities befell our heroines … it should be good clean violence.

James was by now something less of a journalist than a picture editor. His job was to explain, in all its gory detail, the current atrocity to the company's artists so they could draw pictures to match the story. His enthusiasm for the cover story of 'The Man with the Glaring Eyes' almost had him fired.

There had been a series of brutal murders of young women in the city and James was asked to supervise a suitable drawing. What came back from the artist pleased him immensely. It portrayed a deeply sinister dark alley, lit only by a baleful gas street lamp whose sickly beam shone on the body of a young girl whose throat was cut from ear to ear, the tendons severed, her blood streaming into the rain-swept gutter. James thought it did complete justice to 'The Man with the Glaring Eyes'.

But his editor tore the drawing from his hands and was speechless with rage.

> 'For God's sake boy', he shouted at me, 'It's not a bad scene but look at the lassie's skirt; it's away above her knees.' Abashed, I realised what rule I had broken. I took the drawing away and had the hemline lowered a modest inch or two and the drawing was accepted, slit windpipe and all.

It was decided to move him sideways and he became (as I became, working for the same newspaper many years later) the anonymous author of many and varied Sunday favourites. One week he would write two hundred words as 'The Henpecked Husband'; the next might be 'Always a Wallflower' or 'A Bairn Without a Name'. Often, James was obliged to write under the title of an animal such as 'An Unloved Alley Cat' and 'Percy the Poodle'. They were not signed so the author was not identified; a great relief in later life when ridicule might threaten the admiration of fellow correspondents and the respectability of an established reputation.

It was a depressing time for a young man. His father was dying, gradually descending into that conscious coma that was called senile dementia then and Alzheimer's today. James was playing at being a journalist and had become angry and frustrated at the pretence. Then he was ordered to move to the newspaper's Glasgow office on the other side of Scotland and a long way from his beloved Elma. He was twenty-seven and about to reconcile himself to a lifetime of ennui and trite absurdities. The prospect haunted him.

Then came a completely unexpected invitation to join the *Scottish Daily Express* as a sub-editor at the princely sum of nine pounds a week. Glasgow was very much a place to somewhere.

> Suddenly, it promoted my whole life into a new dimension. Elma and I were married in Dundee and I seemed translated into something quite new. We danced around Glasgow as though it was Babylon and at night I would take the tram down Albion Street to the office and fulfil my place in the noble calling of the Fourth Estate.

It was euphoric but it was short lived. His father, no longer recognising James or anyone or anything around him, died in a nursing home. Some months later, James was called to the hospital where Elma was about to give birth. He arrived with a bunch of flowers breathless and expectant but she died before he could reach her bed. He named his baby daughter Elma. It was May 1940 and across the English Channel Hitler's army was already moving into France.

It was an exhausting time, single-handedly looking after his child and working night shifts in the Glasgow office. Then he received his call-up papers for compulsory military service.

He was surprised and relieved when the medical examiners rejected him, having diagnosed organic cardiac disease. They also warned that he should, at all costs, avoid physical exertion and never fly above three thousand feet.

In the years that followed he was regularly seated in airliners flying above thirty-five thousand feet and joined, in one fashion or another, five different armies and two navies.

I had emerged from that medical unnerved to the point where I hardly dared cross the street. But it eventually became clear that I was physically indestructible and in the years to come, in Germany, Africa, India, Malaya, Indo-China, Korea and Japan, I was able to reflect upon the curious durability of the officially infirm!

Then came an offer which, in Lord Beaverbrook's regime, was one you did not refuse. He was to move to the *Daily Express* and its London headquarters in Fleet Street. Baby Elma was promptly sent to her grandmother in a part of Aberdeenshire that James calculated was the least likely to be bombed in all of Britain. Then he started on his journey south and the beginning of a momentous life.

I could not think of any of any trade or calling that would have accorded a fairly young and earnest person like myself, the same extravagant resources to examine the planet. I went every-where in the world and I rejoice that I went when the going was good.

He describes his ten years with the *Daily Express* as wild, violent, obsessive, exasperating and full of mad unpredictable movement, chasing from one manifestation of human error to the next. But it began, as careers mostly do, in a very humdrum way. He became a night sub-editor on the paper and despite all his excited expectations in Glasgow, he loathed it once he came to London. He spent his nights working and his days trying to sleep. Days off meant travel-ling the hundreds of miles by train to Aberdeen to see his Elma and every visit was a reminder how little he belonged to her and how her childhood owed less and less to him. Then, a day later, the long return journey back to London and its nightly air raids.

It was at this time he was asked by the BBC to write and record short pieces on his personal reflections of life in wartime Britain. After ending a night shift sometime after midnight, he would leave his office in Fleet Street and walk to the studios, often composing his script on the way. They were directed at the North American Service and were in effect gentle propaganda. But that was the accepted necessary cliché; Britain was fighting for its survival and needed as much help as it could get and the Americans should not forget it.

He met Elizabeth O'Conor while she was working in what passed as the newspaper's art room. It provided the maps and diagrams as the newspaper attempted to explain the intricacies of the war in Europe.

> She was both kind and tranquil, she was beautiful and generous; she was as vulnerable as I but more composed and she did what I supposed impossible; she took me over the barrier between the past and the present and opened all the closed doors. When we were married it was like entering a theatre in the second act; we united our children, my daughter and her son and for the first time in three despairing years, there seemed some point in establishing a root in life.

Elizabeth gave him the confidence and ambition that had slowly drained from him and she encouraged him to return to the one job in newspapers that made sense, the only one he knew would complete him. He asked, and finally demanded, that he become a reporter again and to his surprise the management agreed.

When the war ended Cameron's roving nomadic life began. It was a time when the company's accountants did not rule the roost, a time when editors did not hesitate to send a reporter to the furthest ends of the earth simply to find out if there was anything of interest there. And James invariably did. He wrote feature articles about the surf boats swarming around the ships in Ghana, the lotus lakes in Kashmir, the extraordinary Tung-tan market in Peking, the windmills of Mykonos and Halong Bay in Tonkin. The labels on his suitcase overlapped: India, South America, South Africa, Siam and Burma, Indonesia and the Caribbean, Patagonia and Afghanistan.

Like every foreign correspondent since, he spent much of his waking life belted to an uncomfortable seat, peering through a perspex window at the world below and with that nagging doubt familiar to all reporters, that on this one you would fail.

'You are only as good as your last story.' That was the catch line, the one that kept you anxious but also the one that kept you cautious, meticulous and your own guardian.

> All I know is that, however long you've been at it, one never sits down at the typewriter, in the dreary hotel bedroom or the press room, or the rooftop or the dugout or the office desk, staring at that ghastly blank paper, but what one says: brother, this is it; this time they will find you out. And if you feel it with enough doubt and worry and misery and fear – somehow, they don't.

It was a world of air schedules and time zones, careering around the world at ridiculous speeds, traversing hemispheres from the cold to the hot and back again in the space of a day.

> You could cross the Date Line and have a week with two Tuesdays or indeed no Tuesdays at all. I once crossed the Line on my birthday, which meant it vanished, the day disappeared completely. If I did it on that same day every year would I never grow older?

A correspondent's travelling life is like any drug, addictive and destructive. Wandering the globe with no permanent anchorage creates a sense of not belonging, a depressing anonymity. Home is where the passport takes you. On arrival, the identity-cum-accreditation card is the official authorisation for being there; name, photograph, date of birth, colour of eyes, even a thumb print. The cards come in all colours, sometimes bedraggled, seldom laminated and usually endorsed by the undecipherable signature of an unknown bureaucratic scribbler.

You are what it says you are. Cameron was a man of many descriptions.

I have one from an Asian country calling me a 'Sojourner', another, with cryptic intent, calls me 'Male, for one week'. A South American passport clerk stamped my page, 'Admitted he is passing on'. The worst is a document from Ethiopia cataloguing me for all time with the chilling phrase, 'Temporary Person'. I feel these things to be true.

In the summer of 1946, Cameron was selected in a random ballot to be one of three official British observers to witness the twin atom bomb explosions on a tiny atoll called Bikini, ten thousand miles away in the Pacific. Following the annihilation of Hiroshima and Nagasaki, the Americans wanted to test the bomb's further potential. Even as he prepared to leave England, he had a premonition that he was about to witness something physically and spiritually disturbing. And so it proved to be.

The experiment was called Operation Crossroads. Two bombs were to be exploded on a collection of obsolete warships in a lagoon within the island, one from the air, the other under water. On board them in cages and pens was a variety of animals, goats, cows, pigs, rats and mice. Why they were there was a question from the assembled press that nobody among the assorted experts cared to answer. It represented the Noah's Ark of crazed American scientists.

Crossroads was intended to establish the thoroughness of the destruction of metal and life of the new, improved weapon. The only way that could be done was to explode one bomb over the aged battle fleet and the second under it. The derelict battleships *Nevada* and *Arkansas* were their twin bull's eye and in a typically American bizarre touch, the face of the Hollywood actress Rita Hayworth was painted on both bombs.

James, along with hundreds of military observers and international press, stood waiting eighteen miles away from the target.

> At a few minutes to nine o'clock that morning, we caught the voice of the bomb-aimer over the loudspeakers, tinny and remote like an old gramophone record. 'Listen World, this is Skylight ... this is a live run ... coming up on thirty-five miles off target ... adjust goggles ... standby ... fifteen miles ... standby ... standby ... standby ... Bomb gone! ... Bomb gone! ... Bomb gone!'

It was hypnotic. Hundreds of observers were transfixed. No effort was made by the newspapermen to write down what they were seeing. Like James, they knew the image would remain indelible.

> In that first fine edge of a second it might have been a sudden start low down on the horizon. Then it grew and swelled and became bright and brighter and pierced the goggles and struck the eye as a crucible does. Now standing up steadily from the sea, was the famous mushroom. It climbed like a fungus, a towering mound of firm cream shot with veins and rivers of wandering red. It mounted tirelessly through the clouds. The only similes that came to mind were banal; a sundae, red ink in a pot of distemper. Yet it was beautiful in its monstrous way, a writhing mass, over four miles high and two miles across. From behind me I heard the frenetic ticking of typewriters and very soon I was fumbling for my own. The reportage had begun and many of us will never live it down.

James, horrified by what he had seen, appalled at the implications, on his return to England became a founder member of the Campaign for Nuclear Disarmament. 'I think now that neither democracy, nor fascism, nor communism, nor religion, nor anything else, justifies one man pushing a button and killing thousands of total strangers. Nothing is worth that.'

It was settled in Paris. It had taken five years of bargaining since the end of the war but the victorious Allies had at last ended their haggling and agreed on those parts of the world that needed reconstructing. What to do with liberated territories that had no sovereignty to be reinstated, no obvious identity to be repaired, no democracies to re-adjust. So the arbiters in 1950 rearranged the map, just as Africa and central Europe had been dissected willy-nilly at the end of the First World War. With one exception. What to do with Korea?

It had been a Japanese colony since 1910 but since the surrender, Korea was the orphan child and both Russia and America wanted to adopt. So it was decided to cut the country in half – equal shares at the 38th parallel. The division had no political, ethnic, geographical, economic or military sense and it was later disclosed that the Americans had agreed to that line because they only had a small-scale map available at the time. So Moscow installed its communist puppet Kim Il Sung in Pyongyang and the Americans, at a loss to find anyone better, selected the only Korean politician who spoke English and placed a right-wing reactionary, Syngman Rhee, in the Presidential palace in Seoul. To speed the process and to do its bidding, Washington handed him $500 million as a down payment.

But as might have been predicted, North and South were not content to stay apart and the 38th parallel rapidly became a frontier at war. On 25 June 1950, President Harry Truman announced that the South had been attacked and that the communists were preparing to invade. He was the first though not the last American president to invoke the 'domino theory' as the reason to go to war in the Far East. If Korea fell to the communists, he warned, then neighbouring countries would follow one by one until Stalin captured his biggest prize, Japan. From the Oval Office of the White House, he said it was time 'to start rolling back communism'. The American crusade to stop the East going Red had begun.

James Cameron was now working for *Picture Post*, a respected weekly that had successfully combined superior writing with superior photographs. It was ideal for him, with no more agonising deadlines, no more frantic last-minute excursions. The *Post* provided a civilised routine, time enough to write and space enough for his kind of writing.

He and photographer Bert Hardy landed in South Korea at a small airstrip at Taegu close to the most southern and vitally strategic port of Pusan. They were told that the enemy was only eleven miles up the road and, if they captured Pusan, they would have taken all of Korea. Only the arrival weeks before of American troops of the 24th Division, backed by the UN, was stopping them.

> It was clear that something had changed since yesterday. It is not always necessary to know a place to realise that some immediate factor has altered it. The airfield had a disrupted, despairing look, the roads were already choked with refugees, the white anonymous ragged multitudes moving off, bent under their loads, columns of dusty misery on the endless road to nowhere. Taegu was secure but the ragged people did not believe it. They were practised refugees who were always first away; they now had nothing to leave behind.

The war grew gradually around Taegu until it was besieged. The communist army was on three sides and the sea was on the other. All the Americans could do was to hold the line until something happened and they could not think what until US Air Force Sabre jets came screeching in from carriers in the Sea of Japan rocketing communist positions. They came in unopposed because the communists had yet to be supplied with aircraft by Moscow. Clinically and casually they dived in on their enemy and blasted the earth to pieces where a town had once stood.

The bombers followed the fighters, the artillery followed the bombers and the infantry followed them. And there was no reply.

What remained was a heap of ashes and North Koreans sprawled among the debris in unreal tangled postures, with limbs projecting in impossible attitudes. The only visible body that still bore resemblance to a man remained sitting upright in a pile of still redly glowing cinders; for a startling moment he looked not like a dead Korean but a living yogi. The rest were carrion, the smell unendurable and the marching men hurried past gagging.

He saw an old man, one typical of old men in Korea with a face like Buddha. He had let the battle catch up with him and had not been able to cope with the commotion. He lay beside the road quite still but he had not been hit or hurt in any other way. James held his head and gave him water but it dribbled down his beard. Then he died without fuss, without a sound and with grace.

James wanted to stay to write and photograph more but they could already hear the snap of sniper fire. The Marine sergeant warned that if they delayed there was a chance of an ambush and there was nowhere to hide except in the filth in the ditches. 'You gotta make up your minds quick. A mouthful of shit or an assful of lead.'

Given the warning no one hesitated. A week before, a jeep carrying five correspondents had been ambushed and two were killed. The bodies of two British correspondents had already been flown back home. The war was barely three months old but twenty-one international correspondents and photographers had already been killed. Some bodies were never recovered.

The land smelt of war because the land smelt of death and putre-faction. The Americans only collected their own dead; the rest, North or South Koreans, were left to decompose where they had fallen, to rot in a rotting country.

James and Bert drove carefully, careful to obey the rule of the war-reporting road – be sure there is always enough room for an emergency about-turn. Sometimes they would drive for a day and see not another living soul. They came to what had once been a town called Pohang. Shells, bombs and napalm had reduced it to a plain of ashes.

Then we saw a strange thing. One solitary old man, alone in all the blackened emptiness. He was raking and groping among the ashes of what must have been his house, actually sifting his home through his fingers. Now and again, he would find something which he laid aside, a tin can or a nail or two. He was a relic, like the last man in the world.

The Americans could not hold their line and the communists were now only five miles away. A train full of casualties was leaving Taegu overnight for Pusan and James and Bert Hardy were on it. Nine hours later they arrived at the port and what appeared to be an American evacuation camp. There they could contact London and wait for the order to leave. It also gave them both the opportunity to do what the frantic activity of the past weeks had stopped them doing: to write the broader overview and find the picture that told all.

James walked through the camp that morning and chanced upon a scene that would later change the course of his life.

This terrible crowd of men was worse than anything I had so far seen. After so many weeks of seeing many distressing things, this might have made little impression on me if the condition of these men had not been quite sensationally appalling.

There were about 700 of them and they had been in jail long enough to have reduced their frames to skeletons, puppets of skin with string for sinews, their faces a translucent grey and they cringed like dogs. They were manacled with chains or bound together with ropes and compelled to squat, foetal position, in heaps of garbage. Sometimes they moved enough to scoop a handful of water to drink from the black puddles around them. Any deviation brought a gun butt to their heads.

Finally they were herded, the lowest common denominator of human degradation, into trucks with the dumb air of men going to their deaths. I was assured that most of them were.

It was medieval yet American soldiers watched and photographed them for their own amusement. These men were not prisoners of war. They were not convicted criminals. They had had no trial. They were political prisoners, suspects, accused of being agitators, even covert communists plotting against the regime of Syngman Rhee, the man who had the nomination and support of the West. It seemed that his brand of democracy was no less vicious than the atrocities committed by his opponents in the North. Yet these men had been imprisoned and tortured within full view of the grand villa housing the United Nations Commission. James protested to the Commissioner and was told that it was indeed rather disturbing but 'Nevertheless, you must remember that these are Asiatic people and congenitally different and their standards of behaviour are quite different from ours.'

James wrote all that he had seen in his dispatch as dispassionately as he could. He did his best to drain it of emotion but it was documented in detail. Bert took photographs should some people doubt it and demand evidence. There would be repercussions for both men but that would come later. Now was the time to leave Pusan for their next destination. It would be well behind enemy lines at a place called Inchon and the Americans were going in by sea.

> They were serving cakes and coffee in the wardroom, of all the things to start an invasion with; the stomach contracted at the thought. We had learnt the drill or hoped we had. The Marine has said, 'When you gentlemen hit the beach you'd better run diagonally for one fifty yards and then get your goddam heads down behind a tussock and wait until somebody does something.'
> 'Till who does what?'
> 'Till somebody does anything, for Christ's sake. What am I, a fortune teller?'

And so began the biggest amphibious landing ever assembled since D-Day. Two hundred and sixty-two war ships and three hundred thousand American and Commonwealth troops commanded by General MacArthur, the hero of the Philippines. James sent this dispatch to London that night. Was ever an invasion described in such a way?

> We saw the floating tanks, the grotesque sea going masses of amphibious ironmongery. They crawled out of the hull of the mother ship, she spawned them out in growling droves ... they were surrealistic and terrifying, ludicrous and dreadful at once, like a flock of rattling tortoises as they lurched out of the womb of the ship and began to crawl over the surface of the water, their treads spinning, with the heads of their little men growing from their carapaces. As the light faded, the noise rose in key, soared in volume, the intervals shortened between the explosions and from over the south, the aircraft came, steady formations, everything very neat. The din was hypnotic.
> At last the hundreds of troops began to surge towards Inchon, row after row of craft, line abreast, like a cavalry formation. Now the

twilight was alive with landing craft, tank loaders, things full of guns and Marines, forty thousand to be put ashore with the tide.

The landing craft carrying the press was suddenly enveloped in heavy black smoke and when it cleared, they saw there were no beach, no diagonal run and no tussocks to hide behind. Just a wall, ten feet above high water mark. And by some absurd miscalculation, landing craft carrying Marine assault troops were behind them and so close they could not turn. So James landed ahead of them.

My feet were numb, I lost my grip on the slippery wall and slid down to my waist in the sea. For a moment there was more terror from the roaring landing craft that were slamming into the wall than from the enemy on the other side. I scrambled over the parapet and fell into a North Korean defence trench, happily empty of North Koreans.

That was the Inchon landing, the day MacArthur and his international army started to push the communists back over the 38th parallel and restore the division of the country, North and South. But he was a famously extrovert, ambitious and aggressive general, bounding with self-esteem and not known for his respect for his political masters in Washington. Encouraged by his easy success at Inchon, he went a parallel too far and took his army over the 38th and right into the North and as close to the Chinese border as he dared. That autumn the Chinese responded, entering the war with a half a million troops, attacking in suicidal human waves. MacArthur was sacked but it did not end the fighting.

It ended three years later when President Dwight Eisenhower threatened to use his atom bomb and only then did they try to count the cost. Two million soldiers, North and South Koreans, were killed or wounded; a million Chinese troops. The Americans sent some fifty-four thousand body bags home. Civilian casualties were never counted.

It was the first post-war military confrontation with communism. One American newspaper headlined it: 'The Cold War Has Turned Hot'.

James returned to London as the *Post*'s rotogravure presses were preparing to print his story of the Pusan prisoners. He had been congratulated by his editor, Tom Hopkinson, and Bert Hardy's accompanying startling photographs were explicit enough to need no captions. It was an exposure of such cruelty that it could not be opposed by anyone of goodwill. It seemed right then that it should also be published by a magazine of established liberal and humane pretensions. All agreed except the one who mattered more than the collective editorial opinion. He was the proprietor, Edward Hulton. Without any consultation or explanation he ordered the story off the presses and forbade its publication.

He had succumbed to pressure from on high, pressure from the United Nations, whose Commissioner in Pusan had seen it all and had turned a diplomatic blind eye, and from the Americans, who were bruised by the implicit criticism of their endorsement of Rhee, their South Korean puppet.

Hopkinson resigned and James followed him soon after. Such was the public furore over the affair and such was the contempt for Hulton that *Picture Post* never recovered and in time closed. But James's story and Bert Hardy's photos were published. They appeared in the socialist, quasi-communist newspaper the *Daily Worker*.

⁂

Two atom bombs with the painted face of a Hollywood actress exploding on a tiny Pacific island remained indelible images. What had been post-war scientific experiments had since become a cold war threat of apocalyptic dimensions. The A-bomb was now the H-bomb, a simple advance in the alphabet but a new weapon of such destructive proportions it would enable the world's two superpowers to destroy each other within half an hour. Sir Winston Churchill had warned that the war of the future would differ from anything known in the past and each side would suffer what they dreaded most – their annihilation. The bomb that destroyed a city called Hiroshima in 1945 killed eighty thousand people. Only fourteen years on in 1959, the Federation of American Scientists, among them the bomb's makers, warned that their new invention constituted a threat to the existence of all the people of the world, perhaps even to the world itself.

The Campaign for Nuclear Disarmament was formed that year and James was among its founder members. Others supporting it included Bertrand Russell, J. B. Priestley, Ritchie Calder, the historian A. J. P. Taylor and the Labour activist Michael Foot. It was imposing company. The movement began as a cause but in time it became a major factor in the politics of Britain. The initials CND entered its vocabulary and its marches and sit-ins were soon part of the country's established protest agenda. Cameron wrote:

> We believed that Britain's pretensions to a nuclear policy were economically unsound, militarily a fallacy and morally an abomination. We asked no partisan allegiances, no local loyalties and demanded no personal surrenders. Our badge became a stark symbol.

It was a badge that was pinned to hundreds of thousands of lapels by people of all parties or of none, from every religion, work place and office and from every walk of life. Only the British press seemed to ignore or ridicule it. But the campaign grew and it prospered. The young found in it something not provided by the Church or Parliament. The unions began voting specifically for CND policies, which in turn forced the Labour Party officially to adopt them too. It was not all peaceful. Protests became demonstrations and they often became riotous. In December 1982 thirty thousand women joined hands around the Royal Air Force base at Greenham Common in Berkshire to protest at the government's decision to allow the American Cruise missile to be sited there. A year later that figure had doubled, with the protesters living in a vast tented camp. The highlight of the CND calendar was the Easter March from the Atomic Research Establishment in nearby Aldermaston to London, fifty miles away.

But the movement slowly fell apart as its ambitions became fragmented and internecine struggles for power began at the top. Its sole purpose was to ban the bomb. If it failed in that it did succeed in its second aim, which was to ban the testing of the bomb. The CND was a brave attempt to slow down the snowballing pace in nuclear weapons research and in that it succeeded. James believed it to be a good thing in a discouraging world and it earned its place in the records with honour.

Cameron was a relentless critic of Americans and their foreign policy or what he preferred to call their 'malicious imperial adventures'. He enjoyed nothing more than shredding their precious icons. It was a love–hate relationship that endured.

> They are wonderful, terrible people presiding over a new undeclared empire, so rich, so strong, so vulnerable, so generous, so blind, so bountiful, so clumsy, so kind, so perilous, so unmanageable in their simple minded craftiness and the brutal innocence of their lethal benevolence. They are the people with whose good intentions the road to hell is so painstakingly paved.

Was ever a nation indicted so caustically and so lyrically? He savaged them further in his reporting of the Vietnam War, which he covered for the *News Chronicle* from the day the conflict first began in 1965.

He became, like so many correspondents there, an emotional casualty, and for many years after it had ended he found he could not write or speak of it dispassionately.

> Nothing in my life, and I have seen too often the corruption of the well intentioned and the destruction of the innocent, has been as lowering as this uniquely brutal and muddled war. Every day I was there it grew more and more vile and crude and senseless, driving more and more to a despairing end. It came to exercise and concern me and it sometimes seemed that I wrote and spoke of little else. I hated it then. I hate it now. I have said so much about that unlucky place that I am embarrassed to say more.

As the multitude of contending international correspondents swarmed into South Vietnam in those first months of the American invasion, James typically looked elsewhere. He was determined to go to the communist North, to the capital, Hanoi. But the chances were remote. For many years the communists had stubbornly refused all requests for entry and relied instead on their own crude propaganda to contest the repetitive and questionable material that was coming from the vast and efficiently run American propaganda machine in Saigon.

It had been twelve years since any correspondent from the West had been allowed to enter the North and James was not optimistic. An application for a visa had been made and reminder after reminder had been politely sent but after months of waiting, he was ready to accept that it would never happen. But late in 1965, permission suddenly arrived, the gears had meshed and he began the long circuitous overland route to the communist capital, via Pakistan to Ceylon, from there into China and Canton, Peking, Nanking and finally across the final border into Hanoi. He took with him a television cameraman.

We were received initially with marked coldness which grew gradually into cordiality that eventually permitted us unprecedented travel throughout the country and culminated in an unexpected invitation to dine with the Prime Minister Pham Van Dong and President Hồ Chí Minh, the revered leader of Vietnam's thirty-year long struggle for independence.

Vietnam's whole history is that of fighting and losing to intruders. First the Chinese, on and off for a thousand years, then the French, with the interregnum of Japanese occupation during the Second World War. When that war ended, it was decided that Vietnam should be allowed free elections to decide its future. But the French reneged and remained for another nine years. Finally, came the Americans.

As a young man, Hồ Chí Minh learnt his Marxism in Moscow and as a revolutionary, touring the capitals of Europe. For a while he worked in the kitchens of the Carlton Hotel in London.

He had initially declined James's request for an interview but he was curious to see a visiting Englishman and wanted to speak English again.

His first words in hesitant English were, 'Tell me, what does the Haymarket looks like these days?' He poured some beer and lit his fifteenth cigarette from the stub of the old one and laughed. He was, in fact, rather funny, the only top level communist I have ever met who had a recognisable sense of fun.

He could even be sardonic about the holy writ. When I asked him a political question, he smiled; 'You ask the Prime Minister that. He's a better Marxist than I am. After all [pause] ... he has to be!' With his wispy Asian beard and glinting eyes, he had the air of a gnomish ivory miniature, the elusive father figure whose unseen presence dominated every move in this most brutally tragic situation of our time.

James spent three arduous weeks compiling unprecedented material on a country that for so long had been closed to outsiders.

He wrote a five-part series for the London *Evening Standard* and not, as one might have expected, for his favourite newspaper, *The Guardian*. America's prestigious *Time* magazine published all five reports, although reticently. It explained that it had tried to get its own man into Hanoi and failed and, anxious to report both sides in the war, felt obliged to use Cameron's reports. The magazine protected itself from domestic criticism with a withering leader article.

> Cameron is a tireless, didactic liberal of the ban-the-bomb breed. His report is a rare eyewitness account by a western journalist but it leaves little doubt of his own emotional commitment; he firmly believes the U.S. has no business whatsoever in Vietnam.
>
> Cameron vividly captures much of the flavour of that tense troubled country but he is less of a reporter than a conduit for North Vietnamese propaganda. He writes that it is a land 'where everyone considers it necessary to live in disguise, to inhabit his own country pretending he is not there.'
>
> His articles are full of personal prejudices, all anti-American and pro-Hanoi. He is constantly outraged by American action. He calls U.S. air raids an 'impertinence, what arrogance, what an offence.'
>
> Cameron is a receptacle for some masterly public relations work by Hanoi. Period!

He made a short film for television and a book was rushed to publication and both were enthusiastically applauded in Britain and Europe. But he was not prepared for the reception it got in America. He was reviled, ridiculed, accused of being a covert communist and a less than subtle conduit for Hanoi's propaganda. He was labelled the bitter antagonist of America's good intentions to preserve the integrity of what they insisted on calling the democratic South. As far as America was concerned, James had committed an offence simply by being in the North and to argue the possibility that the people there were made of flesh and blood and capable of pain and anger was heresy. To the American public he was nothing more nor less than a *Commie bastard*.

To sell his book, and to some extent himself, his publisher persuaded him to enter the lion's den. It was a turbulent, exhausting itinerary and a hostile experience. New York, Boston, Philadelphia, Washington, Chicago, California, Miami, at the mercy of cross-examinations by impudent television pundits and facile newspaper columnists who, presuming to speak on behalf of their audience and readers, asked why, if he was not a communist, he had been invited into the very headquarters of America's enemy. Did he not know that good American boys were dying out there for a very noble cause? James had already argued his case before he left England.

> Despite all Washington's arguments, North Vietnam is inhabited by human beings. Americans insist they are a race of dedicated card carrying Marxist monsters. But I had seen them as shy, decent people and they appear to differ in no perceptible way from anyone else. And to destroy their country and their lives with high explosive and petroleum jelly is no way to cure them. They have an obstinate belief in their right to live.

At the beginning of the tour, he felt as if he was being intellectually lynched but gradually he began to win his corner. His sincerity and in no small way his charm took some of the anger out of his challengers; chips were slowly removed from their shoulders. Hostility was gradually replaced with inquiry, suspicion with questioning and resentment with regret. It seemed that he had soothed the savagery and he left America with a tinge of optimism that many there might already be questioning their own assumptions about Vietnam and their military involvement. If such was the case, then they remained very much the thoughtful minority. The war was to last another ten years and it grew more brutal, more destructive, more lethal and more costly by the day. James did not go to another war. Vietnam was his last. His next assignment decided it.

In October 1970 I was sent by ITN to East Pakistan. My foreign desk had dithered on whether to send or not, which was, in the event, understandable. A cyclone had hit the Ganges delta and news agencies were reporting enormous casualties. Reading the reports, the death toll was simply not believable. Perhaps noughts had mistakenly been added somewhere along the 6,000-mile telex journey from Dacca to London. Perhaps it was just another charity's exaggeration to get the aid chain into motion. But there was no mistake.

The final count of the drowned and mutilated was never officially agreed. Possibly it was never compiled. Who knew for sure just how many people lived on the Bay of Bengal? But it was reported that the winds that brought the swollen waters of the Ganges and the Brahmaputra to the sea killed upwards of two hundred thousand people. I was a young reporter seeing devastation and the perverse variety of death for the first time. I did not know then that James had witnessed much the same tragedy three years before in exactly the same place.

He was reporting for the London *Evening Standard* on the exodus of refugees escaping the havoc following the same floods that I was to witness. Cholera and dysentery added to the misery and suffering of millions of people fleeing the diseased areas and taking the disease with them. The Pakistani President, Yahya Khan, despised the Bengalis in the Eastern Province and openly referred to them as *maccbar*, the Urdu for mosquito. 'Stamp on them before they bite, squash them before they take your blood.'

Many millions had been sent by international charities to help the refugees but Khan put the money into his own bank account. Instead he sent his troops to harass them and gave his commanders explicit instructions that those who delayed should be raped and shot.

Already some four million had crossed the border into India, coming over at the rate of an estimated fifty thousand a day. There was no noise, no commotion; they were numbed by exhaustion and despair. The young carried the old on their backs but as their strength left them, grandfathers and grandmothers slipped from them and the young men did not look back. Slowly the monsoon rain overwhelmed them all, the mud now too deep, too heavy, and long columns suddenly sat down in it, abruptly, as if they had been ordered to. Mothers dropped their babies in the mud between their knees and watched them drown.

The very old lay on their backs in the brown mess, closed their eyes and disappeared beneath it. Cameron saw it all as if in slow motion.

He was motoring along the Indian–Pakistani border close to the crossing to Calcutta, in a military jeep accompanied by an Indian officer. The journey was to end his assignment and almost his life.

I had seen the collision coming but when it happened the impact was so abrupt that it shocked the sense out of me. For a while I sat quietly among the broken glass of the jeep as though I had been sitting there forever. In any case I found I could not move because of the dead weight of the soldiers on either side of me. We had hit the bus head on. The front of the jeep was embedded under its bonnet, and the crash must have somehow distorted the wiring apparatus because the first thing I was aware of was a curious metallic howl from the horn that nobody tried to stop. It seemed as though the machinery itself was screaming in pain, while all the people involved were spellbound and silent. Suddenly the braying horn stopped, and then there was nothing to hear but the thudding rain. Sitting there wedged in the front of the jeep I found at first that I could hardly stir. The driver to my left was apparently dead; the Colonel on my right nearly so.

They were both big and corpulent men and they lolled against me, jamming me between their khaki tunics and spilling blood into my lap. The colonel's face was a makeup of fantasy; he had been scalped and as fast as the wound soaked him scarlet, so the rains washed away the blood and diluted it.

The refugees walked around me. We offered no threat. They offered no help.

By and by a police truck came by and helped me into Krishnanagar, and from there another truck lifted me the ninety miles back to Calcutta. It was not a smooth road and by now the pain was very bad. I had two broken legs and a small dislocation of the spine. Or rather I thought that was all I had ... I was rather amateurishly strapped together and shipped back on a plane to London, though I recall little of the journey.

James had predicted that the floods and Yahya Khan's cruelty would result in the break-up of Pakistan and the birth of the Bengali nation. He was right, even if it did take another four years and an even greater natural catastrophe. In the spring of 1971, after the floods that killed nearly a quarter of a million Bengalis, Yahya Khan began his genocide against them. He was determined Pakistan should remain intact and to do that he had to wipe out those who resisted him. India went to war against Khan to prevent it and nine months later India won.

It was then, in that second week of December, I went to Yahya Khan's killing fields and this was my report for ITN:

The morning after the surrender, the Indian army arranged to take journalists and cameramen to the dykes about five miles outside the city boundary. I walked the last few hundred yards along the dyke walls. There was a warm, light breeze from the sea and I smelt them. Only then did I know what to expect.

Below the walls hundreds of rotting corpses were laid out in a line. Someone counted two hundred and ten though I shall never know how it was possible to count accurately, because bodies had been torn apart by packs of ravaging dogs. An Indian soldier scattered them with rifle shots but they soon came skulking back like hyenas.

Jacques, my cameraman, began to film it but I knew we would never show it, not in that gruesome detail. This was West Pakistan's final outrage in the closing days of the war. Determined to bankrupt the newborn Bangladesh of its intellectuals, professionals, academics and last remaining politicians, people the infant country would so desperately need, Khan had them rounded up and brought here to be shot and left in the swamps to rot. A new word had entered the vocabulary of war: elitocide.

Since his visit to Hanoi in 1965, James had been fascinated by television. Its crossbred culture was more potent and its scope provided him the space and time to write at length. He saw it as a moving *Picture Post*. He was relaxed in front of camera and he adapted to the discipline of matching words to pictures without effort. He was commissioned by the BBC to write and present a series called *Cameron Country* and followed its success with *Yesterday's Witness*. He wrote and presented a number of one-off documentaries, including one on the Spanish Civil War. He wrote two plays for BBC television; one titled *Sound of Guns* was based on his own frustrating experience stuck in Cyprus during the Suez Crisis in 1956.

Such was the ease of his success on television that he joined the mini pantheon of that medium's trusted voices and faces in company with Richard Dimbleby, David Attenborough, Charles Wheeler and Huw Weldon. Men who represented integrity, honesty and hunger for the truth; men millions of viewers knew they could trust.

In between this workload, he wrote fourteen books. On his seventieth birthday he said he was not ready for retirement. It was not an option. Retirement would be announced by the Grim Reaper himself.

It is not common for philanderers to boast of their affairs. If they are celebrities they are hyper-sensitive to public opinion. Don Giovanni is a notable wicked exception. Journalists are even more cautious because of the dangerous, often vindictive 'dog-bites-dog' relationship that exists among them. Which explains why James was doubly shy at even obliquely referring to his extra-marital affairs in his letters and memoirs. It is said that he had a lady friend in every port, or perhaps waiting at every airport, given the amount of time he spent flying from one to the other. It remains only frivolous hearsay.

His marriage to Elizabeth had lasted nearly thirty years. She had been supportive throughout, caring for their three children, Elma, Desmond and Fergus, attempting to create and maintain as normal a family life as her husband's erratic and unsettling demands permitted. It could not have been easy; wives of such men know that it is wearisome, depressing and very lonely.

In return, they expect a modicum of domestic duties from their man when he is home. They may even demand emotional support. If they have any suspicion that he may, on occasions abroad, be tempted to do what faithful husbands are expected not to do, they cope with it on condition that it is never admitted or referred to. What they cannot accept is it becoming known to everyone and that was something James could not prevent. Too many of his fellow correspondents knew of it. Stories trickled back as they were bound to do, accidentally, even maliciously and in 1970 Elizabeth, despite her continuing love, divorced him. There were no recriminations from either side. James did not blame or excuse his infidelities for the break-up but rather the long periods he was away from Elizabeth and the children. In his autobiography, *Point of Departure,* he uses one simple and immensely sad sentence to explain it.

'The habit of loneliness over a long period engenders the wrong responses to love and there is nothing, whatsoever it may be, to compensate for that.'

Perhaps it was the habit and damage of loneliness that persuaded him to travel less and search for other security. During his frequent visits to India he had met Moneesha Sarkar and in 1971 he married her. His book *An Indian Summer* is dedicated to her: '*To Moni. Who gave me her heart's blood and life's hope.*'

She was his rock and, in his declining years, his comfort. His final book, *The Best of Cameron*, a compilation of his lifetime's writings, is dedicated to the family he had, with her help, assembled, near and far.

> My family is a living testimony to the truth that humans of different backgrounds, races, colours and cultures can be a real and living entity, not just in peace but in love. Elma, Sabita, Fergus, Kiron, Nicholas, and Margaret.

> Outside my window now lie forty feet of rock and grass and the escarpment to the sea and the point where the sardonic seabirds sit like sentinels guarding the ocean. The cottage hangs on the edge of Ireland with its fading white face lashed by the wind, in the howling empty solemnity of west Cork. From here only the Atlantic threatens me. I love this place but it will not last long. Nothing lasts long.

James wrote that, resting in a rented cottage, knowing he had not long to live. For over forty years he had lived the life of a chain-smoking, hard-drinking, workaholic globe-trotting nomad. All that time ago, at his call-up medical, the doctors had warned him to be gentle with his body or he would not survive. He had indeed lived long and lived it his way.

But there had been too many journeys, too many years of stress and neglect. His mind was, as ever, critically alert but his body was weary and there was no time for repair. He had been diagnosed with cancer, he found it painful even to eat and he regularly passed blood. He joked that his liver had become a pathological curiosity, a candidate for the Hunterian Museum.

It was soon made clear to me that most of it was due to the old mistaken belief that I could live forever sustained on high hopes and alcohol. It was not shocking but it was saddening. This had never occurred to me as a serious danger. I did indeed drink too much but always, it seemed to me, for good reason; it was after all, said to be the occupational hazard of the trade.

This could not have come at a worse time and it was no way to behave for one who had newly become a grandfather.

I went to hospital for some time and thereafter for a while, I was very nearly well.

The tale is told. I am loaded with memories of good times and rotten times, of strokes of good fortune and some terrible flops. I wouldn't have had it otherwise. Hope subsides but curiosity remains. Every day is, necessarily and even now, a point of departure. We shall see.

He died of throat cancer, complicated by pneumonia, on 26 January 1985. He was seventy-four. From her home in India, Moni recalls that day:

It was our wedding anniversary and he asked me to open a bottle of champagne. We drank a sip or two, then he closed his eyes and did not regain consciousness. He died during the night.

He loved the Salvation Army brass band that played near our house every Sunday morning and I don't know how or why but as he was taken away, for some reason the band went off their usual route and they marched past our house belting out their hymns. I remember the sun shone brightly and there was a lot of laughter and tears.

The Golders Green crematorium was packed with masses of people from all walks of life. I was truly surprised at the response. The Post Office delivered the mail in sacks and it continued for weeks. The Crown Prince of Jordan wrote and so did Indira Gandhi.

I scattered his ashes in Scotland and India.

Of all the tributes, and there were many, there was one he would have appreciated most:

HE RAISED JOURNALISM TO THE HIGH POINT OF LITERATURE

Clare Hollingworth

EIGHT

CLARE HOLLINGWORTH

S he was the first to report the outbreak of the Second World War: a 27-year-old debutante with the biggest scoop of a lifetime.

She joined Martha Gellhorn in breaking the taboos that outlawed women from the front line and, in time, became one of the world's great war correspondents.

'I can do anything a man can do, use a man's loo, sleep on the floor, sleep in the car. All I need is a toothbrush and typewriter.'

She was the doyenne of the British foreign correspondents, the supreme professional, tenacious, ascetic, self-reliant and fearless in the line of fire.

'When I'm on a story, I'm on a story and to hell with anyone else.'

Blessed with exceptional good luck, she was respected by her male colleagues as an intrepid, bloody-minded workaholic. 'She was such a warrior. It was a curious thing about her. She actually enjoyed war. She was not bloodthirsty, she was actually very humane and kind. But she got a big kick out of it.'

She reported the world's conflicts for over half a century: the Balkans, Egypt, Algeria, Aden, Greece, India, Pakistan, China and the Second World War desert campaign in north Africa.

In Algeria, she walked through a minefield to get an exclusive interview and in Jerusalem was only yards from her hotel when it was blown up by Irgun terrorists, killing ninety British soldiers.

Vietnam was the war she relished most, flying in attack helicopters, sitting defiantly on her flak jacket, carrying her typewriter up to the front with the Marines.

'I enjoy action. I'd try to go to the most dangerous place. It always made a good story. I'm not brave, I just enjoy it. I don't know why but I'm never frightened. God just made me like this.'

She toured the capitals of the world, argued with the Shah of Persia, interviewed Farouk, the last King of Egypt and was a personal friend of King Hussein of Jordan.

As a daughter of the Empire she was at home with the ways of the British elite, giving her easy access to the high and mighty. Her connections led her to another world scoop: her acquaintance with Kim Philby allowed her to expose him as the 'Third Man' in Britain's biggest spy scandal.

Her first marriage was a failure. She said she was married to journalism and nothing should get in the way.

> It died of mutual neglect and separation. I'd quite liked to have had a casual boyfriend from time to time, for a trip to Timbuktu or Togoland, that sort of thing. I never wanted children. My career was much more important. It was much better not to have any and I made sure I didn't.

Her last posting was China. She lived in Beijing during the Cultural Revolution and interviewed the Premier of the People's Republic of China, Zhou Enlai. She said it was the hardest but most satisfying assignment of her entire career.

After more than sixty years 'on the road' she retired to live in Hong Kong and took up daytime residence in its Foreign Correspondents' Club. She made it a very English corner of a foreign field, reading her English newspapers and listening to the BBC World Service.

She braved many battlefields but she has lived to be a hundred, acclaimed around the world. On her birthday she received the Queen's congratulations. But age, she insisted, was an irrelevance.

Whenever someone asked Clare Hollingworth why she went to war, she answered 'Naseby and Bosworth'. When she was a child, her father took her on outings to the nearby Civil War battlefields, close to where they lived in Knighton, a suburb of Leicester. She listened, enthralled, as he told her about the Roundheads and Cavaliers, describing their uniforms, their heraldry, their plans of attack, their successes and the reasons for defeat. He explained to her that war was an extension of politics and the failure of statesmen to keep the peace. As a little boy plays with toy soldiers, so the child Clare relived those battles in her imagination.

Her favourite was Bosworth Field where Richard III had deployed his men along Watling Street. She loved to act out the drama of his last desperate fight and shout his Shakespearean 'A horse, a horse, my kingdom for a horse'. Legend has it that when Richard rode out from Leicester to meet Henry Tudor's forces at Ambion Hill, he crossed the river Soar. On one of the bridges that spans the river, he met a witch who warned him that on his return his head would sink lower than his spurs. After that battle he was indeed carried into Leicester on a horse, his head hanging lower than his feet.

When she was older, father and daughter went to France to visit Crécy, Poitiers and Agincourt. They could still see traces of the trenches King Henry's men had dug to topple the French cavalry. He was passionate about the skill of the English archers and the deadly accuracy of their longbows, and why the French crossbowmen could not return fire because their strings were wet from a thunderstorm.

At the outbreak of the First World War, the family moved into the country at Bodkin Farm near Charnwood Forest. It was an idyllic childhood for her and her sister Peg.

> We children had a wonderful life, playing in the brook, exploring the farm, watching the cows being milked and the pigs born. We joined in the haymaking and harvesting and watched sadly as the rabbits were shot as the corn was cut. Mother churned the milk on Wednesdays and took the butter to market on Thursdays in a small trap pulled by Polly our pony.

Her first experience of war, or the threat of it, was the sight of one of the Kaiser's Zeppelins coming to bomb Leicester. But it overshot and hit Loughborough instead, another ten miles further on.

At seventeen her father, who believed that a woman's place was in the kitchen, sent her to the city's domestic science college. She very reluctantly learnt to fry an omelette and little else. Determined that she would not spend her life as a suburban housewife, she skipped lessons; but her days were not wasted. To fill the hours before she was due to return home, she read books and magazines on world affairs and politics. She converted to socialism and joined the Labour Party as a canvasser for the local agent.

At twenty, she won a scholarship to the School of Slavonic Studies at London University and graduated from there to Zagreb University. Mixing for the first time with people of so many nationalities, she became involved in the League of Nations Union and when she returned to England became a full-time organiser. She wrote her own publicity pamphlets and articles for local newspapers, her first for *Berrow's Worcester Journal*, the oldest newspaper in England.

On her visits to the League of Nations Union's London headquarters she met professional journalists and began to learn something of their trade. She also met Vandeleur Robinson, a regional LNU organiser from Surrey. It was not, she admitted, a romantic encounter but more a meeting of minds; their socialism, their shared dedication to the League and its ideals, their fears at the disintegration of Europe and the rise of Nazi Germany. Odd credentials for a marriage, perhaps, but marry they did. For their honeymoon they toured central Europe and continued to spend their annual holidays there. In Romania they heard the news that Hitler had taken back the Sudetenland; while they were in Bulgaria he annexed Austria and when they were in Serbia the swastika was raised in Prague.

Vandeleur encouraged her to write articles about their travels and she sent to them to Kingsley Martin, editor of the *New Statesman*. Not only did he publish them, he asked for more and she was no more the fledgling reporter. Her passion for central Europe and her new-found talent was the beginning of her remarkable career.

As a result of what she called 'a series of administrative errors', she was sent to Warsaw and put in charge of an international fund for Czechoslovak refugees escaping from the Nazis, mostly Jews, gypsies and communists. She took the decision on who should stay in the Warsaw camp and who should be sent to England. Most had crossed Czechoslovakia's northern border with Poland at Katowice and Kraków. In those months she became very familiar with those cities and the lands surrounding them. Very soon she would find that knowledge invaluable.

In July 1939 she was abruptly recalled to London and told the fund had closed and her work in Poland had ended. The threat of war loomed. Hitler was looking to his northern border and Poland promised to be his next conquest.

Whenever Clare told the story of how she began as a war correspondent, her audience would listen in barely concealed disbelief. Careers, and certainly one such as hers, simply did not happen that way. She was accused of stretching credulity. Yet, for over the seventy years of the telling, her version never altered. It happened just as she said it had. She had been invited to a meeting in Fleet Street.

> Arthur Watson, editor of the *Daily Telegraph*, regarded me from his chair on the other side of his large oblong desk. His office was spacious and the atmosphere contemplative, reflecting the mood of the portraits of his predecessors that decorated the oak panelled walls. He had heard of my work among the refugees in Poland and had read my articles.
>
> I told him I was twenty-seven and that I knew Poland very well.
>
> He said: 'We would like to take you on if you are willing to go back.'
>
> 'Delighted,' I replied.
>
> 'Then get back there quickly. I would like you to go as soon as possible. Tomorrow! Report to our man in Warsaw, Hugh Carleton Greene. But first talk to Bob Skelton, our news editor who will brief you on our requirements, filing times and so on.'

The first flight the next morning to Warsaw was via Berlin. She rushed back to her flat near Buckingham Palace and began packing but it was after midnight before she realised her suitcases were far too large for the aircraft. So she telephoned the night staff at Harrod's, as people like her in those days did at that time of the night. They told her the sizes of suitcases and their prices, and within the hour they were delivered.

The aircraft took off from Hendon at dawn and by midday Clare landed at Berlin's Tempelhof airport. The onward flight to Warsaw was delayed; the entire airport had come to halt, as every German there listened in silence to their Führer's menacing Tannenberg speech. From Warsaw, she caught the night train to Katowice. She felt she had come home but it was now a very different place. At the station, soldiers were boarding trains going west to the German border, and policemen were posting up notices proclaiming the mobilisation of reservists in the Polish army.

There were no vacant hotel rooms in the city but the British Consul-General, John Thwaites, having already evacuated his wife and children to England, offered Clare a room in the Residence. After dinner that evening Clare asked him if she could borrow his car the next day. He asked why and roared with laughter when she said she wanted to do some shopping in Germany. He said the border had been closed for weeks and there was no way she could pass the guards at the crossing.

But he did lend her his car and she did indeed go shopping in Germany.

Next morning, with the Union flag fluttering from the bonnet of the Bentley, she passed through the checkpoints without stopping, and the Nazi officers had saluted her before they realised that they had honoured the British flag.

In the town of Beuthen she shopped for wine, cheeses, ladies' underwear and torch batteries, items unobtainable in Poland. She then lunched on roast partridge and began her journey back.

I drove along the fortified frontier road through Hindenburg to Gleiwitz which had been turned into a massive military base. Sixty-five motorcycle dispatch riders overtook me, bunched together and riding hard. By the roadside were hundreds of tanks, armoured cars and field guns. Screens of hessian that were hiding others blew in the wind and I saw the battle deployment. The German High Command was preparing to strike north of Katowice and its fortified lines.

When she returned, she told Thwaites what she had seen. He did not believe her. He doubted whether she had even crossed into Germany. She opened the boot of his car, filled with her shopping, and said, 'See for yourself!' Convinced, Thwaites locked himself in his office and enciphered his top secret message to the Foreign Office. Clare made her call to Carleton Greene and dictated her exclusive, which made splash headlines in *The Telegraph* the next morning.

As the newspaper's readers opened its pages at their breakfast tables, in Katowice the countdown to war had already begun. Clare was woken by explosions and flashes from distant artillery. From her window she saw the Luftwaffe's Dorniers circling and below her, hundreds of cars in an endless convoy leaving the city.

> I woke up Thwaites and dashed off to telephone Robin Hankey at the British Embassy in Warsaw. 'Robin,' I shouted at him. 'The war has begun.'
>
> 'Are you sure old girl?'
>
> 'Listen.' I held the telephone to my window. The growing roar of the tanks encircling Katowice was clearly audible.
>
> 'Can't you hear it?' I cried.

He heard it and he believed it, and within minutes the British Foreign Secretary in London knew it too. Clare then rang Carleton Greene, who in turn called the Polish Foreign Ministry and relayed Clare's story. The official called it absolute nonsense: his government was still negotiating with the Germans. But even as he spoke the air raid sirens began their wailing and the first bombs fell on the Polish capital.

Clare again borrowed the Consul's car and drove around Katowice. Air raid wardens were on the streets and ambulances were parked in rows by the hospital waiting for the first casualties. She saw a group of young men, all wearing swastika armbands, herded together and guarded by Polish soldiers. They were pro-Nazis and had come onto the streets shouting '*Sieg Heil*' thinking the Germans had already arrived. As she passed them she saw rifles raised and heard the volley but she did not look back. All that afternoon the city echoed to sporadic gunfire as more were summarily executed. There were reports that German stormtroopers had already infiltrated the suburbs of city but she drove on.

> I was not brave. I was not naïve. I knew the dangers. I thought it the thing to do, to witness, to see it for myself. I used to sleep in the car, have a biscuit and a drop of wine and go on … go anywhere with a toothbrush and a typewriter.

That evening, 3 September 1939, she and Thwaites sat together and listened on the BBC World Service to Prime Minister Chamberlain's sombre announcement that, by invading Poland, Hitler had broken the peace treaty and Britain was its guarantor. He had sent Hitler an ultimatum which had been ignored. And so, he said: 'This country is at war with Germany.'

Thwaites told Clare to be ready to leave. German troops would be in the city by evening. She felt sick and had to steady herself against the wall. She wanted to cry but she could not.

> I thought of my years with the League of Nations and helping to organise the Peace Ballot. All we had worked for was now lost. London would be bombed, friends killed and buildings I loved destroyed. And neither Britain nor France could prevent it.

They left Katowice on the road heading south as the first of the German stormtroopers entered the city from the west. Another few hours' delay and they could not have left at all. When they reached Kraków, the centre was already on fire and Polish soldiers were on the rooftops strafing with their machine guns as Dornier bombers and Heinkels came on their bombing runs.

Thwaites ignored the warning shouts of air raid wardens and police and drove on and soon theirs was the only car on the empty roads. At dusk, they were attacked by a single fighter aircraft, its shells splintering a line of trees less than twenty yards away. But they motored on, driving without lights along an invisible road in unknown country. They came suddenly to a road block and a torch blinded them. A Polish officer told them the Germans were only miles away but they were to drive very carefully and slowly over the river bridge ahead because, he said, it was dynamited.

The moon illuminated the vast flatlands and in that brief moment Clare felt the loneliness and the helplessness of a country she had grown to love, now waiting in dread at the approach of the invader.

By the time they reached Warsaw, the Polish government had already evacuated the city and, now that the President had left, every Pole knew their war was over. Thwaites drove on to the safety of the southern town of Lubin but Clare stayed. She had already decided what her next story would be. She would return to Warsaw. 'I was not being brave, I certainly didn't feel courageous; ignorant perhaps and naïve. My overriding feeling was enthusiasm for a good story, the fall of Warsaw to the Nazi divisions. Who could resist that?'

She commandeered a car and for the next three days, drove in and around the city. The roads were jammed with refugees, carrying bits of furniture in prams and dragging children behind them. Children were lost, their mothers zigzagging frantically through the lines of people screaming out their names. Then she heard the sound of aircraft and the splattering of their cannons.

Two fighters, lower than I had seen them before, hurtled towards us, raking the ground with bullets. Confusion, falling shapes, overturning carts and prams, flying skirts, shadows running.

Lying flat in the fields, they covered their heads under coats or sacking, with the ostrich impulse of terror. A horse dropped and lay kicking. When I got to Lubin, the town nearby, it was barely recognisable, just ruins. Flies covered the bodies of men, horses and dogs.

> When it was too dark to drive, I stopped and ate some biscuits, took a pull of whisky and curled up for the night with my torch and my revolver on the seat beside me.

At first light she drove on. Ahead, she saw a column of soldiers coming towards her and assumed they were retreating Polish troops. But these soldiers were marching with a discipline that had nothing to do with defeat. She was driving towards a large detachment of the German army.

> For a moment I was shocked, so instead of turning the car around, I switched off the engine. Then I shook myself, started it up again and drove wildly into the fields, running over meadows, across corn stubble, rolling into rutted tracks, springs creaking. I did not know it then but I had just escaped from German occupied territory.

The experience, not surprisingly, encouraged Clare to abandon her planned stay in Poland. The Germans had all but surrounded Warsaw and there was now only one road out and that was south to Romania. She did not hesitate and, a four-day drive later, she crossed the border to Bucharest for the flight home. The war in Poland was over. For Britain and the rest of the world it was just about to begin.

Clare was now considered to be a central European specialist and she had offers from a variety of newspapers and magazines. She hesitated; she could not make up her mind which one to choose, a very enviable dilemma. Then she chanced to meet Lord Beaverbrook, who persuaded her to join his newspaper, and in late February 1940 she was in Paris reporting for the *Daily Express*. It was a capital a world apart from the one she had so recently left.

Hitler's divisions were moving relentlessly west towards France along the Belgian frontier, yet Parisians were oblivious to their fate.

The cafés and restaurants were full, the haute couture shops displayed the latest spring collections and in Ciro's nightclub and the Ritz bar the wealthy old and the beautiful young continued to drink and dance their way to dawn. Yet soon, Hitler's crack divisions would goosestep down the Champs Élysées and the swastika would fly from the Presidential palace.

Paris irritated Clare. It was the capital of disbelief and she was anxious to return to the countries she knew best. She believed that Hitler was intent on capturing the Balkans, that he had to expand south-east to create a land buffer should Stalin renege on the Molotov–Ribbentrop non-aggression treaty. And the oilfields in Romania would provide essential fuel reserves to keep his war machine running.

The more Clare thought about it, the more pressing it became. In early March she bought her ticket and boarded the train for Bucharest. Her timing was, as usual, impeccable. She would later insist it was entirely accidental.

Romania was in a state of crisis. When it erupted into a civil war, she was the only British reporter in the country to report it.

It was ruled by a fascist regime with the submissive, treacherous, spendthrift King Carol as its nominal monarch. In the summer of 1941 he watched, helpless, as his country was torn apart. Stalin co-opted his northern provinces of Bessarabia and Bukovina, Hungary took Transylvania in the west, Bulgaria grabbed territories in the south and along the Danube valley, the German minority were reunited back into the Third Reich. The king had pledged that not one foot of soil would ever be lost and yet in the three months between summer and autumn, Romania lost a third of its territory.

The king was disgraced. There were attempts to assassinate him and many of his supporters were shot. Maps of Romania were displayed in shop windows swathed in black crepe, restaurants were closed, music was banned. All Romania, or what was left of it, was in mourning. But the outrage could not be contained in black crepe, and Bucharest was suddenly a city of riots. Only the machine guns at the palace gates stopped the lynch mobs breaking through, taking over the palace and hanging the king.

He turned for help to one of his generals, Ion Antonescu, but the general led him to a window, pointed to the mobs below and gave his king an ultimatum.

> In one hour my soldiers will not be able to control them. Their ammunition will run out and the palace will be broken into and your body will receive the same treatment as the Tsar of Russia. If you leave I will guarantee you will arrive safely on the far side of the border.

The king could hardly refuse. There was a tunnel and path that led to a small airstrip where his own aircraft was waiting for such an emergency. But Carol was afraid the flight would be sabotaged so, instead, a special night train took him and his mistress away, and a separate carriage was packed with his baggage, his gold and her jewellery. Once the deposed monarch had crossed the border, General Antonescu promoted himself and formed his own government.

But there was another faction that had already decided it would restore order its own way. The Iron Guard was a paramilitary force of Romanian Nazis keen to ally with Germany. Weeks after Carol's abdication, the guard defied the government and held a rally in Bucharest. Forty thousand of them marched through the city centre fighting off the police and the army. They broke into a prison and killed sixty inmates, set fire to government buildings and firebombed police stations. Then they turned their fury on the Jews.

Clare was the only British reporter in the country to witness it but she could not file. All telephone lines were cut, the airport was closed and the trains had stopped running. So, in that short but very bloody civil war, she kept a diary.

Monday 20 Jan 1941: The civil war began with the round-up of Jews by the Iron Guard. They picked up 500 and did not choose them selectively, they just seized the first men, women and children they saw. They were taken to the abattoir and killed in the manner in which Jewish religion demands that animals are slaughtered. Middle-aged women were hung up by chains and their throats cut and they bled to death while the jeering crowd imitated the prayers of the Rabbi. After fifty had been killed this way the crowd got bored and [the Iron Guard] shot the rest.

There now began daily attempts by the Iron Guard to assassinate Antonescu. He asked for German military support and ordered his troops to patrol the city with machine guns. Field guns were stationed outside his offices.

Wednesday 22 Jan: Noise of machine gun fire and heavy artillery all over the city. The soldiers are only just managing to hold a few streets, the Iron Guard now in control of government buildings. Petrol wagons used by the army as barricades have been set on fire. The German military might take over by tonight. Everyone knows the General has lost, the situation rapidly deteriorates. No one knows the number of dead but it must now be well above five thousand.

Hitler could not allow Romania to self-destruct. The country was crucial to his plan of a Balkan buffer zone. His tanks and infantry were already approaching Bucharest.

Thursday 23 Jan: German planes flying low over the city. At 5 p. m. fifty German light tanks have driven purposely to the field of action. 7.45 p. m. There is still a little fighting for the Germans to subdue. No one knows whether they will take control of the country. Now we are getting figures of those killed. Over two thousand in

Bucharest and some twelve thousand across the country. Large lorries are laden with the dead. I saw six enormous lorries packed high with corpses.

It was still a dangerous city and those who dared to venture out were targeted by Iron Guard snipers or shot at by nervous soldiers. The British Embassy lent her a revolver and she carried it with her everywhere and even slept with it under her pillow. When she was out at night she walked down the centre of streets to avoid being shot by a nervous sentry should she suddenly emerge from the shadows. After some time she discovered that they had orders to shoot on sight anyone who crossed the square in front of Antonescu's residence. And she had crossed it many times.

Once she came close to being killed inside her own apartment. A sniper on a roof nearby shot at soldiers in the street. They immediately opened fire and, as Clare lay on the floor, her windows were blown out and the walls were pock-marked three inches into the brick with machine gun fire. Her rooms were wrecked, yet she survived without a graze.

Attacks on the Jews began again but the Germans, in keeping with their pogroms, did nothing. Jews were strangled in public outside their burning synagogues and those who tried to hide were dragged out and hung from the lamp-posts. Children watching their parents die had their throats cut. The dead were stripped of their clothes and possessions and their naked bodies kicked and mutilated.

27 Jan: Others were packed into lorries and taken out of the city and shot. A reliable witness described how six hundred were shot together. They are still lying unburied by the roadside. But the Romanians are burying their own dead. Where the fiercest fighting took place, flags are unfurled and a stand has been erected on which lie the coffins of soldiers covered in wreaths and wrapped in the Romanian flag.

The British government had at last broken off diplomatic relations with Romania; it was the signal to go. The Embassy staff and other foreign nationals were put on a train for Constanza and Clare remembers crossing German-held territory that night with a gramophone playing Berlin's current favourite dance tunes. When they arrived the next morning, Constanza station was surrounded by German tanks and beyond them in the port Clare saw the cargo ship that would take her home.

On that day, 5 February 1941, over one thousand German troops crossed into Bulgaria. Soon Hungary would be obliged to join the Axis and Hitler's massive Balkan jigsaw would then be complete, just as Clare had predicted.

Clare arrived safely back in England but she did not stay long. She covered the war in Greece and watched the final disintegration of the Balkans from Athens, Sofia and Istanbul. At the beginning of May, she received a cable from her newspaper to make haste to Egypt. Montgomery and his Eighth Army, the formidable Desert Rats, were about to confront Rommel. At the southern Turkish port of Mersin she was told that no ships dared leave port due to German air patrols. But in the harbour she spotted a sailing caïque flying the Palestinian flag.

The captain told her he was going to risk it and was leaving for Alexandria. A price was quickly agreed.

I thought crossing the Mediterranean in a small boat would be something of an adventure and possibly enlivened by machine-gunning Nazi planes. We were shadowed at times by enemy aircraft but our tiny boat was not worth a bomb. When we left Mersin the flag came down and the captain imposed a blackout.

Waves washed over the side, soaking all my clothes and ruining my only expensive garment, a Persian lamb coat. It was impossible to get warm so I just slept and let the fleas and bugs do their worst.

It took her five days and nights in rough seas to reach Alexandria and another week to recover. Her face was blistered by the sun and salt and her entire body sore with flea bites. She bought new clothes and a pair of army boots so she might be suitably dressed for her first foray into the desert and Montgomery's duel with Rommel.

> I arrived in Cairo in 1941 just after the fall of Crete and found little diffi-culty in visiting the 8th Army and attending official press briefings. But my relationship with Monty was not good. I did not get on with him because he would not get on with me. He was something of a woman hater and would not accept the accreditation of British women war correspondents. But he certainly had charisma and the men loved him for demolishing the 'them' and 'us' barrier between officers and men.

In the following months of the desert campaign, she reported the see-saw of battles for control of Libya and eastern Egypt, follow-ing Monty's Desert Rats to Tobruk and El Adem. She was one of the very few who obtained permission to accompany Special Forces operations behind enemy lines. One night she was with GSI, an intelligence unit, on reconnaissance well into German territory. After hours of searching and finding nothing, the unit dispersed and dug themselves into the sand to wait and keep warm.

> In the early hours I heard voices and they were quite clearly German voices. They were about a hundred yards away, a recce party in the sand dunes. I sweated and could feel the sand sticking with perspira-tion to every pore of my body. I hardly dared breathe … a sneeze would have meant death to us all. Then the sound of their engine and the crunch of gears as they went off. Oh! What blessed relief.

She travelled back and forth from the desert operations to Cairo, to file her reports, for a change of clothes, a bath, clean sheets and a decent dinner in the Shepheard Hotel. Waiting for her in the late summer of 1941 was a letter from her husband, Vandeleur. He wanted to marry somebody else and was asking for a divorce on the grounds of desertion. She had not seen him for more than six weeks in the past year, so she could hardly contest it. Not that she wanted to; she too had met somebody else.

Geoffrey Hoare was editor of the *Egyptian Gazette* and freelanced for *The Times*. Clare first spotted him at one of the daily military briefings. She was impressed.

> I was told he was the best bridge player in Egypt. He was tall, blond with an impeccable taste in tropical clothes but far more important, he had a profound knowledge of Egypt and its politics. It was a relationship that took a long time to develop but Geoffrey and I planned to work together and 'live happily ever after'.

Correspondents used their return trips back to Cairo for their 'rest and recuperation', deservedly a time to relax and wind down. But Clare was not one to do either and instead spent her days learning to fly because she wanted to know more about air warfare. She also enrolled on a parachute training course so that she could go on bombing missions with the Royal Air Force. She was nothing if not thorough. In the opening week of the second battle of El Alamein in October 1942, she sent this report on British air successes.

> For the first time in two days of the battle there has been no enemy air activity due to German airfields being waterlogged by storms. But today there were more German fighters in the air than on any day of the battle so far. As many as fifty planes were engaged in dogfights at one time. That the Germans are not writing off Libya is shown by the large numbers of aircraft they have been bringing in from Crete and elsewhere. They are also flying in reinforcements for their land

forces in giant Junkers Ju 52 transports. They may even be withdraw-ing squadrons from the Russian front. The RAF's score since Tuesday is 99 Axis planes destroyed for certain and thirteen more probables. Our losses are twenty-five but many of our pilots have been saved.

When the Americans entered the war she followed their armies across Libya into Tunisia and then on to Algeria, where General Eisenhower had established his headquarters in preparation for his invasion of Sicily and Italy. Monty did not like women reporters. Ike did and personally selected the experienced ones to accompany him. Clare was among them.

But on condition they demanded no special treatment. It was essen-tial to be able to go without washing, sleep and do all the things you have to do in the open desert and live on bully beef and biscuits for days on end. Many male correspondents got themselves back to Cairo because they could not take it.

In May 1943, Rommel and his formidable Afrika Korps were finally beaten; the three-year north African campaign was over and the Allies could begin their invasion into the European mainland. Clare followed them, first to Greece, then Italy and finally Crete to witness the surrender of six entire German divisions.

Clare remained in the Middle East with Geoffrey contributing to various international newspapers and magazines. The story now was of another war, of Arabs against Jews and Jews against the British in Mandated Palestine. Irgun, the Jewish terrorist organisation, led then by Menachem Begin, was fighting British rule and Britain's refusal to form a Jewish Israel in Palestine. In July 1946, Irgun smuggled explo-sives into the King David Hotel in Jerusalem. Clare and Geoffrey had just parked their car nearby.

Suddenly there was a tremendous explosion as the building was torn apart, collapsing in a mountain of rubble. We ran across to the devastation, appalled by the dead and the cries of the injured. Over a hundred people were killed, Arabs and Jews and ninety British soldiers. It was a diabolical statement by the terrorist leaders that the State of Israel would be created out of blood if necessary.

And blood did flow in Palestine before it finally became Israel in 1948. Irgun's atrocities were many and varied. In one of the worst, they captured and hanged a group of British army sergeants by wire from trees in an orange grove. Irgun later reported that it took nearly half an hour for the young men to die. Years later when Clare was introduced to Begin, she refused to shake his hand. It had, she told him, too much blood on it.

President Charles de Gaulle preferred to go to bed early and always with strict instructions that he should not be disturbed until his coffee at six o'clock. So it was an anxious Minister of Defence who woke him at a little past midnight on 24 January 1960, to report the astonishing news that French Air Force jets were about to take off from their Algerian base at Maison Blanche to bomb Marseilles, Toulon and Nice.

The President replied, 'Well, there is nothing to stop them' and went back to sleep. But by breakfast the next morning he had decided that it was time to settle, once and for all, the Algerian mutiny.

Algeria had always been considered by the French as an integral part of the metropolitan motherland. But since 1957 Algerian nationalists had been fighting a war of independence. It was bloody and costly. Many French governments had tried to find a solution, short of ending their colonial rule and handing the country back to whom it belonged. That was deemed to be impossible, with over one million French settlers determined to keep Algeria theirs.

But on 8 January 1959 a new President of the Fifth Republic was elected, the proxy war hero, the man who was seen as the embodiment of France and all its grandeur: Charles André Joseph Marie de Gaulle, the passionate and dedicated patriot. The settlers were confident they were safe with him in charge and nothing would change. But in his inaugural address he spelt out his plan for Algeria and it was plainly a recipe for its independence. There would be negotiations to end the war, and written into the settlement would be safeguards for French property and in particular French ownership of the oilfields. The settlers, known by some as *les colons* and by others as *les pieds noirs,* could remain as Algerians or leave and re-settle in France.

They rejected it outright and rioted in the capital, Algiers, and in Oran, setting fire to government offices and petrol stations. They marched through the streets beating out on their car horns and pots and pans the rhythm of their slogan 'Algérie Française'. There were bomb attacks in Paris and General Raoul Salan, the Commander-in-Chief of French forces in Algeria, and three of his officers attempted a coup. There were wild rumours that rebel French paratroopers were going to land in the capital and lay siege to the Presidential palace. For the first time since the French Revolution, civil war seemed a possibility.

But the war planes did not take off from Maison Blanche and no paratrooper landed in the Champs-Élysées. De Gaulle ridiculed the failed coup as 'an absurd quartet of old retired generals'. Salan was stripped of his rank and went underground, vowing revenge. He emerged two years later having prepared the bloodiest campaign of terror.

Clare came to Algeria in February 1962 when that campaign was well under way. Support for Salan among the settlers was unshakeable. He had recruited many thousands of men under his banner – the OAS, the *Organisation de l'armée secrète.* Their task was simply to terrorise and kill Algerian Muslims, empty their shops and houses, and destroy their businesses. Clare wrote that hatred and violence walked the streets together.

Soon after my arrival I was in the bar of the Aletti Palace Hotel when three men entered. One was wearing the red ribbon of the Legion d'honneur. The other two ordered drinks and then began fingering their revolvers, unloading their cartridges and re-loading them. Then they shouted that they had come to kill a French army captain who was at the far end of the bar. They said he had disobeyed an order from Salan. The young captain turned, bared his chest and shouted to them 'Shoot me now.'

By this time we were becoming alarmed but OAS gunmen at the door prevented us from leaving. The captain was told he had twenty-four hours to report for duty or he would be liquidated without further argument. I never did learn the fate of that captain and I'm ashamed I did nothing.

The settlers lived in the suburb of Bab el-Oued which was surrounded by both regular troops and the OAS. But one morning the corpse of a beheaded white woman was found there and within half an hour gunmen were touring the Muslim districts, machine-gunning from their cars. They did the same killing rounds in the afternoon. Nobody counted the dead.

Clare had valuable Muslim contacts, Algerians she had known from her assignment in Paris. Many were now leaders in the FLN, the movement for independence. But to meet them meant entering the Casbah, the Muslim market and enclave, and the OAS kept watch on any white person entering it, marking them down for later interrogation.

But Clare had a watchman, a shopkeeper at the entrance of the Casbah. He would warn her whether it was safe to enter or not:

I could tell by his smile or his silence or the position of his shutters. Fully up meant there was no tension, halfway up meant he wasn't certain, fully down meant danger. One morning the gunmen shot dead many around the Casbah. My shopkeeper was one of them.

It was a dangerous place for correspondents. Whatever they wrote was bound to anger one side or the other in the conflict, and they were liable to be shot at by both sides. Within a week of arriving in Algiers, Clare's hotel room was ransacked, clothes torn up and her typewriter thrown out of the window. She would answer the telephone and the caller would tell her to leave or she would not leave alive. She found notes pinned to her door with the message accusing her of 'treachery for the *Manchester Guardian*'.

The OAS gunmen especially targeted the Italian press. In March they arrived in their blue and black uniforms to take away the reporter for *La Stampa* saying he would face a special tribunal and, if found guilty of lying about Salan, he would be shot. But, they said, if all the Italian press left Algeria he would be spared. The Italians departed for Rome the next morning all except one, Niccolò Caracciola. He said he would not be intimidated and demanded an apology from Salan.

That evening an OAS commander and his thugs arrived at the Aletti Palace Hotel as correspondents were eating dinner. He demanded to know where Niccolò was but nobody replied. By then the Italian was well hidden. The commander was furious and seized the nearest journalist, John Wallis of the *Daily Telegraph*, and dragged him out into the street and into a waiting truck. Clare was defiant:

Without really thinking I shouted, 'Come on then, let's all go,' and we all poured outside to free John hoping the gunmen would not open fire on a crowd of international reporters. They threw their hostage back to us, the truck revved up and then we heard the click of the safety catches. Someone shouted 'Down! They're going to shoot!' and we all hit the ground together.

Algeria was now under the absolute rule of Salan and his reign of terror. He raided banks to finance his organisation and demanded huge sums from international companies, with the threats of bomb attacks if they refused. His men had free rein to kill who they wanted at whatever time suited them. They smuggled explosives into a prison and blew up over a hundred Muslim prisoners. And all the time the white settlers applauded them.

The Algerian FLN fought back like-for-like whenever it had the opportunity. Clare reported the clashes at the French naval base at Mers-el-Kébir where a mob cornered a white mother and her two children. They cut her down with an axe, smashed the skull of her boy and beat her little daughter to death. She was found still clutching a tiny bunch of geraniums.

Finally came the news that the long-overdue Évian peace agreement had been signed between de Gaulle and the FLN. The eight-year war for independence was over.

> In the Casbah, there was a minute's silence and Muslims stood and covered their head in a gesture of respect for all those who had died but there was no celebration. That would have to wait until the settlers had left and they were free to fly their own flag.

In that third week of March Salan played his last desperate card, ordering the shelling of the Casbah and mortar attacks on government buildings. But he knew he had lost. De Gaulle had ordered his army to end the insurrection by whatever means they thought necessary. The red-bereted paratroopers and commandos were supported by ten armed helicopters. Over the radio Salan appealed for his supporters to come out onto the streets but the doors and shutters in Bab-el-Oued remained shut. One of the bloodiest eras in French history was over.

Salan was arrested and sentenced to be executed by firing squad. That sentence was later commuted by judges citing 'exceptional circumstances'. He was later released from prison in a general amnesty. There were rumours that his coup had received backing from the CIA, on orders directly from President Kennedy, who feared the spread of communism in north Africa.

In time, General de Gaulle kept his promise to visit the independent Algeria. His tour took him to the small town of Tlemcen. Clare was there and she was surprised at the hostility of the crowds of Arabs shouting abuse. It was very threatening.

The General told his bodyguard to open the car door but the officer protested, '*Non! Non!*'

'*Ouvrez la porte*,' the General ordered. '*Moi, je suis le Président.*'

The car door was opened and he strode into the centre of the angry Arabs. Fists were raised. Head and shoulders above the mob, he spoke to those pushing him around. A phrase in French, a few quiet words in Arabic. I could not hear exactly what he said but it was quite plain that the magic of this remarkable man completely calmed and won over the demonstrators. He started to return and the fists that had been shaken against him, now grabbed his hand. When he bent to enter his car I saw it was wet with the spittle of Arab kisses.

My companion on the trip was so overcome by the emotion of it all that he sat on the kerb and burst into tears.

On 25 May 1951, two high-ranking diplomats in the British foreign service defected to the Soviet Union. They escaped arrest after a tip-off from another British diplomat who was also an agent for the KGB. He became known as the 'Third Man'. It was the biggest spy scandal in British history. Clare knew all three.

Donald Maclean was first secretary and head of chancery in the British Embassy in Cairo. He was also a married, cynical, rampant homosexual drunkard. Clare and her husband were his neighbours and frequently met Maclean and his wife Melinda in the social melee of the British expat elite. He complained that the intense round of social obligations bored him. But it was a front, and as a spy, he had many. Mixing with the international strata of Cairo's military and political society was essential in his secret role as a communist sympathiser. By cultivating a personal relationship with the Ambassador, he was able to influence British policy in Egypt in line with Moscow's.

He was competent in all things except controlling his libido. Drunk after dinner, he would chase his young male servants from one bedroom to another and roam Cairo's brothels and nightclubs in drunken orgies. But the British Ambassador knew nothing of it because no one would tell him. He ended his time in Cairo in the most spectacular way but Clare was forbidden to report it.

> He had been invited to an official reception at King Farouk's palace but he did not arrive as expected in white tie and decorations. He wore his scruffiest clothes, stood at the top of the grand stairway lined with the ladies in waiting and then urinated over them. Then he went to the apartment of a young American secretary and tried to rape her. When she fled via the fire escape, he emptied bottles of her whisky and gin, smashed the apartment to pieces and fell across her bed unconscious.

Within days and in keeping with diplomatic protocol, he was discreetly flown home, suffering, in the double talk of the Foreign

Service, 'from stress, on the verge of a nervous breakdown and in need of medical treatment'. Melinda, his wife, left him and his employers sent him to an eminent psychiatrist. Maclean enjoyed his chats on the couch but he always carried a bottle of whisky in his overcoat pocket. In time he persuaded Melinda to come back to him, promising he would reform himself – and she wanted to believe him.

Clare recalls that Maclean never spoke openly about communism or showed any interest in it. But on a visit to his house,

> I noticed that most of the books in Donald's study were about Russia. The subjects ranged over classical novels and histories to the works of Marx and the Revolutionaries. There were books on Soviet architecture, music, the theatre and ballet. There was even one entitled *How beautiful it is to live on a Collective Farm*. They had been well read.

Maclean would not, perhaps could not, change, and disappeared for days with an old friend he had known as an undergraduate at Cambridge. His name was Guy Francis de Moncy Burgess, yet another from the Foreign Service stable of quasi-aristocratic homosexual alcoholics. He had been sacked as second secretary in the Washington Embassy and also sent home in disgrace in another hastily covered-up scandal.

On Maclean's thirty-eighth birthday Melinda baked him a special cake and had planned a quiet evening together. But he told her that he had invited a friend for dinner. He was introduced, she found him charming, the cake was cut and the three sat down to a convivial birthday celebration. Maclean consumed many brandies and instead of bidding his friend goodbye, suddenly announced that they both had to leave on business; he said he would take an overnight bag in case he was delayed. Melinda pleaded with him to stay but the two men left. She went to bed in tears and waited for him until she was too tired to wait any longer. At that moment Maclean and his friend Guy Burgess were already on the cross-Channel ferry *Falaise* to St Malo and the first leg of their long journey to Moscow.

Clare met Kim Philby at one of London's high-society balls at Londonderry House, Park Lane in October 1937. It had been a special occasion and as they danced, her husband Vandeleur had wished her a happy birthday.

> A good looking young man in white tie and well-cut tails was nearby and he approached us and kissed my cheek and said 'Happy Birthday Twin.' He introduced himself and I recognised him as the son of the distinguished Arabist St John Philby. Whenever we met afterwards he would always greet me with the words 'Hello Twin', but I discovered he did not share the same birthday as me. It was a ploy he used to enable him to make useful friends quickly.

Philby was a respected and much-admired agent in British intelligence. He was also a dedicated KGB officer with considerable influence in Moscow. The Russians trusted him completely.

It was not until long after Maclean and Burgess had disappeared that she met Philby again. It was in Beirut. He told her he had left the foreign service and was now freelancing as a correspondent for *The Observer* and *The Economist*. He was not as she remembered him; no longer the flirtatious, debonair man-about-town but a caricature of a middle-class right-wing bigot, openly praising Franco's regime in Spain and Salazar's dictatorship in Portugal. He also said he was a member of the extremist Anglo-German Fellowship. For an active Russian spy it was an impressive and convincing disguise. But there were some present who were not fooled by him and during his stay in Lebanon he was under constant surveillance by MI6 and the CIA. It was only a matter of weeks before he would be arrested and charged with treason.

But Philby still had influential and similarly treacherous friends in high places in the British foreign service, and he was warned that the net was closing rapidly. On the evening of 23 January 1963, Clare was in Beirut again on assignment and on impulse rang Philby's apartment. There was no answer. She tried another number and was told that Philby had not been seen for some days. He had been invited the previous evening to a dinner with the British chargé d'affaires but he had not arrived.

> I telephoned anyone who might have known where he might be. I checked with the Lebanese police and the frontier post and was assured that no Mr Kim Philby had left the country. Then I had a thought. I bought a copy of the fortnightly sheet of 'Le Journal du Levant' which listed ships entering and leaving Beirut. On the night Philby should have been dining with the Chargé d'affaires, a Soviet ship had left for Odessa. Again I checked with the port police who swore Philby was not aboard. But then they admitted they had found a drunken Russian sailor on the quayside after the ship had left and his landing card and documents were missing. Yet the port authorities assured me that all the Russian crew aboard that ship had been accounted for. It was plain enough. Philby had taken the drunken sailor's place and was now on his way safely to his masters in Moscow.

She immediately filed her sensational exclusive to *The Guardian*, reporting that Philby was the 'Third Man', and waited for the editor's congratulations. The hero-gram never arrived. She listened on BBC World Service, expecting her story to lead the news bulletins. She heard nothing. Exasperated, she telephoned her editor, Alastair Hetherington, and demanded to know why her story had not been published. 'Be your age, Clare,' Hetherington retorted. 'Foreign

Secretary Macmillan has told Parliament that Philby is not your "Third Man" and your story would involve us in millions of pounds worth of libel.'

Clare and her newspaper sat on the story for another three months when, with Hetherington away on holiday, Clare persuaded his deputy that she could rewrite her original report in a way that would placate the company's lawyers. Ever so cautiously, it appeared on an inside page with a photograph of Philby:

On an evening in Beirut three months ago, the correspondent for *The Observer* and *The Economist*, Kim Philby, disappeared, and nothing has been heard of him since. Statements made by his wife to the Lebanese police and letters received, though not written by him, suggest that he did not fall over a cliff. It would be difficult for a well-known Englishman to disappear in an Arab country.

Philby knew both Donald Maclean and Guy Burgess and at the time of their disappearance, he was accused of being the 'Third Man' who had warned them that they were about to be questioned by Foreign Office security authorities. The Foreign Secretary Harold Macmillan has stated positively that no evidence has been found that he was responsible.

Philby might be on a secret mission or he might suddenly have grown tired of life in Beirut and rushed off to live with one of the desert tribes. But three months is a long time for a man to hide himself from his wife and employer.

The story shook Fleet Street into action, and shortly afterwards the British government admitted they knew Philby was in Moscow, and had known from the very beginning. There were even rumours that his escape had been organised by British intelligence, to save the government embarrassment when the full facts of Philby's many years of deception became public. At home and abroad, the most damaging spy scandal in British history was given extensive coverage. And Clare notched up a world scoop that almost never was.

That year she was offered the job as *The Guardian*'s defence correspondent, but she hesitated. She was fifty-two years old, fit and as much the rover as ever; the prospect of office life tied to a desk did not appeal. But she loved Geoffrey as she had never loved Vandeleur, and was determined her second marriage would not go the same unhappy way as the first.

> When I was away I missed Geoffrey not only as a husband and companion but also as a colleague with whom I could discuss politics and work in general. I was often away for two to four months at a time and although I was always extremely happy to get back to him I sometimes wondered whether we should have been quite so happy had we been together all the time.

So that they might see each other more often, Clare established strategically placed 'love nests' for their rendezvous. They had an apartment in London's Bloomsbury, a cottage south of Paris and what she called her 'shack' in the hills north of Nice. To be prepared for all contingencies, such as a sudden panic call from her foreign desk, she fitted them all out with her essentials. 'I kept a T and T ... a toothbrush and typewriter in all shacks and flats together with paper, a dictionary, underwear and some old clothes. In London and Paris I kept long dresses and at least one fairly smart outfit.'

As the newspaper's new defence correspondent she was prepared for a dull daily routine, but the next ten years provided a kaleidoscope of new experiences. It took her to the capitals of the world and introduced her to many of its leaders. She wrote about the world's vast armouries, the newest weapons of war and international efforts to ration them. This was the era of gross expenditure on inventions stillborn: there was the oddly conceived Multilateral Force where sailors from many nations were expected to crew the British Polaris submarine, when none of them could speak a common language; the experimental British-built TR2 that never took off; the multi-million-pound development of the revolutionary swept-wing F-111 invented by Barnes Wallis, which the British government abandoned and the Americans took for themselves and made into a formidable and profitable fighter.

Washington, Ottawa, Paris, Athens, Aden, Tehran, Ankara, Singapore, Hong Kong: she was her travel agent's delight. She spent ten years of travelling the globe when she had expected to move no further than her office in Gray's Inn Road, London WC1.

She reported the regime of President Sukarno, dubbed the 'Hitler of Indonesia', as he tried to extend his dictatorship by absorbing oil-rich Brunei. She joined troops of the 1st Battalion Royal Leicesters, fighting Sukarno's communist guerrillas in the mountains along the Brunei–Sarawak border.

Around the fort were Bren and heavy machine guns in well-sand-bagged positions. On the camp perimeter there was an outer circle of barbed wire, mines and booby traps and inside that were sharpened bamboo sticks embedded in the ground. Beyond was a helicopter landing strip. They always flew in pairs in case one was shot down.

There I met Sergeant Harry Rankin who instructed me in jungle lore. He said, 'When all goes silent in the night and the frogs stop croaking, there is danger from someone out there moving.' He pointed to a trench where I would have to take cover if the whistle blew. There was one black soldier called Bert and I said how splendid it was that there were no racial hang-ups and how everyone got along so well together.

He turned on me in a fury. 'If you are suggesting Bert is black you can go back on the next helicopter. Bert is a good Leicester boy just as you are a Leicester girl.'

She went on patrol with an SAS platoon, deep into the jungle along the Indonesian border.

> In single file we followed the tracks, the officer led the way with a map and compass, another man carried the radio set and the others shouldered the weapons and ammunition. We carried our water-bottle, a light groundsheet that could be used as a hammock and five days ration of dates, sweets and dried fish which we slotted into our belts. I discovered that British jungle tactics were straight out of Mao's teachings on guerrilla warfare. Whenever the enemy was near we melted into the jungle, hiding beneath the thick foliage, hardly daring to breathe. We never spent two nights in the same area.

A few months later she was flying over Aden, sitting in the navigator's seat of a supersonic RAF Hunter jet fighter.

Aden is the southernmost port on the Arabian Peninsula and a British colony since 1937. It had been a port of call for ships flying the Red Ensign ever since. After the loss of the Suez Canal in 1956, Aden became Britain's main military base in the Middle East.

There were thirteen different tribes along the coast of the Gulf of Aden, governed by thirteen sheikhs, sultans and emirs, all hostile to British rule and each other. In 1964, to give the region some political and economic stability, an attempt was made to unite the tribes into a Federation of South Arabia and the thirteen monarchs were persuaded to join, encouraged by millions of pounds of British taxpayers' money.

But the Marxist regime in North Yemen had long decided that Aden was to be absorbed into its republic and launched a protracted guerrilla war against the British. Clare had visited Aden many times during the 1950s, when any threat to British rule was unthinkable. Now she was in a British jet fighter as the pilot identified Yemeni guerrilla positions to be bombed later that day.

Wing Commander John Jenner was on a reconnaissance mission over the Radfan Mountains and threw the fighter around like an expert juggler. Flying somewhere between three and four hundred feet, we zigzagged and swooshed between the hills, rolling from one side to the other to identify a truck or see whether a shadow on a rock was hiding a camel or something more threatening. We were well inside the federal border to observe any movement of camel caravans or tribesmen using the wadis. I saw the damage inflicted on them by Hunter rockets some days earlier and quite clearly they had been hit with absolute accuracy.

She accompanied British troops searching for rebel headquarters in the Wadi El Taym area on the plains below the Radfans. The villages were deserted; the women had taken their families, goats and camels into the valleys away from the fighting. British artillery targeted their 105mm field guns into the lower slopes of the mountains where the hard-core resistance was known to be.

At 5 a.m. Operation Newmarket began. Water bottles were filled, orders to the troops were issued and we advanced slowly over country covered in boulders until we reached the steep bank of a wadi. The commander called in an air strike and within minutes four Hunters were rocketing and machine gunning two towers, rebel observation posts, on a mountain two thousand feet above us. The towers disappeared in a cloud of dust. The atmosphere smacked of *Beau Geste*.

But it had all been a great waste of military time and public money. Harold Wilson's election victory in 1966 turned British foreign policy on its head when he announced that, within a year, the British would leave Aden. There was rioting and exchanges of gunfire in the Crater districts, finally subdued by Colonel Colin 'Mad' Mitchell and his Black Watch marching to their bagpipes. By the end of the year, the

Marxist Yemenis took control of the coastal territories, incorporating them into the newly named People's Democratic Republic of Yemen. The thirteen sheiks, sultans and emirs withdrew the gold from their safe deposits, left their tribespeople to the mercy of their new governors and drove their Rolls-Royces and Bentleys across the border to the safe sanctuaries of Oman and Saudi Arabia, careful never to trust the word of the British ever again.

Clare was a 'one off': an outsider with an extraordinary range of insider contacts. Her brusque-brittle attitude upset many, because when she had the scent of a story she had little time for the niceties. Yet, whenever a comforting word or a nudge of encouragement to a young inexperienced newcomer was needed, she could be guaranteed to provide it.

Others before her, like Gellhorn and Nevinson, shared a common feature on how and what they reported. They concentrated on the inhumanity of warfare. They did not catalogue the size and complement of armies and their armouries or the strategies that won or lost battles. Their concern was with the innocents, the deaths and suffering of the non-combatants, the people in between – in the modern vernacular, 'collateral damage'. They wrote not just what they saw but what they felt.

Clare Hollingworth was not from their stable. In all the memoirs and newspaper reports from her sixty years as a war correspondent, there is little that is written, like Gellhorn and Nevinson, 'from the heart'. She preferred to write an overview of what she saw and, like William Russell, to digest and analyse the military and political implications afterwards. She was meticulous in detail and careful to remain unbiased. Nor did she dramatise the dangers that surrounded her in those near-lethal adventures. Sometimes it was quite the reverse. Her colleague and close friend Tom Pocock remembers an incident when they were on their way to Kashmir during the Indo-Pakistan War in 1965.

We were going up to the front in an Indian jeep and we had to get over a bridge that was being shelled by the Pakistanis. Every few seconds there the great whoomp of explosions and clouds of dust rose from the craters. The Indian officer said, 'Let's wait for one and then make a dash for it.' I said, 'Oh dear! Let's cross our fingers.' I remember that Clare turned round, her eyes shining like a young girl going to her first dance, and she shouted, 'Now this is what makes life worth living!'

Correspondents who have worked alongside Clare on assignments all have their own special memories of her, and I have mine. I met her first in 1971 in the second Indo-Pakistan War. Pakistan means 'land of the pure'; it was Mohammed Ali Jinnah's sanctuary for Muslims when religion split India apart. But in an uncomfortable and logistically impossible arrangement, Pakistan was itself split east–west, with a thousand miles of India in between. In 1971, the Bengalis in the East demanded their independence and the ruling military junta in Islamabad went to war to prevent it. What the West Pakistanis then did to them, under the direction of Generals Yahya Khan and Tikka Khan, is well recorded. Yet unlike other grotesque genocides, the Khans' atrocities have been forgotten and, by some, even condoned.

That December I was among a dozen members of the inter-national press corps held captive in the Intercontinental Hotel in Dacca. The city itself was under siege, the airport was bombed hourly by Indian Sukhoi fighter-bombers and all communication was cut. For weeks we lived on boiled rice and scrawny chicken legs, which we suspected were rat. There was an unexploded bomb in the ladies' lavatory and another on the first floor but Gavin Young of *The Observer*, a man of many eloquent words, helped settle our anxieties by playing Gershwin and sometimes Chopin on the piano in the shattered reception foyer.

Clare was our bustling, often bullying matron, our stoic supervisor, our steadying hand. Somebody described her fondly as our Miss Marple. Of all the outwardly brave correspondents there, she was by far the most gung-ho.

Every evening, we congregated in the darkened ballroom and waited for a Pakistani officer to tell us what he would like us to believe had happened that day, brazenly reporting his army's fictitious victories. Clare was at her best.

Clare: You say you killed five hundred Indians today. What are your casualties?
Answer: In our army we believe no soldier ever dies in battle. He goes straight to paradise, so he is not dead.
Clare: Can he still shoot Indians from paradise?

One night, towards the end of the war, the Pakistani Air Force headquarters in Dacca took a direct hit. Early the next morning, I went with my cameraman to film the wreckage and found Clare already there, scrambling across the rubble. I assumed she was searching for any secret documents that might be useful to her – that would be her form. I was wrong. 'Silly boy!' she said in her best schoolmistress voice. 'There's nothing secret here. I'm just looking to see if any bottles of whisky have survived!'

The war in Vietnam was Clare's last, and it was the one she relished most. She arrived in Saigon, capital of the non-communist south, in March 1965. That month 3,500 US Marines came ashore on the beaches of Đà Nẵng: the first American combat troops to set foot in Vietnam. Within a year they were joined by another 200,000, confidently come to win Uncle Sam's war to stop Hồ Chí Minh taking over Indochina. John Kennedy was another President obsessed with the 'domino theory': that if Vietnam fell to the communists, the rest of the Orient and Asia would follow. Kennedy should have read his history and learnt from the French. His obsession finally cost the lives of over 56,000 young Americans and over two million Vietnamese.

Kennedy had used the Gulf of Tonkin 'incident' as an excuse to occupy South Vietnam. In 1964 two American destroyers had opened fire on North Vietnamese warships believing they were being attacked. But there had been no attack. The destroyers' captains had mistaken an electrical storm for shell fire. That was kept a discreet secret but the incident served its purpose.

Clare was just one of the many international correspondents who, like James Cameron, even in those first months of the war, predicted an inevitable American defeat. Her reports were invariably critical, frequently cynical, and her readers were left in no doubt that she considered the G.I.s to be an army of occupation in a hostile country. Their only allies were the Vietnamese money makers and the corrupt political elite.

> It was born during my very first trip for *The Guardian* that this was a war the Americans could never win. Not only were their commanders and troops inept at jungle warfare but the Pentagon itself failed to appreciate and understand that the overwhelming factor against them was one of geography. Even if they had invaded North Vietnam, they would be an army of occupation, constantly harassed by guerrilla action. But over and above this awesome prospect was that China would never have permitted an American presence on her southern border.

She arrived in Saigon to find that it was not one but two cities. It evoked memories of Beirut, Algiers and Tunis, colonial capitals planned by Parisian architects with elegance in mind, graced by tree-lined boulevards, spacious parks and wide streets bordered by gardens and grand white stucco buildings. It had a Gothic-style cathedral and an Art Deco post office and, most essential of all, the tennis club and swimming pool for the French elite, called the *Cercle Sportif*.

None of which was of any interest to the American G.I.s, who strutted along Tự Do Street gawping at mini-skirted dolly girls on hire for twenty dollars a time, plus another fifty later for the doctor. Saigon was dollar crazy and tried to pretend there was no war. But the pavement cafes had begun to move indoors as a precaution against the odd grenade tossed from a passing motorcycle, and there were barricades of barbed wire around the cathedral and post office to prevent a lorry packed with high explosive parking too close. Though everyone was free to go wherever they liked, nowhere was safe. Saigon had long been infiltrated by the Vietcong, the South Vietnamese communist guerrillas, who walked its streets in perfect anonymity, shadowing the Americans they were fighting and killing.

The countryside was theirs too, despite attempts by the Americans to control it on land and in the air. The dense jungles and rubber plantations provided the communists with perfect cover; they could move wherever they pleased undetected. So the Americans decided to take that cover away by the simple and brutal method of defoliation. The chemical was codenamed 'Agent Orange'. It contained large doses of cyanide and was sprayed by squadrons of low-flying C130 aircraft. Vast tracts of luxuriant forests were reduced to a sterile desert, a moonscape where nothing survived, and where nothing would live for another half century. It killed everything but the communists. They not only survived but increased in numbers.

One of Clare's first stories was a river-marine operation in the Mekong delta. The Americans had planned to take sampans loaded with supplies along a canal to a garrison near Mỹ Tho. They were to be escorted by heavily armed patrol boats. But the Vietcong ambushed them.

They ran into heavy machine gun fire and the first American was killed. Then one of the patrol boats was sunk by a mine. Accurate mortar fire rendered movement impossible. They called in air support, twelve bombers and a fleet of helicopter gun-ships that blasted everything in sight. Then they ordered a crack Ranger battalion to join the battle. After it was all over, the Saigon government claimed two hundred and seventy Vietcong killed, six Americans killed and three helicopters shot down. This was described to me as a successful operation although the canal remained in Vietcong hands and the sampans never left their moorings.

Aboard a US Air Force bomber on a raid north of Đà Nẵng, Clare wrote,

There was some fire from the ground but I did not see or hear it hit the aircraft. We had already made one bombing run and we were supposed to make a second raid to blast a Vietcong camp from a mountaintop. Instead we turned away and on the return journey the pilot said over the intercom, 'The United States should be proud and grateful for all you have done today.' What, I queried, had they done? He then told me of the 'great bravery' of all in his plane, which was of course rubbish as we had not known we were in any danger. On our return to Da Nang, he refused to go on a second mission on the grounds of 'the terrible sufferings' of the crew during the trip which I had just experienced myself.

She had not been long in the country when she received a letter from Geoffrey. He complained of pains in his arms similar to those he had experienced before a heart attack some years earlier. He wrote that he was about to visit a specialist for a check-up. Clare did not hesitate. She cabled her editor requesting permission to return. She was on the flight to London the next day.

He had a minor heart attack within hours of arriving at the hospital and had somehow managed to persuade people to smuggle cigarettes to him. He had ten days of treatment but then a massive attack and he died a few hours later. Life has never been quite the same since. I still miss him every night in bed. I'm not talking about sex but we used to have a chat before we went to sleep, with a half a pint of beer or something, about what was happening in the world. Yes! I miss him enormously.

A month later she returned to her story in Vietnam. Mention the name Khe Sanh to correspondents who saw duty in Vietnam and they will have a story to tell. It was a vast American camp under siege, just south of the demilitarised zone that separated the North from the South. In theory, the garrison of six thousand US Marines was meant to prevent the communists moving men and supplies along the Hồ Chí Minh trail, but that theory never became practice. For over six months the communists had prevented the Americans from leaving their camp; the only way out for them was by air or a white flag. They were shelled and mortared day and night and they wondered why. Khe Sanh was a gateway to nowhere, it no longer had any strategic value. But the generals, in customary true grit, had promised their President it would not fall, and American television networks had made it a symbol of defiance and courage. Like the Alamo, it had become an American obsession.

Correspondents considered it the most dangerous place in all of South Vietnam. Only the reckless or those on non-prescription drugs volunteered to go there. Clare, fitting neither description, went of her own accord because that was where the story was. Personal danger was never part of the equation.

She flew in with the Air Cavalry, young men proud of their reputation as the gung-ho derring-dos with a death wish. They painted their attack helicopters with the face of a tiger or a shark and marked up their kills underneath. Clare landed under constant mortar and machine gun fire, yet her report is almost blasé.

> As I arrived, F-100 fighter jets were attacking trenches and dug-outs about two hundred yards from the edge of the camp. The grassless soil was blood red, the trees scorched and blasted amid the shell holes. The North Vietnamese were caught in the attack of rockets and napalm and there was nowhere for them hide.
>
> Later I was taken to inspect their trenches. Each was brilliantly constructed and within easy rifle range of the camp. In the officer's dug-outs, all the American positions were accurately marked on maps. They were stacked with US ration packs and cartons of fruit juice from California which no doubt compensated for the strong smell of the burnt corpses out in no man's land.

A month later, Clare went back again to Khe Sanh for Operation Pegasus, the American High Command's final attempt to break the siege.

> I went in a big Chinook helicopter, packed with troops, 150mm howitzers and boxes of ammunition. Cobra helicopter gun-ships, capable of firing forty-five thousand rounds a minute, escorted us as others prowled the surrounding hills to draw fire from an unseen enemy. Five hundred helicopters had ferried in twenty thousand American and thirteen thousand south Vietnamese troops and under heavy shelling, were pressing forward to within a mile of the beleaguered garrison. Six fighters came in to 'hose down' the enemy but the mortar fire was continuous. It was hitting our positions with remarkable accuracy. I saw a direct hit on a storage dump destroying thousands of tons of fuel.

It was billed as one of the biggest and most concentrated operations of the war, but the communists simply dispersed into the mountains.

Many, many hundreds were killed, but still they did not abandon Khe Sanh.

The Americans did. Despite the months of siege, the months of famous fighting and dying, the generals abruptly evacuated the camp and the first of the Marines left on April Fool's Day 1968. When they were gone, the communists came back, moved in and stayed. Khe Sanh had begun as folly. It ended as just another of America's many Vietnam tragedies.

It was January 1968 and the Vietnamese were about to celebrate Tết, their lunar New Year. No work was done at Tết, shops were closed and in the past, there had even been a pause in the war. But this January the communists changed the rules and launched their biggest offensive, attacking thirty provincial capitals simultaneously. In Saigon, the Americans fought to defend their embassy when a unit of Vietcong, kamikaze-style, penetrated the nerve centre of American's war operation and almost captured it. It marked the beginning of the end of America's Vietnam adventure.

Clare went to Phú Lâm on the western outskirts of the city where the Vietcong were attacking an American radar station.

> I climbed to the highest building where three soldiers lay wounded. Communists were firing from a nearby house and crawling around the roof, it was easy to obtain a view as Cobra helicopter gun-ships dived on a large garage which was the main Vietcong position. The noise was ear-splitting as fighter planes rocketed, setting off fires and I could see the communists quite clearly through field glasses. More air attacks, more fires, more explosions. I decided it was time for me to withdraw and file my copy.

> When the Vietcong were trying to take over Cholon, Saigon's Chinese suburb, I was taken by a friend into the middle of it. We moved from one bullet-pocked building to another, with

gunfire all around us. But there was little danger to worry about because my escort had been a first class house-to-house fighter in the 1939–45 war.

On 2 May 1968, the *Daily Telegraph* published a world exclusive. The American military command in Vietnam, still recovering from Tết, now suffered a second shock. The generals could not believe what they read and promptly and too prematurely rubbished it to the Saigon press corps. But it was true. Secret talks were about to begin between Hanoi and Washington for the withdrawal of all American forces from Vietnam. It was an astonishing scoop and it was by-lined 'Clare Hollingworth'.

The little Vietnamese was very polite. He suggested I might like to discuss a business matter. He asked me if knew of a certain Algerian and mentioned his name. I said I did. He had been a reliable contact of mine during the independence struggle.

Then my visitor said 'We expect to see you at Mass in the cathedral tomorrow', and left without any further explanation.

Next morning I arrived promptly and waited in the pews. Was it a hoax? Presently a man came and sat beside me and after a short prayer, thrust a document into my hand. In the flickering candlelight I saw credentials carrying the stamp of the North Vietnamese.

I followed him into the darkness of the empty Lady Chapel as priests and choir walked in procession to their places. The candles cast dancing points of light on the walls but in our shadowy corner we were just two worshippers with bowed heads.

Then he told me all I needed to know. The American President and the American people were war weary. They wanted out and talks would soon begin in Paris between Henry Kissinger and the North Vietnamese negotiator Lê Đức Thọ.

Within a year the American and North Vietnamese negotiators did indeed meet in Paris, but it would take another five years before the G.I.s waved their final goodbyes and went home. They had fought a vicious, bloody eight-year war of hide and seek, and theirs was an ignominious exit. They had no idea of what winning meant. They only knew what they had lost.

They should have read Kipling:

> *And the end of the fight is a tombstone white*
> *With the name of the late deceased.*
> *And the epitaph drear: a fool lies here*
> *Who tried to hustle the East.*

But what had been agreed in Paris meant nothing. It was not a peace but a piece of paper. The Americans had simply abandoned the South Vietnamese and left them to fight on alone against the vastly superior army of the North. Week on week, that army moved relentlessly south, like a pool of red spreading over the map of Vietnam, until it was finally all theirs.

On Monday 28 April 1975, my ITN camera crew and I sat in our Saigon hotel waiting to be evacuated. The communist tanks were on the far side of the Saigon River only a few miles away. We could hear their engines. Tomorrow they would enter the city victorious. That evening I wrote this in my dairy:

> It is all over and who would have thought it would happen quite this way? This will be our last night. By rights we should all get drunk but nobody wants to chance a hangover tomorrow. It's the end of the war but perhaps not the end of the bloodletting. People fear the worst. Wealthy Vietnamese fathers have been touring the hotels offering wads of dollars and jewellery to any westerner who will take their daughters out. A lot of dollars have been taken. I doubt if many daughters will be.

Today a Vietnamese officer in Lam Son Square stood to attention just below my window, saluted the flag and shot himself in the mouth. One Vietnamese lady along the corridor says she will poison herself tonight. We shall know for sure in the morning.

But Clare was not there that day to witness the end of the war she had so famously reported. She was by then the *Daily Telegraph*'s first resident China correspondent, based in Beijing.

She was now sixty-one and knew that it was probably her last foreign assignment. She also knew it would be her hardest, reporting from a vast country that had been all but sealed off since the imposition of the 'Bamboo Curtain' in 1949.

It was an austere and isolated life. She lived alone in a very bare and inhospitable government-run hotel. As a foreigner she was banned from travelling without a government minder, forbidden to talk to anyone without permission, forbidden even to dine with her interpreter. 'And yet I cannot recall ever feeling lonely. After dinner alone I used to go to my room and sit on the hard chair with its straight hard back and think how lucky I was to be in China.' The interpreter's father had been murdered by the Red Guards and she told a story that has haunted Clare ever since.

Every year, on the evening of their wedding anniversary, the interpreter's parents would drug their children with sleeping pills. Chinese children at that time were trained to report any deviance by the family from the Party line.

When the children were asleep, the couple pulled a box from a secret compartment hidden under the floorboards. Inside were an evening gown and a dinner jacket and they dressed themselves as they had done in their pre-Revolution youth. To do so now in public would have meant certain death. In the silence and darkness of the room, the couple danced and embraced in their few minutes of happiness and freedom. Then they hid the clothes away for another year.

After three exhausting but exhilarating years, she returned to London to become the *Telegraph*'s defence correspondent. She had just celebrated her sixty-fifth birthday, and it was suggested that it was time for her to end her global travelling and remain firmly and safely anchored to her desk. But her appetite for foreign news was insatiable. There is a story that when news was slow, she would come into the office with a bedroll and demand to be sent to the latest trouble spot.

In 1981, aged seventy, she 'officially' retired. At her farewell party, along with many fond speeches, they gave her a toy pistol. Her era had passed and she tried hard to think it had not. She left for Hong Kong and wrote occasional articles for the *Sunday Telegraph*. She bought a small apartment close to the Foreign Correspondents' Club and, as she found it more and more difficult to walk, it became her daytime home. In her favourite chair where no one else dared sit and in a corner of a foreign club that would remain forever England, she continued to worry about the world and its troubles, reading her newspapers with a magnifying glass and listening to the BBC World Service with headphones. She would often telephone the *Telegraph*'s foreign desk with advice or a warning, or even a reprimand about something she had read and did not like in the day's edition.

In the club and in the company of visiting journalists, she is comfortable and respected, and no visiting foreign correspondent misses the chance to sit with her and listen to her reminiscences. Her eyesight has all but failed but her memory, her power of recall, like the surfeit of luck and good fortune that has accompanied her all her life, remains infallible.

On her eightieth birthday she wrote that she was still planning new adventures.

I must go back to Egypt to see how my old friends regard Muslim fundamentalism and I've developed a strong desire to return to my old haunts in the Balkans, to my old stamping ground, Bucharest, Sofia, Belgrade, Athens, Albania. And what is the future of Asia? There is still so much to do and write about. So much to do.

Her nephew Patrick Garrett in his biography writes this:

> There are correspondents who can take a minor scrap and turn it into a second Stalingrad. And there is Clare who can turn out a very matter-of-fact account, however dramatic it was. She never dressed up the mundane. So what made her such a legend? It was a mixture of her focus on the facts and her sparkling personality and her unstinting energy and commitment to the story.

She was one hundred on 11 October 2011; she was feted internationally and the Queen sent her the congratulatory telegram. But she finds few consolations in old age.

> It's extraordinary being old. I just dream of being young all the time. I'm still very much a youngster.

EPILOGUE

For over forty years I have been one of Russell's 'luckless tribe', reporting wars and other inhuman tragedies for British television news. Yet none of my television contemporaries feature in my list of great war reporters. Nor should they. We cannot equal the lives of those you have read about. Nor can we compete with newspaper war correspondents. We are of the same trade but not from the same mould.

In his self-deprecatory way, James Cameron wrote that journalists 'splash in the shallows, only occasionally applauded to the rare heights of mediocrity'. It hardly describes him, one of Britain's greatest. It fits us better, we who skim the surface of a story.

Our television reports can impact spectacularly and create momentum but, given the tyranny of our medium, we have time to tell only a fraction of what we see and hear and feel. We are governed not in column inches but in seconds. Our stories are never complete and there remains a residue of guilt.

But we do all share something: a common ambition. When we begin our careers we think of ourselves akin to crusaders, that what we write, what we report, the power of photographs and the television images, might somehow change the world for the better. That it might even end war.

But does anything change, anything that matters? Despite all that is written and every word that is broadcast, do we not simply advertise the evils of our world, do nothing to end them and perhaps even make worse its miseries? Is that our epitaph?

The doubt festers.